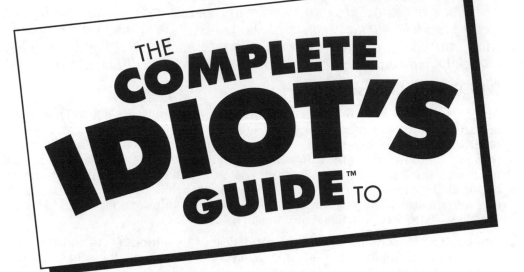

THE COMPLETE IDIOT'S GUIDE™ TO

Assertiveness

by Jeff Davidson

alpha
books

A Pearson Education Company

This book is dedicated to my wonderful cousins and relatives Dr. Jay and Craig Mandell; Sheila Persky and Diane Brody; William, Sylvia, Bobby, Alan, and Richard Leader; George, Hannah, Jackie, and Roy Leader; Dr. Nancy Davidson; and Richard, Janice, Jimmy, and Jill Davidson.

©1997 Jeff Davidson

This publication contains the opinions and ideas of its author. It is intended to provide helpful and informative material on the subject matter covered. It is sold with the understanding that the author and publisher are not engaged in rendering professional services in the book. If the reader requires personal assistance or advice, a competent professional should be consulted.

International Standard Book Number: 0-02-861964-1
Library of Congress Catalog Card Number: 97-073152

03   02   8   7

Interpretation of the printing code: the rightmost number of the first series of numbers is the year of the book's printing; the rightmost number of the second series of numbers is the number of the book's printing. For example, a printing code of 97-1 shows that the first printing occurred in 1997.

Printed in the United States of America

Brand Manager
Kathy Nebenhaus

Executive Editor
Gary M. Krebs

Development Editor
Jennifer Perillo

Production Editor
Carol Sheehan

Copy Editor
Lynn Northrup

Cover Designer
Michael Freeland

Book Designer
Glenn Larsen

Illustrator
Judd Winick

Indexer
Nadia Ibrahim

Production Team
Tricia Flodder, Mary Hunt, Megan Wade

Contents at a Glance

Contents

6   Increasing Your Vocal Self-Confidence   57

7   Self-Confidence Tips You Can Practice Today   67

Part 5: Assertiveness in Your Personal Life 179

17 Special Assertiveness Situations for Women 181

22 Who's the Boss Around Here?   249

23 Assertiveness with Your Peers   263

Foreword

I've been called an assertive's assertive. You know the adjectives: forceful, strong, firm, compelling, forthright, direct, straightforward. I thought that I could write this foreword on the strength of my personality alone. Fortunately, as one author's compliment to another, I read Jeff's book first and learned a great deal.

Jeff is able to raise to a conscious level what so many of us feel viscerally, but can't explain. He helps us to articulate our own successes, strengths, and special talents. I always viewed assertiveness as a double-edged sword, which meant that I had to be careful or else the "negatives" would outweigh the positives. Jeff teaches us, however, that there is no negative connotation to assertiveness if we view it correctly and use it appropriately.

He helps us understand—on a conscious level—that assertiveness is central to self-actualizing, self-confident, constructive people. Moreover, Jeff is able to transcend the stereotypical, and help us to become more assertive in a wide variety of environments and encounters. Some of us find it easy to face up to a bureaucrat, but difficult to confront a loved one. For others, the reverse is true. This book helps in all cases.

I'm a consultant, speaker, and author, and I work with some of the finest organizations and most talented, competitive, and dynamic people one could meet. Yet I also have to deal with support people, "backstage" people, passive people, and difficult people. Jeff helps us modulate our approaches so that we can be effective with virtually anyone, simply by being our naturally assertive selves. With Jeff's help, your professional and personal life will become easier.

The secret to high self-esteem and strong motivation is to adopt specific skills that generate results, continue to use them, continue to be successful, and continue to see ourselves in a positive light. That dynamic becomes both crystal clear and immediately accessible through the techniques and approaches of this book.

Jeff explores areas you simply don't visit in other works, discussing a variety of other critical but often-overlooked areas. As an entrepreneur, however, what I really enjoy about all of Jeff's 25 books, and particularly this one, is his unflagging focus on self-confidence, poise, and dignity. He eschews the belligerent and the manipulative, and despises the passive-aggressive. His approach is one of human worth, individual rights, and common sense. And he does this with an economy of language and a flair for pithy examples. What more can one ask for in a self-help book?

I've benefited from Jeff's advice, and I'm a recognized cynic; I wasn't even paid for this contribution to what will undoubtedly be thousands of additional book sales for him. More power to Jeff, and to you for being wise enough to select his work as a learning tool. Read and enjoy!

Alan Weiss, Ph.D., President
Summit Consulting Group, Inc.
Author, *Million Dollar Consulting*

Introduction

Have you ever felt like no one was listening to you? Or if they were listening to you, they didn't act on what you said? Do you find it hard to get people's attention? Do you find yourself saying yes when you would prefer to say no? If these and related issues have been tugging on your mind, perhaps you need to be more assertive.

Many people mistake being assertive with being overly aggressive, overbearing, or tactless. Some think that to be assertive you have to nag. Some people associate assertiveness with defensiveness. In truth, assertiveness need not encompass any of these things. Assertiveness, defined in simple terms, is nothing more than compelling self-assurance. Assertiveness as I refer to it in this book means an ability and willingness to easily speak up for yourself, and to make your viewpoint heard and known, without trampling on the rights of others.

If you feel as if you need the extra edge in day-to-day situations with others, you've come to the right place. *The Complete Idiot's Guide to Assertiveness* focuses on helping you develop positive assertiveness, actually enabling you to program—or reprogram—yourself for interpersonal and professional success.

Serious, but Light

Unlike other books on the topic, *The Complete Idiot's Guide to Assertiveness*, in the tradition of the *Complete Idiot's Guide* series, is humorous throughout, while delivering sound advice. I'm hoping you'll enjoy every page and want to keep reading. After all, it's no secret that we live in an over-communicated, over-informed, overly noisy society where practically everyone is having a harder time getting the attention of anyone else.

Kids have greater difficulty getting the attention of their parents. Employees have greater difficulty getting the attention of their boss. Spouses are finding it increasingly arduous to get the attention of each other. The need among many people to be appropriately assertive has, perhaps, never been greater.

As such, I've written *The Complete Idiot's Guide to Assertiveness* to cover effective methods for developing positive assertiveness, including where and when to be assertive, with whom, and why. If you want to improve your career prospects while avoiding dead ends, have a happier home life, and in general be more effective and persuasive in interpersonal exchanges, you've got the right book!

What You'll Find in This Book

The Complete Idiot's Guide to Assertiveness is divided into six sections. You can read the book from cover to cover, or you can browse through the Table of Contents to find the particular topics that interest you most. Here's how the book is organized.

In Part 1, "A Little Attention Please," I'll address general issues about assertiveness—what it is and what it isn't.

In Part 2, "A More Self-Confident You," I'll focus on a key component of becoming more assertive—increasing your self-confidence.

In Part 3, "I Assert, Therefore I Am," you'll find pivotal information about how to assert yourself and to get increasingly better at it.

In Part 4, "Assertiveness in Your Home Life," you'll learn all about being assertive at home—no easy feat!

In Part 5, "Assertiveness in Your Personal Life," I'll discuss assertiveness in everyday personal situations, including some special advice on assertiveness for women.

In Part 6, "Assertiveness in Your Professional Life," you'll discover how being assertive can make a difference in the workplace.

Extras

To guide you through the book, refer to the icons that contain boxed tips and information.

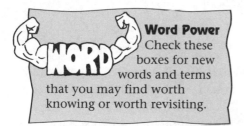

Word Power
Check these boxes for new words and terms that you may find worth knowing or worth revisiting.

Make It So
These boxes contain highly practical ideas and information that you can "run with."

Handle with Care
Check these boxes for suggestions on handling situations that require a sense of diplomacy, tact, and consideration for others.

Just the Facts

Longer factual material that may be of interest to you is presented in these boxes.

Acknowledgments

A profound thanks to all the talented crew at Alpha Books, who picked me once again to be an author in their hit series.

Thanks to Gretchen Henderson, Gary Krebs, Jennifer Perillo, Carol Sheehan, and Lynn Northrup for their guidance, careful editing, and excellent performances.

Thanks to Jeff Jackson in International Sales for getting this book translated around the free world. Thanks to Rachel in Subsidiary Sales for making sure that excerpts are printed everywhere it counts.

A big thank-you to Margaret Durante in Promotion for getting newspapers, magazines, and TV and radio stations to give me a call. Thanks to Gardi Wilkes for booking me on shows where the hosts were enthusiastic and supportive. Thanks also to my agent, Trent Price, for his endurance and fortitude.

I'd also like to thank my two part-time editorial assistants, Mittie Jones and Erika Meyers, for their talents, insights, and energy. I would also like to thank Sandy Knudsen for her lightening-fast fingers that glide over the keyboard like quicksilver. Last and most important, a special thanks to Valerie Anne Davidson, age 7, who knows how to stand up and speak up for herself anytime, and has given me a lot of pointers.

Trademarks

Part 1
A Little Attention Please

If it's always been hard for you to get the attention of others, to be heard, or to be followed, take heed. You're not alone. Millions of people feel the same way. In fact, even people who have considered themselves to be assertive most of their lives are finding themselves being increasingly unheeded. Why? Because we live in an over-communicated, over-informed, overly noisy society in which everyone is having a harder time getting the attention of everyone else. I believe, and evidence is piling up in abundance, that we've reached the point in our socio-cultural evolution where people have too many things competing for their time and attention and that this diminishes their ability to effectively interact with one another. In English, it means you've got to be more effective at being heard and being heeded. The chapters in this section all focus on a central theme: the growing importance of developing effective assertiveness skills in a world that is increasingly unable to offer its full attention.

Chapter 1

What Is Assertiveness and What Isn't?

In This Chapter

➤ Developing effective assertiveness techniques

➤ Why assertiveness has gotten a bad rap

➤ The difference between assertiveness and aggressiveness

➤ Learn why there's no need to nag

➤ How being assertive can help those around you

"Wow, you really asserted yourself when that guy at the auto repair shop suggested you might need hundreds of dollars worth of new parts."

"Gee, maybe I ought to take an assertiveness training course. I get such a hard time when I'm out at night."

"I'd like to be more assertive with my boss, but I'm afraid I'll end up getting fired."

Although you may hear language similar to these examples, what do such statements really convey? More importantly, if you learn to be assertive, will you save more money, keep creeps away, and gain a better bargaining position at work?

Will your whole life improve if you learn how to be assertive? Increasingly, the answer is YES! Being assertive is a valuable skill in a world where people don't listen to you; listen, but don't understand; or understand, but don't respond. In this chapter you'll learn what assertiveness really is, and how it can help you.

What Does it Mean to Be Assertive?

Assert, *assertive*, *assertiveness*, and other derivative words have many different meanings in many different dictionaries. In a nutshell, you have a fundamental right of sorts as a human being to express yourself, if in doing so you don't trample on the rights of others. You also have the right to make your needs known, and to say no and feel good about your decision.

Word Power
Being assertive means to speak or stand up for yourself or others without diminishing someone else's rights.

One school of thought is that there are three human response styles: passivity, assertiveness, and aggression. Assertiveness is the mid-level response. What do each of these response styles mean?

➤ *Passivity.* In this behavior, you confine your actions to certain narrow borders. For example, someone asks you to accompany them when you don't want to. You go along, but are inwardly resentful for having to do so.

➤ *Assertiveness.* In this behavior, you speak up or stand up for yourself or others without diminishing someone else's rights. For example, an assertive response to an unwanted invitation would be: "I appreciate the invitation, but I'll have to pass on it."

➤ *Aggressiveness.* In this behavior, you diminish someone else's basic rights, communicating in an uncivil or disrespectful manner. For example, an aggressive response to an invitation would be: "I would never accompany you. Disappear!"

Another school of thought holds that assertiveness is a multi-faceted, multi-dimensional element of behavior that has three main characteristics:

1. Conveying appropriate self-interest
2. Maintaining integrity
3. Upholding rights

Conveying Appropriate Self-Interest

When you display a capacity for determining what merits your time and attention, be it engaging in conversation or spending time with others, you are conveying appropriate self-interest. Other instances include pursuing your education or career, establishing priorities (see Chapter 3), forging relationships, and joining organizations, as well as following your own inner-wisdom and drawing on your ability to seek input from others. These are all basic, if less recognized, forms of assertiveness.

Maintaining Integrity

There's a kind of integrity that goes along with assertiveness—meaning what you say, when you say it, in the way that you say it. It is being free to effectively rebut and refute, or support and enhance other's views. While many people equate assertiveness with the ability to say no, it is more than that. Assertiveness is also having the ability to say yes, or saying yes within limits. It's having the ability to say maybe because you mean maybe, not because you're putting somebody off for fear of saying no.

Maintaining integrity encompasses dealing with others' judgments, disapproval, or hostility as it may arise.

Upholding Rights

Assertiveness is recognizing your rights as a person, taxpayer, consumer, group member, audience member, and the like to voice your opinion, observation, or concern without impeding the rights of others.

In this book, whenever you see the word "assertiveness" or any root words, consider it shorthand for "the process of exhibiting effective assertiveness techniques"—in other words, the ability to skillfully and tactfully ensure that you are heard, understood, and heeded. After all, why attempt to be understood if you can't get the other person to respond or act on what you said?

At no time in this book will assertiveness connote anything negative, such as being aggressive, overbearing, hostile, argumentative, angry, manipulative, or pushy. When I mean to convey those terms, I'll actually use them!

Why this distinction? Because many people associate assertiveness with negative behavior, such as being overbearing or rude.

A Positive Term

If I say it once, I'll say it a thousand times: assertiveness is a positive word. It relates to a skill that will enable you to:

➤ Feel better about yourself.

➤ Minimize any unpleasantness you may experience during a day.

➤ Potentially have better relations with others.

➤ Reduce stress.

➤ Potentially propel your career.

➤ Possibly vault yourself into a leadership position.

Not bad for a single skill, heh?

But slow down, speedo—being assertive won't guarantee success in life, love, work, or any place in between. It does aid enormously in establishing a climate in which effective relationships can flourish.

Physical Versus Vocal Assertiveness

Okay, so you know that assertiveness means standing up for yourself, maintaining your personal rights, and making your views heard and understood. It also means acknowledging the rights and feelings of others. Assertive behavior can be both physical (see Chapter 13) and vocal (see Chapter 6), and often, in the most effective cases, both dimensions are employed.

When it comes to safeguarding your space, your possessions, or even your own body, almost naturally you find yourself sitting or standing more erect. In essence, you're conveying to others through your body posture that you mean to stand your ground. You then use your voice in a manner that's honest and open to relate to others how you feel and what you need.

Developing or Exhibiting Effective Assertiveness Techniques

There are signs that tell you if you're being effectively assertive (hereafter simply referred to as being assertive):

➤ You get more of what you want.

➤ While others may not agree with you, they tend to respect your position more often.

➤ You don't feel as frustrated or irritated as you might otherwise feel.

➤ Situations that previously represented roadblocks no longer appear as such.

In general, more of your interpersonal communication and relationships go more smoothly more often than you previously might have thought possible. Why? Because you're able to impart to people what you want or feel in a manner that is direct yet tactful, forceful yet not demanding, captivating, and perhaps even motivating.

Nature or Nurture?

Is assertiveness something that is inherent among people to a greater or lesser degree? It seems as if every human characteristic can be traced to a gene these days. In recent years, scientists have found genes for hostility, risk taking, obesity, and, still in the research stage, neuroticism, which one researcher has dubbed the "Woody Allen Gene."

Perhaps you have a sister who, when younger, was ready to kick derriére at the drop of a hat, and a brother who would just as soon not rile anybody's feathers. Undoubtedly, some people, either at birth or along the way, did receive some extra assertiveness coupons. Today, among others, they serve as:

➤ Sales representatives

➤ Police officers

➤ Lawyers

➤ Reporters

➤ Disc jockeys

➤ Politicians

And the list goes on, but not necessarily in that order!

The Meek Shall Inherit...

Even if you've always been the shy and retiring type, you can learn to be assertive—certainly more assertive than you have been in the past. And with the purchase of this book, your chances just improved dramatically.

Assertiveness is not dependent upon your size, weight, gender, ethnic origin, or any of that jazz. People of all sizes and shapes and from all walks of life are assertive (just as people of all sizes and shapes from all walks of life are *not* assertive).

While size, musculature, articulation, vocabulary, and being male all tend to increase the probability that one is assertive, none of these factors needs be present for a person to be assertive. What's more, there are ways to be assertive without the benefit of these apparent natural advantages.

Assertiveness Has Gotten a Bad Rap

Within at least the last generation or so, people have associated assertiveness with other behaviors. For example, flying into a rage or treating others in a demeaning way is sometimes regarded as assertiveness. Yet, controlled or uncontrolled aggression is generally disruptive, not effective, and if anything, unassertive.

JUST THE FACTS MA'AM. **Just the Facts**

Aggressors may appear to get their way, at least in the short run, but generally they fail to win long-term cooperation. Consider the world's dictators and how often the people from their own countries rejoice once the dictators are deposed.

Aggression, Grrr!

Aggressiveness often encompasses manipulation. Aggressive people use anger, guilt, and reproaches to get their way. The other party feels the manipulation. They may give in to it, but they don't feel very good about it. However, when you encounter someone who uses assertive behavior, you don't feel as if your rights or feelings are being tread upon. When you consider the hundreds of potential interactions you have with people all day long, it becomes easy to understand why assertive behavior is vital for balanced, healthy relationships.

Think of it this way—being assertive gets you what you're seeking, or at least more of it more of the time. Being aggressive yields resignation or compliance at best, resistance and hostility at worst. With aggressiveness, you decrease rather than increase your chances for getting what you want.

Assertiveness Feels Good!

When you act aggressively, you actually lower your brain serotonin level; whereas when you act assertively, you increase your brain serotonin level. This results in that deep-down good feeling, what some people call the "warm fuzzies."

Because there is a physiological effect in the brain following an action, you can literally determine whether you were assertive or aggressive largely based on the way you feel. If you feel good, chances are you were assertive. If you feel bad—angry, upset, stressed, or depleted—chances are you were aggressive. In plain English, aggressiveness, volatility, or hostility exacts a toll.

If you find yourself overreacting in some situations, you may be releasing adrenaline, responding as if you're in a life-or-death situation. Your brain may be receiving external messages to respond with anger. Yet, if you're able to postpone taking action for even a few moments, other parts of the brain can receive signals that enable you to respond in a more balanced, rational way.

When you encounter someone who is assertive, you don't feel put down, manipulated, or dominated. If anything, you feel positive about the encounter, or at least neutral. Why? Because the respect that the other party has for you is evident.

There's No Need to Nag

Nagging can be seen as a way to manipulate others by using guilt with repetition:

> "You told me we were going to leave by 11:30."

> "You said you would make the phone call."

> "Did you get the newspaper like I asked?"

In each of these cases, the party making the statement is drawing on the emotions of another to accomplish something:

"You said x."

"You didn't perform x."

"Apparently you need reminding that you said x."

"I want to know when you're going to accomplish x."

In contrast, by using assertiveness in the same situations, neither party feels overly emotional:

"I'd like to leave at 11:30 as we agreed. Is that still doable?"

"Could you make the call now?"

"I'm looking forward to reading the news. Will you get the newspaper?"

Why do people nag? Perhaps they saw a parent doing this as they grew up, or they fell into a pattern and simply don't realize there are more effective ways to impart their wishes.

Handle with Care

Nagging, like aggression, may be effective in the short term, but it's not efficient. If you have to ask somebody repeatedly to get something accomplished, you're expending more energy than if you have to ask only once. Also, even if you get the other person to do what you want, you may do it in a way that alienates that person.

There's No Need to Be Offensive

People who haven't learned the fundamentals of being assertive often end up being offensive. Offensive behaviors incorporate everything we've discussed so far, such as aggressiveness; nagging; manipulating emotions; drawing on guilt, anxiety, and shame; being overly vocal; appearing threatening; and, in general, acting "not nice." Unfortunately, when it comes to human interaction, too often it's an either/or situation. You're either assertive or you aggravate, offend, or bore the other party in some way.

Assertiveness comes in handy, particularly with those with whom you'll be dealing on a recurring basis. It's one thing to let a poor customer service clerk have it when his or her company lets you down in some way. It's quite another when you're dealing with co-workers, spouses, and friends whom you will see again.

While it's sometimes difficult to know whether you have been assertive, it can also be hard to tell if you've offended someone. Fortunately, the clues you need to assess your effectiveness may be readily visible:

Word Power

To respond *vociferously* means to do so with gusto—a clue that you may have been regarded by another as aggressive, not assertive.

➤ Is the other party doing what you ask?

➤ Does he seem offended or angered?

➤ Is she responding vociferously rather than in normal tones at a normal amplitude?

➤ Does the conversation continue on an even keel rather than the other party clamming up?

➤ Does the level of cooperation increase following your request?

➤ Do you feel good about the interaction rather than experiencing an increase in stress somewhere within your body?

➤ Has the other person made an appropriate request in turn, usually following something that you've asked?

➤ Is it relatively easy to move on to other topics?

If you can answer yes to most of these questions, you've probably been assertive, not offensive.

Assertiveness Is Not the Opposite of Passivity

Because assertiveness has been misunderstood and perhaps incorrectly applied, some people (gasp!) go out of their way to actually avoid being assertive when the situation merits it. The passive person thinks, "If it ain't broke, don't fix it." This kind of person may hope that:

Handle with Care
Don't confuse passive behavior with *passive-aggressive* behavior, which involves cloaking one's feelings while seeking ways to "get even."

➤ Things will go his way.

➤ Others will correctly interpret what she wants.

➤ He can get through a day without having to confront others.

This kind of approach to interpersonal encounters often leads to frustration and disappointment rather than actually having yourself heard, understood, and heeded. Passivity leads to stress and anxiety because those who display it don't get their needs met.

A Different Animal: The Passive-Aggressive Type

Passive-aggressive individuals, like passive individuals, also prefer not to confront others—apparently never having learned assertive behavior. Yet, while they may not like what's happening to them, they do intend to get even, another time, in another way.

Just the Facts

Passive-aggressive types may deal in back-stabbing, spreading rumors, or being silent at opportune moments. If you ask them what's wrong, they're likely to say "nothing," because their real goal is not to resolve any potential conflict, but rather to inflict some sort of emotional pain or suffering upon you. They're hoping that you'll figure out what you've done wrong and not do it again in the future! Wow, and you thought life was tough enough to figure out as it is.

The problem with the passive-aggressive person's "lessons" is that you're rarely able to determine what he wants you to do, and instead experience other confrontations with him.

Unfortunately, identifying passive-aggressive behavior is tough. Passive-aggressive types use a subtle form of sarcasm, reproaches, manipulation, and even sabotage. None of these tend to be overt because, after all, they can't bear to confront you, so they stealthily put their "strategy" into place. Predictably, things seldom work out for the better.

Here is a summary of the behaviors we've covered thus far:

Assertiveness Versus Other Behaviors

Behavior	Seeks Objective Through...	Tends to Make the User Feel...	Makes the Other Party Feel...
Assertive	Direct communication	Good about the situation	Good about the communicator
Aggressive	Fear, threats, hostility	Anxious, bent out of shape, stressed	Angry, resentful, preyed upon
Manipulative	Emotional appeal, guilt	Ashamed of having to rationalize	Jerked around, used, taken advantage of
Offensive	Whatever it takes, immature behavior	Attacked, annoyed, "on the defensive"	Upset, put down, disrespected
Passive	Going along, not making waves	Powerless, lethargic	Domineering, imperialistic
Passive/ Aggressive	Teaching you a "lesson"	Victimized, wronged	Confused at first, then angry

Being Assertive Can Also Help Those Around You

Fortunately, you can identify someone who is aggressive, overly physical, nagging, offensive, or passive, and by being assertive, actually benefit the other party.

> **Make It So**
> When you communicate with others so as to draw them in and enlist their support, you've increased the probability of achieving what you were after.

When you're assertive, you stay in control. You draw on elements of effective interpersonal communication (the focus of most of this book), and you enable the other party to feel good about the encounter as well.

Think of assertiveness as having a goal that you're trying to achieve and setting up the groundwork for its realization. If you put down or turn off the other person when he could have helped you more easily achieve the goal, then you're engaging in self-defeating behavior.

Your assertiveness can help the other party in a variety of ways for a variety of reasons:

1. The way you communicate indicates that you respect the rights of the other party. Who doesn't like, want, and deserve respect? Consider people that you like. Chances are they convey some measure of respect to you, virtually every time you encounter them. So it is with those who are assertive.

2. Being assertive gives the other person room to maneuver. If you ask something of me, even something I don't expect or want to do, but you do it so that I feel good about your request, I have options. I can respond to you, perhaps handle your request, and not feel as if I've been collared. I don't need to get defensive or confrontational. Indeed, in honoring your request, I may be able to complete a promise I originally made to you.

3. Assertive behavior provides a model for effective responsiveness. If you've approached me in a way that appropriately gets my attention, implores that I listen, and urges me to act, you've also given me a formula for being assertive myself. Since much of the behaviors that we exhibit come as a result of what we see in others, it's advantageous to spend time around people who are assertive and pay attention to how they behave.

4. Being assertive is efficient. I find it ingratiating when somebody beats around the bush before making a request of me. You can see it coming from a country mile, and you almost want to say, "Out with it already."

   The beating-around-the-bush method of making requests between intimate partners or friends can, on occasion, be amusing. On a habitual basis it comes across as, at best, being wishy-washy and, at worst, manipulative. The assertive communicator gets right to the heart of the matter without being coarse or abrasive.

The Least You Need to Know

➤ In this book, assertiveness and all its root words mean developing or exhibiting effective assertiveness techniques.

➤ With assertive behavior, your brain experiences an increase in pleasure. With aggression, your brain experiences a decrease in pleasure and an increase in anxiety and stress.

➤ Assertive behavior helps both parties in a conversation feel good.

➤ Assertiveness can be learned.

➤ Being assertive helps those around you as well.

Chapter 2

The World as We Found It

In This Chapter

- ➤ Why it's harder for you to get anyone's attention
- ➤ The decline of service and attention
- ➤ Couples in crisis
- ➤ The decline of accessibility

Remember when the people at the supermarket checkout counter actually greeted you as a fellow human being? Remember when the tellers at the bank actually knew your name? Remember when you could call a company and actually speak to a real person who, more often than not, could actually put you in touch with the proper party? These are remnants from a world that used to exist but is rapidly disappearing.

In this chapter, I'll explain factors that make it harder for you to get anyone's attention, let alone get them to act on what you've said. Once you understand what the challenges are and the societal changes that have caused them, you'll be better able to manage your behavior to get the results you want.

Press "Two" for Service, Press "Three" for Returns...

If you've been hiding in a cave in France for the last 16 years, you're probably unaware of the emergence and dominance of voice-mail systems in western societies. Otherwise, undoubtedly, you've listened to more menus with more options and more numbers to press than you had ever wanted to or believed would be requested of you.

Technology can be a wonderful thing. For example, people don't have to go deep into mine shafts to dig because machinery can do it. Most people would agree that this is a benefit to society. Sure, some jobs may be replaced, but who wants to work deep in the mines anyway?

At organizations throughout the world, telephone receptionists and customer service representatives are being replaced. At the current rate of replacement, they one day will be as rare as dodo birds. From a profit and loss standpoint, it's easy to understand why organizations would rather have robots answer their phones than people. A whole year's worth of salary and benefits that the company doesn't have to pay, no vacation time, no sick time, and no complaints can be quite attractive.

> **Just the Facts**
>
> Whatever the technology costs, it's usually far less than having a person in that position. Studies by prominent management magazines have borne this out time and time again. The cold reality in industrialized nations is that machines often replace people, whereas people rarely replace machines.

> **Word Power**
> When you use an expression or example to refer to something that it does not literally denote in order to suggest a similarity, you're using a *metaphor*. Metaphors add power to your speech by evoking associations that make other people respond more strongly or more quickly.

Even if the company installs an 800 number so that customers call at the company's expense, the overall cost of handling calls in this manner is still bound to be less than installing one person in the same position. The underlying philosophy is that as long as callers eventually reach their destination, all is fairly well. Never mind if the callers were frustrated, had to listen to eight inane choices, and even then didn't get the service or satisfaction that they wanted on the first couple of tries.

The metaphor of voice-mail systems—what you have to endure to reach your party—typifies developments throughout our society. No one is listening, or if anyone is, it's because they've figured out ways to harness technology so that they don't have to actually deal with you.

Start the Revolution Without Me

Fine, you say; as consumers we'll revolt. We won't do business with people or organizations that subject us to endless decisions via voice mail. What happens when, say, all airlines put you on hold, when all retail stores have switched to voice-mail systems, or when one industry after another subjects you to a voice-mail system?

16

Technology designed to aid interpersonal communications, business efficiency, and dispensing of products and services, is often used as a screen, mask, dodge, way to hide, way to delay service, way to screen calls, and, if you're in the federal government, a way to ignore citizens altogether. Because it's not likely that this trend is going to reverse itself soon, people have already begun to develop strategies to effectively get their messages through in spite of having to cope with endless voice-mail selections.

Many books on marketing, for example, now suggest that you have a 30-second message rehearsed so that when you encounter voice mail or an answering machine, you'll be able to succinctly fire off everything you want to say with one breath, leave your phone number, and get off the line before you hear that irritating recording, "Your message has exceeded the limit," if you hear it at all.

Such books also offer alternative ways of getting your message through (such as using fax and e-mail), most of which are probably familiar to you. In fact, texts on this singular phenomenon—getting through to prospects who have arranged their work and home life so as to not be reached easily—practically represent their own genre!

> **Word Power**
> When your speech or actions are *succinct*, they proceed in a brief and efficient manner. Being able to state your position or make a request using succinct language improves the response you get, because you've made yourself clear and haven't wasted anyone's time.

Just the Symptom

If the inability to reach others via the telephone and other readily available technology was the core of the problem, and not symptomatic of a much larger issue, I could devote all of my attention to assisting you in this narrow realm and I would only need about 20 pages. However, the challenge of getting through to others is much larger.

Whether you're a naturally assertive person, shy and retiring, or somewhere in the middle, increasingly, in all arenas of society in which you interact with another person, it's becoming more difficult to be heard, understood, and heeded. To understand why, let's explore other converging issues.

A Quarter-Million More People Per Day and Counting

Suppose I told you that every four days, there are one million more people on earth?

Suppose you learned that every two years and nine months, the world gains a population count (live births minus deaths) equal to the current population of the United States—275 million people? In fact, every decade, the earth gains four times the current population of the United States.

Would such information shock you? Would you be upset? Would you begin to understand the ramifications of a world facing exponential human population growth?

As you've guessed by now, everything I just said is true. I don't wish it to be this way. You probably don't wish it to be this way. Reality being what it is, however, you and I are part of a world population growing to 10.5 billion people by the year 2050 or so. At that point, demographers say that the population will level off.

From the standpoint of supply and demand, some areas of the world are certainly going to be in dire need of food, water, and natural resources. History tells us that in cases of severe overcrowding, calamities such as fires, flood, typhoid, viral and bacterial breakouts, and other phenomena that you wouldn't even wish on your mother-in-law, have a vastly improved chance of occurring. Keep in mind that for everyone, not just you, it is harder to be heard, understood, and heeded now than perhaps at any time in at least the last century.

High Density, Low Manners

New York City, with its eight-million-plus population, is often regarded by outsiders as a place where people are brusque, uncaring, and constantly in a hurry. It would be easy to pick on New York as an example of how the individual is quashed in a densely packed environment, so let's begin.

Make It So
To thrive in a densely populated western urban environment, you have to be assertive—there isn't much way to get around it.

When you live and work in an overcrowded area where traffic is a mess all the time, long lines are the norm, and many people perceive they have to fight tooth and nail to make it through the day, it's predictable that the quality of responsiveness among service providers, even to their key customers, might decline.

Walk into a typical New York City bank. Even if you have a million dollars invested there, the teller is not likely to know your name and in many cases won't even look it up during your entire transaction. In an environment where you're a number, not a name, or where so many people are prostrate on the sidewalk that you can't stop to deal with them all, it's understandable that individuals feel depersonalized.

If you live in New York or Los Angeles or some other teeming metropolis, all other things equal, your need for this book is likely to be somewhat less than that of other people. Not so curiously, when New Yorkers are out of their native environment, visiting other parts of the country, it's often easy to spot them. They have been politely characterized as loud, pushy, and abrasive. At least that's the way it seems to the folks in Podunk or Pocatello.

Your environment can have a profound effect on how assertive you need to become in this life. At the tail end of that observation is another—as all rural, suburban, and urban areas increase in population as a natural function of simply being in such an environment, most everyone feels an enhanced need to assert themselves more often than previously to continue to be heard, understood, and heeded.

Numbers Don't Lie

You can't fight the sheer numbers; in a world of six and one-half billion people and counting, where exponential population growth since the 1960s has been the norm (incidentally, there were only three billion people in the world in 1960), and where the population density has more than doubled since 1962, each person's ability to be heard is challenged.

Here's a recap of how much the population density per square mile has increased in this century:

➤ 1936: 38

➤ 1966: 59

➤ 1996: 100

➤ 2026: 160?

This Update Is Brought to You By...

If you thought advances in technology that enable people to screen themselves from others and an ever-increasing world population density weren't enough, you neglected to consider a third factor. The sheer volume of information that you're exposed to also has significant impact on your ability to catch the attention of someone else.

If you travel for your work, you know that there's a CNN monitor about every 50 paces in just about every major hub airport in America. These ill-placed television sets bring you the "up-to-the-minute news" so you won't be "deficient" or a couple seconds behind the rest of the world in terms of what's happening. The only problem is that these updates don't represent news.

Handle with Care
Most of the information that you get today via news and information services is from carefully crafted packages paid for by the organization or person featured. So think twice before believing anything vaguely resembling a "news feature."

By some estimates, at least 75 percent of all the features and profile pieces you read in newspapers and magazines have been "placed." The features and profiles you see are part of a coordinated effort, undertaken and funded by the company or individual publicized.

"Notice Me." "No, Notice Me."

Because publishers have long known of the healthy number of executives and entrepreneurs in their community who wish to be written about and who have the funds to commission an article, they often get their material for free.

If you're not aware of this phenomenon, it may seem to you that others in your industry or profession do so spectacularly well that they generate spontaneous press coverage. Hmmm…wonder why the roving reporter never makes it to your door? Unless your house is on fire, pal, nobody's coming to interview you, until you partake of the process and get yourself a PR agent!

The small percentage of items broadcast and printed each day that do actually represent news are presented to us in endless variations. It's not enough that xyz candidate is charged with campaign donation irregularities, then you and I have to hear about it all day, all week, all month, from every conceivable angle and news source.

Would you believe there are 1,800 reporters who cover the White House on a daily basis? Couldn't, say, 300 reporters do the job and maybe share their insights with everyone else?

The volume and quality of information we're all subject to beyond news and attempts at portraying information as news is staggering. The typical issue of *Orbit* magazine, which carries television programming for people who have satellite dishes, lists more than 61,000 television programs a month. To give you an idea of how much programming 61,000 shows is equal to, if you watched six hours of television a day every day for 31 years, you would have watched 61,000 shows.

Direct to Your Living Room: The Average Number of Programs Listed in *Orbit*	
Within 60-minute period	84 shows
Within 24 hours	2,006 shows
Within 7 days	14,046 shows
Within 1 month	61,000 shows
Within 1 year	732,000 shows

Deluged Around the Clock

Obviously, no one person on earth is subject to this amount of information. The magnitude of information to which we are all exposed vastly exceeds that of any previous generation in the history of the earth. You live in a world where more information is generated in an hour than you could take in the rest of your life.

JUST THE
FACTS MA'AM.

Just the Facts

I calculated the volume of broadcasts and publications presently available and added a conservative growth factor over the next several years. The conclusion: Within a few years, more information will be generated in one minute than you could take in the rest of your life.

Think about this; every minute, more than a lifetime of information is generated. Thankfully, you're not exposed or impacted by 99.9 percent of it. The dramatic effects, however, are readily abundant. Drop too much information in the lap or the mind of anybody and he or she will become overwhelmed, agitated, perhaps even disoriented. Spew a constant stream of news and information at everybody throughout society all day long in all directions, and you'll end up with a population that has an increasingly difficult time with the following:

➤ Determining what's important

➤ Interacting with others

➤ Achieving agreement or consensus

➤ Simply being heard

The State of the Union

Consider how difficult it is for the man who is arguably the most powerful person on Earth to be heard. I'm talking about the president of the United States. Findings from the U.S. Election Commission, League of Women Voters, Nielsen's Rating Service, and Library of Congress reveal that most people:

➤ Do not vote in elections.

➤ Do not watch the Inauguration or Inaugural address.

➤ Do not watch the State of the Union addresses.

➤ Do not read *The Federal Register*.

➤ Have no idea what executive letters have been signed.

When the President and (for now) his spouse want to convey a message, it often has to be simple, short, and pounded into the heads of targets. Consider Nancy Reagan's "Just Say No" message. You can scoff at it, and say it was or wasn't effective. It's one of the few things, however, we remember about the Reagan administration.

The very reason why we pay so much attention to the phenomenon of sound bytes is the resulting hyper-explosion of information that infiltrates every corner of our society. In a world where so much data is thrown at so many people for so many hours each day, the 30-second sound byte, predictably, is all, if anything, that could get through to the electorate.

Hence, a "thousand points of light," "building a bridge to the 21st century," or other equally inane, meaningless drivel are often all that linger in one's memory following four- and eight-year presidential administrations.

If the commander-in-chief has a hard time getting through, what chance do you and I have? Fortunately, with the help of this book, your chances have dramatically improved. I've got to give it to you straight, though; this will take some effort on your part. As sure as your eyes are glancing across the words on this page, it's getting more difficult for people to simply hear each other.

Six Minutes of Quality Time

The steady stream of books coming out in the last decade or two about making relationships work is testament to the fact that men and women are having a harder time being understood. Whether it's *Men Are From Mars, Women Are From Venus*, or *You Just Don't Understand*, the market for such tomes seems to be insatiable. People want to know how to get along, particularly in an intimate relationship.

You've probably encountered articles stating things such as, "The typical couple spends only six minutes together each day in conversation," or "The average couple has only a minute and 30 seconds of quality time each day." I don't know how anybody can come up with such information, unless they have built hidden video camcorders into the walls and ceilings of every place a couple might go in the course of a day, and have monitored the couple's conversation for weeks on end, along with several thousand other couples, to derive an average. It's a little like the Ann Landers observation a few years ago that the typical woman kisses 65 men before she kisses the man she's going to marry. I mean, how absurd! How could anybody generate such data?

Handle with Care

Whether it's a minute and 30 seconds, six minutes, or 40 minutes, if your partner is tired, frazzled, over-informed, and feeling lucky just to make it back home, it's unlikely that he or she is going to be in a highly responsive mood when you're ready to pour out your heart.

Like, take Stat 101!

Nevertheless, even if observations and "calculations" about the amount of time couples spend actually conversing with each other are off by a factor of five or six, we're still talking about people who are in intimate relationships and only converse with each other for less than 40 minutes a day.

You can't force "quality time" (if there even is such a concept) in between long stretches of frenzied activity. And, if you happen to be in a relationship with a workaholic, overachiever, or someone who is simply stressed to the max, how effective do you think anything you say to him is going to be? How effective would you be if your partner was rested, balanced, and in harmony with nature? I rest my case.

Even Your Mother Has an Answering Machine

Now for an easy quiz. Please get out a number-two soft lead pencil and answer the following four questions. Please be sure to keep your eyes on your own paper; otherwise, you're only cheating yourself.

1. In the future, will there be more technology in our lives or less?
2. Will there be more people in the future or fewer?
3. Will we be besieged by more information or less?
4. Will intimate partners face more impediments or fewer?

How to grade your score: If you answered "less" or "fewer" from one to four times, immediately reread this chapter. If you wrote "more" for all four questions, give yourself an "A." Your grasp of reality is sufficient to continue on to the next chapter.

You see, when even your own mother has an answering machine, it's a safe bet that before too long, everyone will be "wired." Then, your machine will call my machine about the message your machine left for my machine last week, and you and I will be out of the loop altogether! The only people who will encounter each other will be sleep-walkers, and they won't have much to say.

Tell Me to My Face

You could make the argument that no matter how technological the world becomes, how many people are added to it, how much news we're hit by, and how many impediments to being heard develop, there will always be situations in which people converse with one another. I agree. From employees responding to their boss, to a teacher lecturing her students, to a father and son on a fishing expedition, to a baseball manager in sight of an umpire, we will always have things to say to one another on a personal, face-to-face basis.

What will be the quality of the interaction, however? Will the parties actually listen? What's the quality of your interaction with others today? Has it been improving in recent years, staying the same, or declining? I'll bet it's slightly declined, perhaps through no fault of your own.

I'll bet you're finding it harder to get people to return your phone calls, harder to get the IRS to respond to your tax question, harder to have your children do what you say, and harder to have your co-workers understand you.

If any of this is true, even a little part of it, you're probably going to want to know how to be more assertive. With that, let's turn to Chapter 3, on when to be assertive, so that we can get you back into the winner's circle.

The Least You Need to Know

➤ Communication technology designed to enhance peoples' ability to contact one another more often is used as a screen to avoid contact.

➤ Human population is experiencing exponential growth, resulting in an increased population density in virtually every corner of the planet.

➤ More information is generated in an hour than you could ingest in the rest of your life, and too much information in your life in general decreases your ability to respond to others.

➤ Couples and intimate partners today face major impediments to communicating effectively with one another, and this is perhaps unprecedented in at least the last 100 years.

➤ When your own mother has an answering machine, it's a sign that it's going to be tougher to reach anyone, let alone be heard, understood, and heeded.

WHO DO I HAVE TO
KILL TO GET MORE
BREAD!!

Chapter 3

Where and When to Assert Yourself

In This Chapter

➤ Knowing what you want

➤ What's worth fighting for

➤ A short course on decision-making

➤ Identifying priorities and supporting goals

You're standing in a bank line waiting to take care of some routine matters when the customer ahead of you gets into a spat with the teller. It seems that this customer's checks will be put on hold for a few days before he'll be able to receive cash for them. He's not happy about it and makes his opinion known. Meanwhile, you're waiting and starting to feel irritated. Do you speak up? After all, you've got other things to do today.

You're meeting your fiancée's parents for the first time at a dinner they're holding in your honor at their home. You're seated at the table when you notice a dead fly in the potato salad. No one has been served. No one else seems to notice. Should you sound the alert?

Your co-worker is making a presentation to your team. He's doing a good job and everyone is impressed. After about five minutes, however, you detect a major problem. You know for certain that one of the assumptions upon which he heavily relies is wrong. Therefore, he needs to redirect most of his presentation. Do you say something? If so, when, and to whom?

In this chapter you'll learn to recognize when it's important to assert yourself, and when it's better not to.

What's Worth Fighting for and What's Best Left Alone

In the first scenario I described, when you're standing in the bank line, there are some compelling reasons for you to say nothing:

➤ You know when you enter a bank that there is a good chance you will wait in a line. No surprises here.

➤ Although you may be irritated, feeling that the customer in front of you is causing an unnecessary delay, chances are that even if you decide to say something, you won't finish up any more quickly than without speaking up.

➤ The unpleasant feelings that you may experience as a result of your speaking may not be worth speaking up in the first place.

Soon it will be your turn. Then you'll be out of the bank, and the delay will be forgotten. Maybe another teller will come on duty, or you'll put your time to better use by focusing on what you want to accomplish that afternoon or how you want to feel in general.

In the second scenario, when you're at dinner and you spot the fly, you have a variety of options.

➤ You could say something diplomatic and slightly amusing, such as, "Oh my, it looks like we have an unwelcome visitor in the potato salad." Since you're new at the table, you want to keep things light. Undoubtedly, your fiancée's parents will feel a bit embarrassed. Think of it as an opportunity for you to play the diplomatic, charming, future son-in-law.

➤ You could nudge or make eye contact with your fiancée, directing her to the tainted plate. Undoubtedly, your fiancée will take over, and your job is largely done. After everyone joins in the discovery and expresses their embarrassment, you could say something such as, "Oh yes, that happened to us once," or "Well, it's a good thing we found out now, rather than later."

There are two more options, neither of which is recommended:

➤ You could not say anything and hope that someone else makes the discovery. But, you run the risk that no one else makes the discovery, and someone ends up ingesting a dead fly.

➤ You could wait until the potato salad is parceled out, wait to see who receives the ill-fated portion, and hope that he or she notices.

In the third scenario, when a co-worker is about to lead your team down the wrong path, the need to assert yourself seems pretty clear. It's simply a question of how. The most tactful way would be to get your co-worker's attention and ask if you could speak to him for a minute. You can do this by using a look, a nod, a whisper, or a note. If you have a break coming up, then that is your best opportunity.

Handle with Care
It's never a good idea to just say something if you might humiliate someone.

Your goal is to stop the presentation as politely and unobtrusively as possible for the sake of your co-worker, if not for the sake of the entire team. Once he has the same information that you do, he'll want to postpone the meeting for now, or if he's quick on his feet, perhaps redirect the remaining portion of the presentation.

It behooves you to make a move. Otherwise, you're wasting everyone else's time and setting up your co-worker for embarrassment later.

The $64,000 Question

In the three earlier scenarios, I advised saying nothing in the first instance and speaking up in the latter two. None of these situations is necessarily crucial to your long-term health or well-being or to the other parties involved, although the co-worker making the presentation based on a wrong assumption could potentially suffer some repercussions.

So, what's a nice reader like you to make of this? Here are guidelines for asserting yourself when the issues confronting you are not earth-shattering:

1. *Respect the position and feelings of the other parties involved.*

    The man ahead of you in the bank line is already flustered because the teller won't cash his checks. His actions are relatively understandable. After all, hasn't this ever happened to you? By speaking up, you will not improve his situation. You might give moral support to the teller, but you could always do that after the first customer leaves.

    In the dinner scenario, your immediate goal is to make sure that no one ingests a dead fly and that any embarrassment anyone might feel is minimized.

    Likewise, with the co-worker making the presentation, you wish to unobtrusively get his attention, so he can make a decision as to what to do, given the information you have to impart.

2. *Remain in balance.*

    In the bank line, you're better off waiting the extra minute or two, even if you are a little flustered, than to let your emotions get the best of you and speak out when it's the teller's responsibility to handle the situation.

At dinner, obviously you wouldn't want to say, "Oh my God, look at the dead fly in the potato salad. How disgusting!" Even if this is what you really feel, expressing yourself in this way would come across as too strong. You'd disrupt the atmosphere at the dinner and put the onus on the others to restore it.

In the case of the co-worker's presentation, it's easy to understand how you might feel excited once you hear him going down the wrong path. However, blurting out what you feel and potentially disrupting the meeting, especially in the case where you have respect for your co-workers, would create a undesirable situation. Keeping your emotions in check is related to the third element: with malice toward none.

3. *Proceed with malice toward none.*

Certainly in the latter two cases, there's no reason for you to act with anything less than concern for the others. In the first instance, the bank line, you may have no concern for the customer in front of you, but unless this customer is blatantly abusive and the teller ostensibly lacks the skills to handle the situation, you're better off saying nothing. Even if the situation turns out to be horrendous, you're still better off saying nothing. After all, there are other tellers, the bank manager, and who knows who else who could step in if the situation merited it. It's simply not your place either to say something or display malice.

4. *Make a time check.*

Ask yourself, "How will I feel about the situation tomorrow, in one hour, or in even five minutes?" Chances are, five minutes after departing the bank, you won't even think about the delay. So, your decision to say nothing is well advised. At dinner, since you're the only one who can see the fly in the potato salad, a day, hour, or five minutes later you'd still feel bad if it was served to someone. Your decision to speak up is clearer. The same is true with your co-worker making a presentation based on a false assumption.

The common denominator to these three scenarios is that they all represent minor situations that are likely to pass quickly. Now to a larger concern: You might be good at both holding your tongue and speaking up as the situation merits under such scenarios, but how are you when pursuing larger, more important issues?

Before You Can Assert Yourself, You Have to Know What You Want

By establishing priorities in your life, you more readily know when to speak up and when to let things ride, what's worth fighting for, and what's best to walk away from. Let's focus on clarifying what's important to you, and how prioritizing helps you in your decision-making, which, in turn, helps you stand up for yourself, your family, your organization, and your community.

Too Many Priorities Equals No Priorities

When asked to list their priorities, most people end up listing too many. Suppose you compose a list of 19 areas in your life that are most important to you. By definition, they can't all be priorities. Why? How can you, or anyone for that matter, closely pay homage to 19 different aspects of life? I'm not saying how many priorities you need to have to be realistic, but for most people the number is somewhere between four and nine.

> **Make It So**
> Whatever you do when selecting priorities, remember to keep the number manageable. The fewer the priorities, the more energy and effort you lend to each of them.

When assessing what's important to you in life, here are some potential category headings. Later you can modify these or pick entirely new ones. For example, your priorities might come from one or more of these basic areas:

➤ Personal: health, welfare, finances, intellect, interests, recreation, love, sexual fulfillment

➤ Family: health, welfare, lifestyle, children's education, recreation, enrichment, reverence

➤ Friends, relatives: health, welfare

➤ Community, region: appearance, prosperity, schools, institutions

➤ Country, fellow citizens: security, quality of life, freedoms, pursuit of happiness, opportunity, justice

To further clarify, the things most meaningful to you in life are, by definition, your priorities. Priorities are broad elements of life, so broad that they often become misplaced somewhere within your daily high-wire balancing act. Remember, if you have too many priorities, you're not likely to respect each of them. Now then:

➤ List everything that is important or that you wish to accomplish.

➤ Hours and even days later, go back and assess your list. Drop the nice, but on second inspection, not-so-important items.

➤ Combine any items that are similar in nature. Having too many priorities leads to frustration and despair.

➤ Rewrite, redefine, or restructure any of your choices. If you're not sure of an item, feel free to delete it.

➤ Put your list away for another day, then review it again.

➤ Delete, combine, or rethink any of the items remaining. If something seems less important, drop it. You cannot afford to have more priorities than you can support.

➤ Complete your list, for now—priorities can change.

Here are some examples of priorities you might choose:

"Provide for the education of my children."

"Achieve financial independence."

"Maintain my loving, happy marriage."

"Work for world peace."

Your priorities may change radically as the years pass. They are always based on deeply felt needs or desires, usually representing challenging but ultimately rewarding choices.

It helps to boil everything down to what I call Your Priority Card. For maximum benefit, I suggest that you write or print out your priorities on small business-size cards. Keep one in your wallet, one in your appointment book, and one in your car.

Read your priorities list as often as you can. As you'll see, reading this list frequently contributes to your sense of staying in control—it's invigorating when you're actively supporting what you've chosen as important.

It isn't overkill to review a list of your life's priorities EVERY DAY. Now, armed with a concise list or card of those things you identified as important in your life, it's easier for you to proceed through your day, week, and year, knowing when to assert yourself and when not to. The criterion becomes this: Is the situation confronting you directly related to one of your priorities? If so, you have a good indication to speak up in this situation. If not and you choose to say nothing, it's likely that "This too shall pass."

A Short Course on Decision-Making

Even if you're totally clear about your priorities, one issue after another, big and not so big, will arise to challenge you. My friend has a poster on his wall that reads, "Not to decide is to decide." If you haven't made a decision, that alone is a form of decision—a choice *not* to take action.

Decisions worth making are not always apparent. Is it important to decide the color of the next toothbrush you buy? The next movie you see? It may seem important at the time, but of all the movies you've seen, how many have had a profound impact on you? What about attending the next PTA meeting? If your children are doing well, or the school system is strong, it may not be necessary to go. While the big, important decisions to make in your life may be readily identifiable, there will be a host of decisions of varying degrees of importance that will only be important for a fleeting amount of time.

Most decisions you make are of no long-term importance—in many instances, they're not even of short-term importance. It may be hard to grasp, but even with career decisions, you can sometimes go back and change something. Even if you make a fundamentally bad decision to assert yourself over something at work, it won't be so bad if you're generally producing good work and doing a good job. Most decisions have no significant impact.

You Make the Call

Here are some situations that you might encounter. In each instance, would you assert yourself or not?

1. You make an appointment with a doctor. You specifically make it for early in the morning because you're told that at that time there will be the shortest delay, if any. You're kept waiting for more than 15 minutes. When you finally get to see the doctor, should you say anything? Should you say anything to the office staff?

   Personally, I would comment to the office staff after about 20 minutes. I have a friend, however, who has a unique approach to waiting for others that you might want to employ. He says, "If a doctor keeps me waiting for more than 15 minutes, I send him an invoice for my time, usually based on $75 an hour. My invoices don't get paid, but I never have to wait again."

2. The coach of your son's little league team doesn't seem to have his act together. For one thing, he doesn't let your son play often enough, even though your son objectively is a better player than some of the others. Do you speak up about this?

   This is a tough call, but my advice is to not interfere. Your son may feel disappointed, and the coach's decision not to play him often enough could be detrimental to the success of the team. There are, however, overriding factors. You can't fight your son's battles, at least not all of them. Also, parents, in general, do too much meddling when it comes to their kids' affairs, particularly in regard to the little league. In some cases, it's outright embarrassing to everyone concerned.

Handle with Care
Helping your child emotionally will better prepare him for different coaches, teachers, bosses, and others in life who may not always give him a fair shake. In perspective, this is just one coach and one season in your son's baseball "career." There will be other coaches, other sports, and other seasons.

You can work with your son both on his baseball game and his emotional development. Helping him to become an even better player will increase the odds that the coach will notice him in practice and let him play more often.

What if other parents are speaking up to the coach about their sons' playing time? Now, you think, you have a perfect right to speak up as well, but don't. Human nature being what it is, the coach may let your son play more often if other parents speak up about their sons! The coach may resent meddling by outsiders.

JUST THE FACTS MA'AM.

Just the Facts

When University of South Carolina basketball coach Eddie Fogler was subjected to squabbling by the relatives of players on his team, he took the only route a coach could take. Mired with a 5-5 record, including some losses to traditionally weak teams, Fogler told the relatives point blank to butt out. He then reshuffled his lineup in accordance with what he felt was best. The team went on to win 18 out of the next 19 games and captured their first-ever Southeastern Conference Championship, beating the highly ranked Kentucky Wildcats.

3. You're good friends with the couple that lives down the block. You conclusively discover that one spouse is cheating on the other. What do you do?

   By now you're thinking, here's a time when I'm going to speak up. I need to let the spouse who's being cheated on know what's happening.

   I recommend you say nothing. Spouses have a way of knowing when all is not right between them. It's not your place to step in, even to send an anonymous note.

4. You're playing in a pickup basketball game with some regulars when two of them collide going for a rebound. They get into a heated exchange that may escalate. Should you step in?

   Keep watching. You'll know in seconds whether the incident will conclude or turn in a nasty direction. If it's getting worse, assert yourself. You don't want the people involved to start fighting and perhaps get thrown out of the gym. Also, since you're part of the game and what's taking place is disrupting the game, you have an "athlete's right" of sorts to get the game back on track. (By stepping in, however, you do run the risk of getting slugged yourself!)

   As a legitimate third-party observer to the spat, however, if you forcefully say something like, "C'mon, let's get back to the game," or "All right, let's keep this in perspective," your input may help to alleviate the situation. Moreover, it's not likely that either of the participants is going to have any lingering negative feelings toward you. This kind of stuff happens, and the quicker it's over with, the better.

5. You learn from a co-worker that the boss is going to choose someone else for a promotion you've had your eye on. You're meeting with the boss this afternoon about something else. Should you speak up?

   Yes. Take advantage of the opportunity with your boss to present or reiterate your case. The best approach is to ease into the topic area and try to get the boss to tell you the same thing you heard from a co-worker.

   I'll cover professional assertiveness in Chapter 21.

6. You walk into a sandwich shop and you see one counter person working with a customer. Another worker is at the drink machine, and a third is in the back slicing up something. A fourth worker is cleaning tables at the far end of the establishment. You've been standing there for at least two minutes now, and none of the four employees seems to notice or acknowledge your presence. Do you say, "Ahem," or "Excuse me," or do you simply wait like a good soldier until it's "your turn"?

Forget speaking up; practice restraint. You want to speak up in those situations where it's clearly called for. In this one, I would pick a time limit, say another minute or perhaps two minutes, whereby if someone didn't tend to me, I would simply leave the establishment. Given it's not the only sandwich shop in town and you're not dying of hunger, vote with your feet.

If enough people were to leave under the same circumstances, management might get the message. Even if others don't do what you do, you get the opportunity to find another establishment that offers more responsive service.

> **Make It So**
> In work-related situations, particularly in relation to promotions, assertiveness is the order of the day. You don't get ahead by sitting back and being meek and mild. This is the time to toot your own horn. You're even *expected* to do this.

> **Handle with Care**
> Attempting to train employees that customers such as you keep a restaurant in business is futile. If they're not aware of this fundamental truth of business life before you walk in, why would they understand only minutes later?

Self-Confidence Is the Key to It All

In each of the situations I've discussed, the more self-confident you are (the subject of Part 2 of this book), the clearer it becomes whether you need to assert yourself. There's almost an inverse relationship between self-confidence and the need to be assertive. In other words, the more self-confident you are, the less often you need to be assertive. The highly self-confident person who experiences a put-down may not feel compelled to respond in kind.

Concurrently, the highly self-confident person knows when to speak up and can do so rather easily. As you learned in Chapter 1, it's a pleasure to be around people who are assertive, because they know how to state their case in a manner that makes other people feel good about it.

It's painful to be around people who feel compelled to assert themselves all day long, because they don't have a clear idea of what merits their speaking up and what doesn't. In that respect, understanding your priorities, maintaining self-confidence and self-control, and achieving an "assertive balance" is probably the most admirable combination of traits you can have.

The Least You Need to Know

➤ Most issues in which you feel you may need to assert yourself, in retrospect, are insignificant and are best left alone.

➤ Before deciding to assert yourself, make sure that you respect the feelings of others, are not overly emotional, have no malice toward others, and are speaking up over an issue that will have some impact five minutes, an hour, or a day later.

➤ By identifying the handful of priorities you have in life (knowing what you want), you have a clearer indication as to when to assert yourself.

➤ Most people have too many priorities and, hence, an unclear idea of what's truly important to them in life.

➤ You're going to encounter an endless variety of situations in which you'll have to decide whether or not to assert yourself. A surprising number of times, the best route may well be to *not* assert yourself.

Chapter 4

Assertiveness Through the Ages

In This Chapter

➤ Assertiveness in recent history

➤ Assertiveness in religion

➤ Assertiveness in the arts

Throughout history people have asserted themselves at critical junctures and become immortalized for it:

➤ Moses told the Egyptian pharaoh, "Let my people go."

➤ Jesus told an unruly crowd, "Let he that lives without sin cast the first stone."

➤ Martin Luther nailed his 99 reforms to the door of the Catholic church knowing this would set off a landslide of controversy.

➤ George Washington confessed to his father that he did in fact chop down the cherry tree, saying, "I cannot tell a lie," (or at least that's how the story goes).

➤ Martin Luther King, Jr. delivered his famous "I Have a Dream" speech but, of equal note, endured many years in jail and discrimination for what he believed in.

We tend to admire those who are assertive, especially in support of broad sweeping causes such as freedom, truth, and human rights. It seems as if bold and assertive statements and bold and decisive action have been the rallying points for followers to take up the lead.

They are certainly turning points that historians dutifully record. In this chapter we'll look at a specific instance where one person's assertiveness had dramatic impact.

I Came, I Saw, I Made My Wishes Known

Even people who are assertive for less than noble reasons tend to stand out in history. Indeed, the Latin phrase *veni, vidi, vici* ("I came, I saw, I conquered") lingers in memory for its sheer audacity, if nothing else.

The German philosopher Johann Wolfgang von Goethe once said, "Boldness has genius, power and magic in it." In an overly communicative society, assertiveness, in the form of boldness and brashness, is often the key to notoriety, wealth, and even acclaim. For example, while there might be eight, 12, 15, or several dozen female singers with the range, voice quality, and talent equal to or exceeding that of Madonna, she has captured the most headlines in the 1980s and early 1990s, sold the most albums, and has consistently sold-out concert tours.

Andre Agassi may not be the most talented player on the pro tennis circuit, but he's the one who most people remember. He has starred in camera commercials saying, "Image is everything," and for many years has flashed a rather sporty image himself.

Name that Person

I'm going to describe two inventors. The first still owns the record for holding the largest number of U.S. patents. He is the widely celebrated inventor of the phonograph. He is commonly regarded as the inventor of the light bulb, although he merely improved on it. He also made dozens of improvements to other existing products. Can you name him? Undoubtedly you can, since he's Thomas Edison.

> JUST THE FACTS MA'AM.
>
> ### Just the Facts
>
> Thomas Edison was not the original inventor of the light bulb. He improved on a principle that others had already discovered. For example, in 1802, Sir Humphrey Davy produced an arch light, a crude, carbon-based method of illumination. He was followed in 1844 by Jean Foucault, who made an arch light strong enough to light up the Plaza de la Concorde in Paris.
>
> By 1860, Sir Joseph William Swan had devised a crude light bulb, and 18 years later he demonstrated a successful carbon filament lamp at Newcastle, England. This was ten months before Edison "invented the light bulb."

An inventor of equal brilliance and contribution to society revolutionized the automobile industry. He's credited with having ushered in a new era of ignition systems, vehicle performance, and vehicle safety. He patented a painting process that prolonged the life of cars by reducing the incidents of rust.

With four hundred million vehicles in America alone and more than a billion throughout the world, surely you can name this hallowed inventor. He also became a philanthropist, and to this day his name is part of one of the foremost cancer research and treatment facilities in the world, which he helped found. Who is he? Give up? He is Thomas Kettering, for whom the Sloan-Kettering Institute is partially named.

Why does virtually everyone know the name of Edison, and nearly no one knows the name of Kettering? Okay, perhaps Edison's inventions were more consumer-oriented or impacted more people more quickly then. After all, 100 years ago, everyone was likely to turn on a light switch, but not everyone owned a car.

Edison, as it turns out, relentlessly promoted himself. He constantly talked to the press and gave interviews. He always issued pithy quotes. He went out of his way to grand-stand. He often bragged that he got by on very little sleep per night, a claim later proven to be untrue. Edison was socially assertive, always looking for opportunities in which to get into the news.

> **Make It So**
> Two performers, alike in all major respects, with a similar array of accomplishments, may have vastly different experiences in terms of what they earn, how they are perceived, and how they are remembered, based on their levels of assertiveness.

Kettering was not a meek or mild lab scientist. He was a strong leader within the organizations he formed. He also gained a reputation as someone with a quick wit who could both give and take a joke. Yet, unless there is some dramatic, Oscar-winning movie about Kettering in the future, it's not likely his name will ever be known on the magnitude of that of Edison.

So it is in many arenas of life.

Assertiveness in Recent History

Prior to the modern era, in which reporters cover virtually every corner of the globe, it was hard to know the specifics of when one leader stared down another and, hence, avoided war, disaster, or what have you.

In recent American history, particularly in regard to the affairs of presidents, there are several instances we can draw on in which an individual's assertiveness resulted in an outcome not otherwise predictable.

And We're Keeping the Dog

When Richard Nixon ran for vice president in 1952, he was accused of irregularities on his personal financial statements. He went on national TV and gave what became known as the "Checkers Speech," in which he defended his finances, his wife's right to wear a good "Republican cloth coat," and the fact that his family was going to keep the dog named Checkers given to him as a gift.

Nixon's ability to assert himself at this critical juncture, winning over the hearts and minds of enough of the populace, enabled him to stay on the ticket and carry Dwight Eisenhower into office. What would have happened if his speech hadn't gone over well, and Eisenhower had to replace Nixon on the ticket? History suggests that when a presidential candidate is forced to change his running mate, the results are a loss in November.

We Showed Them, or Did We?

Some ten years later, President John Kennedy faced the Cuban Missile Crisis. The Soviet Union planned to fortify Cuba with a ring of Soviet missiles. Kennedy told Khrushchev that he simply could not allow Soviet missiles in the Western hemisphere. The situation got extremely tense, and many people feared war would break out. Eventually the Soviets backed down, and Kennedy was hailed as a hero for this episode.

The full story, however, has never been widely understood by Western governments. I toured the Soviet Union in 1984. Visiting some of their state museums, I learned that at that time, because the American president, Kennedy, had the power to command the Soviet Premier to remove the Soviet missiles, the Soviets vowed they would never allow themselves to be in that position again.

Since he did not allow Khrushchev to save face, Kennedy actually precipitated a massive arms buildup in the Soviet Union. The Cuban Missile Crisis, in perspective, led to an escalation of the arms race in both the East and the West that exhausted and drained both economies for the next 27 years.

The Soviet Union eventually fractured from within, and in 1989 disbanded. Since then, there have been some notable reductions in the scale of Eastern and Western expenditures.

So, on one hand, Kennedy was hailed as assertive by Americans. But on the other hand, Russians viewed him as aggressive, because they felt backed into a corner, which further fueled Cold War hostilities.

Go Ahead, Make My Day

Though in retrospect a small event in the course of history, when U.S. President Ronald Reagan stood up against the air traffic controllers in 1981, he took a major risk. He told the strikers that what they were doing was illegal, and that they would lose their jobs. For weeks, there was actually a chronic shortage of air traffic controllers.

If a major air disaster had occurred during this time, Reagan's entire administration might have fallen under scrutiny. Had this happened, it certainly would have harmed his chances for re-election in 1984.

Of all the groups that you could go up against head to head, I would think the air traffic controllers would be the ones to avoid. After all, if sanitation workers go on strike, a city may stink for a while, but it's not likely a plane is going to crash because of it.

Thankfully, no major air disasters happened during Reagan's confrontation with the air traffic controllers. This result, combined with some other early wins in his administration, helped Reagan have a far easier administration with Congress and the electorate than many of his contemporaries had enjoyed.

Reagan appeared assertive, but actually was aggressive. If anyone had sabotaged the system, the repercussions might have rained down on Reagan.

Time will tell if the decisions these presidents made and the actions they took proved beneficial or detrimental to society.

One thing appears certain: The American public approves of bold and decisive action and supports a president who appears to assert himself at critical junctures. Even if he turns out to be wrong or the other side regards the gesture to be aggressive, the public admires that element of his personality.

By contrast, presidents who have acted with indecision, such as Jimmy Carter during the Iran hostage crisis, are not looked upon in the same light.

> **Make It So**
> Whether in interpersonal circles, at work, or in your community, taking a stand and asserting yourself for what you know or believe is right tends to win you, at the least, the approval of an otherwise silent mass.

Assertiveness in Religion

In recent years, Pope John Paul II has made proclamations re-enunciating the Catholic Church's official position on abortion and women in the clergy. Many people don't agree with his views and see them as outdated. Ever-growing numbers of Catholics find themselves in opposition to what this religious leader is saying.

Yet, he is held in high esteem, perhaps more so than his recent predecessors. Certainly, he has personality and charm. But why is Pope John Paul II endearing to so many of his flock, even those who disagree with him? Is it possible that his self-assured assertions win admiration, if not capitulation?

For five decades, the Reverend Billy Graham has been seen as one of the most prominent religious leaders in America, if not throughout the world. Yet he had no formal religious training, no advanced degree in theology. He was not even an ordained minister. He used innovative techniques to summon the masses to his rallies.

He also lived his life by a credo, so that others could see that he was true to his word. He abhorred marital infidelity, and although he had numerous invitations from female admirers, he steadfastly refused to engage in extramarital affairs. He demanded the same of his closest associates.

Many religious leaders give powerful, moving performances when on the pulpit. Of the televangelists, Dr. Robert Schuller comes to mind among those who have maintained the straight and narrow course and not fallen prey to that which they preach against. Yet, even those who have been subject to scandal still seem to maintain a loyal following. Often, they emerge from their turmoil with a clear, bold, new direction, and as seemingly better people for having had the experience. The assertive leader on the pulpit or platform wins followers.

When I was growing up, the religious leader of our congregation was an eloquent speaker, but a crusty old soul who could sear a hole through your brain at 50 paces with just a glance. And this was years before light sabers were introduced in *Star Wars*.

One time, he stopped in the middle of a religious service and peered out over the audience to say to someone, "Yes, you!" In a room with hundreds of religious students in attendance, the impact was clear and indelible: "If you come into this house of worship, you come to pray; you don't come to converse with your neighbor. And when I'm leading the service, mine is the only voice I want to hear." (Except maybe for God's.)

I can tell you that I was never one to talk during the service, nosiree.

Assertiveness in the Arts

Everywhere you look, the bold are favored over the bland. Mozart's music was considered too innovative and too radical for its day; whereas his rival, Solare, was hailed as an accomplished composer. As time passed, Solare's compositions have been forgotten while Mozart's are played throughout the world.

As for the fine arts, if you walk into any major museum today, on the walls you'll see the bold departures of some artists of an earlier era. Monet and Manet, Cezanne and Degas, and the Cubists and Impressionists invariably are some of those whose work have been hailed as genius, no matter how obscure some of these artists may have been during their own lifetime.

The Martha Graham or Alvin Ailey dance troupes, in demand all over the world, reflect the innovative movements, techniques, and radical departures that their creators infused into the performances.

Surely, many innovators in the arts quickly vanished from the scene when their assertive forms of expression did not find favor with audiences. On balance, assertiveness in religion, the arts, and other arenas of human endeavor is what makes life different and often better, and certainly more interesting.

The Least You Need to Know

➤ History reveals that leadership and assertiveness go hand in hand.

➤ People who are more naturally assertive in their personal lives are better remembered than those who are not.

➤ People seem to have a need to believe in the assertiveness of historical figures.

➤ Assertiveness helps you stand out, whether in religion, the arts, or other arenas.

Part 2
A More Self-Confident You

A major key to developing effective assertiveness skills is becoming more self-confident. Self-confidence is nothing more than that deep-down feeling that you're basically a good person, deserving of what you have in life and of what is rightfully yours to earn. While it's possible to be assertive without being self-confident, being assertive when you're self-confident comes much more naturally and easily. In a nutshell, self-confidence radiates power and health. Others want to be around you and to be like you. Fortunately, you can increase your self-confidence.

The self-confident are those who walk into a job interview knowing that they have the skills and knowledge to handle the position being offered. Self-confidence is embodied by the woman who asks to be promoted based on her assurance that, because of her previous efforts, she deserves the promotion. The chapters in this section all focus on helping you become someone who is naturally and easily influential to others, more visible, and yes, even more attractive, without getting cosmetic surgery.

Chapter 5

Why Self-Confidence Is So Important

In This Chapter

➤ Changes you can count on

➤ Finding opportunities in the face of uncertainty

➤ Where do and don't you shine?

➤ How to talk to yourself

➤ The mindset of the confident

Everywhere you look, there are lifelong career professionals losing confidence in their ability to stay competitive in a rapidly changing society. At the same time, no one in society has a long-term lock on any market niche, and no body of information affords a strategic competitive advantage for long. The reality of our times is that everyone is feeling at least a little unsure of himself, and in that sense everyone is in the same boat.

So, in this chapter, we'll explore the ever-vital concept of self-confidence. Whatever level of self-confidence you currently maintain, I promise that even greater potential awaits.

It's Normal to Be Confused Today

You and your contemporaries face more challenges, more complexity, and more change than your counterparts of any other generation. No matter who you work for, including yourself, to stay competitive you have to constantly:

➤ Upgrade the product or service you are offering.

➤ Keep a sharp eye on ways you can innovate.

➤ Give more value to the customer.

➤ Deliver your product or service faster.

Whatever targets you or your organization serve, you can be sure that your constituents are more sophisticated or knowledgeable about substitute goods or services and, hence, more demanding.

The Unique Challenges of This Age

Your grandfather and possibly even your father, in their early twenties, learned job skills that may have served them for their entire careers. This situation is not likely available to you. As you've learned, the volume of new knowledge generated in every field is enormous; it easily exceeds anyone's ability to keep pace. As a result, everyone feels underinformed, despite their absorption of an unprecedented volume of information.

JUST THE FACTS MA'AM.

Just the Facts

Today, an entire workforce faces the specter of living in a society in which potentially:

1. No job is secure.

2. No product or service has a sustained, competitive advantage.

3. No one can accurately predict how a new technology may impact existing markets.

In combination with the factors you read about in Chapter 2—exponential human population growth, exponential growth in information, and in some respects, the breakdown of human inter-connectedness—it's easy to understand why you're part of a generation that's facing unprecedented challenges in human experience. Against such a backdrop, it's understandable how you, I, or anyone else could feel a little shaken on occasion, if not routinely stirred.

Social and Technical Changes You Can Count On

The following chart offers a few of the social and technical changes—the "new reality"—to which you are subject. If only one, two, or a handful of these types of changes occurred every couple of years, it would be relatively easy to take them in stride. Unfortunately, that's not the way the future is unfolding. Soon, you'll face more social and technical changes annually than people used to encounter in a decade.

Reality Changes

Old Reality	New Reality
Nine-to-five workdays for the rank and file	Variable hours
Central business district	Satellite cities, superstores, cyberstores
Family-held or long-term business ownership	Conglomerates, joint ventures, limited partnerships
Brick and mortar organizations	Cyber, mobile, fluid, and temporary organizations
Clearly defined work roles	Changing, one-time, team-related, and temporary roles
Long-term employment in paternalistic organizations	Uneven employment patterns, less core staff, more part-time staff
Producer versus consumer differentiation	Blurring of the lines between producer and consumer
Slowly emerging markets	Rapidly to instantly emerging and dissipating markets
Brand versus brand competition and relative customer loyalty	Product/service substitutability; customer loyalty suspect

Along with tumultuous change come changes in expectations concerning how long things ought to take, how well products ought to perform, and how effective services ought to be. Once the Pandora's Box of expectations is open, it never returns to the previous level. Hence, everyone in every profession faces increasing demands from customers—it's enough to shake anyone's confidence.

As a case in point, would you buy the world's best TV, with super-quality, high-screen definition (with Bruce Springsteen's 57 channels and nothing on!) if it did not come with a remote channel changer? That is, if you had to get up and change the channel by hand each time you wanted to see what else was on? My guess is that 99.9 percent of the population would not purchase such a product. So it is in all other aspects of our society.

Once a time-saving, labor-saving, complexity-reducing product or service is widely introduced, everything that came before predictably meets its demise in short order.

Word Power
The term *Pandora's Box* springs from mythology relating to the notion that once a box, gate, door, or other structure symbolizing the introduction of change is opened, the status quo is irrevocably altered (such as a customer constantly expecting more).

I am not a purveyor of doom; nevertheless, it's unlikely you'll be able to "coast" for the rest of your career. You'll continually have to be in a learning mode, stay flexible, and find new ways to confidently face the future.

Don't panic! No world leader, CEO of a multinational corporation, head of an organized religion, Nobel laureate, university chancellor, senator, or multimillionaire has got it made in the shade.

The Importance of Self-Confidence

Against such a backdrop, in many business circles there is a growing realization of the connection between:

➤ Self-confidence and effective decision-making

➤ Self-confidence and effective supervision

➤ Self-confidence and appropriate risk taking

The CEO of one large, multinational company believes that self-confidence is a fundamental prerequisite for his managers in today's chaotic, ever-changing business environment. This company recently introduced a new evaluation procedure in which their key staff members are assessed according to such qualities as self-confidence, candor, courage, and openness.

Whew! And you thought getting to work on time, making quota, or filling out the monthly report were the keys to succeeding.

Increasingly, the self-confident executive is being asked to make the right choices, assemble the right team, marshal the appropriate resources, articulate his vision, and see everything through to successful completion.

A manager was once deemed worthy if he or she understood and faithfully executed the age-old functions of analysis planning, implementation, delegation, control, and so on. Today, it's more likely that such managers are required to share power with and empower others; assume the role of follower as needed; all the while maintaining enthusiasm, energy, and confidence.

Feeling More Confident Even in the Face of Uncertainty

There's an old story about an owner of a vegetable stand along the side of the road during the Great Depression that occurred in the U.S. throughout the 1930s. His business was doing quite well. Yet, day after day, he encountered travelers who told him to be wary because many people were out of work in the big city.

After hearing this message repeatedly, the owner cut back a little on his product offerings, lowered his prices, and reduced his business hours. Sure enough, within a few weeks, what had once been a thriving business became one that was just hanging on.

This tale illustrates how the Great Depression for some was a mindset, not an economic reality.

Opportunity Knocks

There are people who find opportunities in the face of uncertainty, and who feel more confident even as the masses are feeling less so. There's a clever scene in the movie *Peggy Sue Got Married* in which Kathleen Turner as Peggy Sue tells a classmate how everything in the future gets smaller except for radios, which get much, much larger. Boom boxes were a highly visible example of a growth industry that bucked the trend for a while. Ultimately, they are being replaced by miniature systems with even greater power.

Make It So
Despite the rapid pace of change in society, and perhaps because of it, new opportunities are always emerging for entrepreneurs and executives as well as for people from all walks of life, including you.

No matter how the future unfolds, keep in mind this general principle: Needs don't disappear—they shift.

Consider the following:

➤ A rise in car thefts spawned a huge anti-car-theft device industry.

➤ The reduction in permanent staff has spawned a huge temporary-help industry.

➤ The rise of PCs on nearly every desktop has spawned a new generation of ergonomic office furniture.

➤ The increased threat of terrorist attacks has spawned a sales surge in portable airline luggage carts, because travelers can no longer leave their luggage unattended.

➤ The increase in divorce has spawned a huge dating-service industry.

➤ The increase in the number of families with dual working parents has spawned a huge child day-care industry.

➤ The continuing fitness craze has spawned a huge increase in sales of workout clothing and equipment.

In short, look for opportunity in change.

What About You, Shortcakes?

What do Tom Cruise, Paul Newman, Arnold Schwarzenegger, Sylvester Stallone, Robert Redford, and Dustin Hoffman, as well as movie greats from yesteryear such as Humphrey Bogart, John Garfield, and Kirk Douglas, have in common? They are all short, most standing less than 5'9". Although society tends to value the tall athletic look (like me!), these Hollywood screen actors are among Hollywood's great action and romantic leads.

On a personal basis, what are some of the obstacles, challenges, or impediments you face that you could "turn around" and use to your advantage? For example, Spud Webb lasted more than ten years in the National Basketball Association. He was listed at 5'8" tall, but his real height is closer to 5'6". Yet he won the NBA slam dunk contest in 1986 over a field of superstars eight to 14 inches taller than he is.

The conventional wisdom in basketball at the time was that a 5'6" player simply could not compete, let alone be a slam dunk champion. Nevertheless, Webb changed the rules for himself and others, such as 5'3" Muggsy Bogues—shorter than your grandmother—who also lasted more than ten years in the NBA.

Webb, Bogues, and the growing number of shorter players who have followed compensate for their lack of height by working out and doing various exercises to build their leg muscles. They use blazing speed to drive past taller opponents. Because they are shorter, and therefore closer to the floor, their ball handling is surer. When they hunch over while driving to the basket or passing to a teammate, they force opposing taller guards to look down at an uncomfortable angle.

In the great game of life, you may be dealt a different set of cards than everyone else. However, there are ways to play those cards to your best advantage.

Building Blocks

Make It So
Eleanor Roosevelt once said, "Nobody can make you feel inferior without your consent." The first step in feeling more confident is to assess the basis for any lack of confidence you may experience.

Okay, so you don't want to launch a new product line and you have no chance in professional sports. You're just trying to keep your job or maybe get a raise.

If you want a promotion or a raise but are not confident that you deserve it, you're likely to let your doubts get in your way. You may be reluctant to be assertive—to directly approach those in charge of promotions. Or you might couch your request in a vague, indirect manner, using terms like "maybe," "if," and "sometimes."

A vital component in building or rebuilding self-confidence is to take a good look at the basis for your lack of confidence:

➤ Where does it come from?
➤ In which situations is it more of a problem?
➤ In which situations do things seem a little better?

Finding the answers to questions like these can help you dispel personal myths, emphasize positive occurrences, and begin a realistic program to build your confidence.

The Basis for Your Lack of Confidence

In your heart of hearts, when no one else is around, how do you feel about yourself, and how might that contribute to feeling less confident than you otherwise could? For example, do you think that you are:

➤ Too short?
➤ Too heavy?

- ➤ Unattractive?
- ➤ Unintelligent?
- ➤ Lacking in imagination?
- ➤ Lacking in creativity?
- ➤ Lacking in energy?
- ➤ In the wrong social circle?
- ➤ In the wrong professional circle?
- ➤ Lacking the proper education?
- ➤ Too impatient?
- ➤ Too easy?
- ➤ Too many of the items above?

Do You Believe the Ads that Say You're Inadequate?

A major polling company surveyed a cross-section of American men and women in the 1980s. The company found that two out of every three adults in the United States report that they "fidget, fuss, take furtive glances in windows and mirrors, and study other people's reactions to the way they look." A solid majority of people are almost obsessed with their physical appearance. All indications—cosmetic sales, cosmetic operations, the rise of the image industry—are that this obsession has reached new heights.

While it might be hard to overcome the pull of a society that bombards you with messages that you are inadequate, the quickest way to develop rock-solid self-confidence is to determine where you shine and where you don't.

Where Do You Shine, and Where Don't You?

Rene Hodges (fictional) is the type of individual to whom other people readily respond. There's something about her; perhaps it's in her eyes or her ready smile. She's attractive, but not a "knockout." When you meet her, she gives you her full and undivided attention. When you're speaking to Rene, you get the notion that at least for the moment, you are the most important person in the world. She listens to you carefully, never trying to butt in with her own comments. She waits until you're through before responding.

Rene has a sense of self-acceptance that seems to come from a place deep within her. This self-acceptance manifests itself in the form of self-confidence. When you encounter her, you feel it immediately, and you even feel a bit more confident yourself.

No, Rene is not perfect, far from it. She has her fears and concerns, irritations and frustrations, shortcomings and blind spots. Yet you can see that she enjoys her life. She's willing to share her experiences. There are many people like this in the world, although, unfortunately, they are too few in number.

JUST THE FACTS MA'AM.

Just the Facts

It was said of Jacqueline Kennedy Onassis that when she conversed with you, it was a unique experience. Ms. Onassis' biographers and many admirers observed that one of her most outstanding traits was the ability to offer her full and undivided attention to the party with whom she was speaking.

"When she spoke to you," noted one recipient of her attention, "it was as if there was no one else in the world." This capability often made others find her immediately endearing.

Rise and Shine

One of the secrets about radiant, self-confident people is that they know where they shine and where they don't. Either through logical analysis or intuition, they've determined when and where they're at their best and how to be at their best more of the time.

I attended a seminar in which an instructor took us through a series of visualizations. Asking us to close our eyes, she then said to think back to the times when we were vibrant, a magnet to others. This was an enjoyable exercise for me, as a number of thoughts and images came rushing forward.

I was at my best, I ruminated, in situations where I was known in advance, or where at least the other party or parties knew something about me. The room or place of encounter was well lit if inside or sunny if outside. I was dressed well; had recently worked out and, hence, was feeling quite fit; and was someplace where I wished to be as opposed to had to be.

Where Jeff Shines

➤ He's known in advance.

➤ He's well rested.

➤ He's prepared.

➤ There are bright lights, or it's a sunny day.

➤ He's recently worked out.

➤ He's feeling fit.

➤ He's dressed appropriately.

➤ He wants to be there.

From this simple exercise, I further identified the factors that increased the probability that I would be at my best, and, hence, more self-confident:

1. I had recently shaved (don't laugh, many days I don't).
2. I was color-coordinated (don't laugh, most days I'm not).
3. A member of the opposite sex whom I found attractive attended the seminar (hey, we're talking reality, and this is true for me).
4. I was prepared for dealing with subject matter with which I was comfortable.
5. I was not hungry or thirsty.

Where doesn't Jeff shine? The answer to this is relatively simple—largely the reverse of the factors above. More specifically, I determined that I predictably experience low self-confidence under the following circumstances:

Where Jeff Doesn't Shine

➤ When he's underdressed for the occasion.
➤ When it's past 11:00 p.m.
➤ When his blood sugar is dropping.
➤ When his bank balance is low.
➤ When he's eaten too much refined sugar.
➤ When he hasn't worked out in days.
➤ When his hair looks too thin.
➤ When too many deadlines have emerged around the same time.
➤ When he's unsure of the value of the project.
➤ When he's confronted by too many instructions at once.

The presence of one or more of these factors increases the probability that I might experience self-doubt, the enemy and lack of self-confidence.

Nipping Self-Doubt in the Bud

One prominent psychologist likened self-doubt to a living death. He said it could consume so much of your energy and exuberance that you spend unending hours seeking to correct whatever supposedly isn't working in your life. You then engage in self-management and self-improvement campaigns and are nearly left apart from yourself, constantly battling your innermost thoughts and emotions, striving for some unattainable notion of perfection.

You Shine When...

It's time for you to determine where you shine and where you don't, so that you can eradicate any self-doubt that may block your self-confidence and, hence, your ability to be assertive.

Where Do I Shine?

➤ _____

➤ _____

➤ _____

➤ _____

➤ _____

Go ahead and fill in all the blanks above. Then revisit this roster in a couple of days. Undoubtedly, you'll think about other factors that are present when you shine.

Now, where don't you shine? Try to make the list as long as possible. I assert that by identifying as many factors that up until now have potentially contributed to your lack of self-confidence, you'll have a clear roadmap as to how to be more self-confident more of the time.

Where Don't I Shine?

➤ _____

➤ _____

➤ _____

➤ _____

➤ _____

Revisit this roster in a couple of days and add any other factors you considered.

An Easy Game Plan

Your assignment is to increase the probability that those factors where you're likely to shine are present, and to decrease the incidents of the impeding factors. Yes, it may sound simplistic, but there are deep-seeded reasons as to why you're effective when the first set of factors are present, and why you're not when the second set are present.

In a nutshell, if you don't shine, say, when you're in a large crowd, you can work on that from now until the end of your days. However, you'll still probably never be comfortable in large crowds. If you're far more effective on a one-to-one or small-group basis, cultivate that.

Not in 20 More Years

In the 1996 U.S. presidential elections, Republican candidate Bob Dole proceeded under the illusion that he could be as effective in front of large crowds as incumbent Democratic challenger President Bill Clinton. Unfortunately for Dole, if he had 20 more years to practice, he probably still wouldn't be as effective in that arena. It's not in his nature. Rather, he could have:

> **Make It So**
> You want to look for venues where enough of your "shine" factors are present so that you can be at your best more comfortably, more naturally, more of the time.

➤ Accented his strength in dealing on a one-to-one or small-group basis.

➤ Arranged his campaign appearances to more closely ally with his ability to impact people based on his interpersonal skills and charms.

➤ Had his spin doctors and handlers set up more situations in which he met with a handful of key leaders from a community.

➤ Held one-on-one interviews.

➤ Arranged his affairs so that reporters and others sought him out, rather than attempting to barnstorm around the country as is the contemporary norm among U.S. presidential candidates.

What Do Others Observe About You?

Seek out others who know you well. Ask them where and when they think you're at your best, and where and when they think you're not at your best. You might be surprised by the answers, and you might gain highly valuable insights.

If you can readily accept some of the input others give you, add it to your list. If you're not sure, check out what they've told you. Notice how you feel from a self-confidence standpoint the next time one of the factors that someone pointed out about you, either pro or con, is present.

Where Others Say I Shine

➤ _____

➤ _____

➤ _____

➤ _____

If their observation seems to hold merit, then add it to the appropriate list. If not, check it out a couple more times to be sure, and then drop it.

Where Others Say I Don't Shine

➤ _____

➤ _____

➤ _____

➤ _____

➤ _____

How to Talk to Yourself to Create Results

"What's come over me? I feel like I'm losing control."

"What a dummy I am. How do I manage to say the wrong thing at the wrong time so often?"

"For crying out loud, when am I going to get my act together?"

"Maybe I just don't have what it takes. I once thought I did, but now I don't know."

Do statements like these, or anything even remotely related, ever creep into your head? If you say no, you're lying! Abundant research shows that most people engage in negative self-talk.

Amazingly, based on some studies, the typical adult engages in negative self-talk as much as 80 percent of the time. If you're at all typical in this respect, and I can vouch that you are, your internal dialog about what you do in life, your performances, and who you are dwells heavily on the negative, four times as much as the positive self-talk you give yourself.

The Mindset of the Confident

If I asked you right now to list ten good things that you've done or that have happened to you over the last ten years, could you do it? Undoubtedly, ten good accomplishments or ten good experiences represent only the tip of the iceberg of what you could name if you had total recall. For example, if you're still in your twenties, you probably graduated from high school, perhaps from college, maybe aced some courses, and perhaps were accepted to graduate school.

If you're in your thirties or forties, you perhaps:

> ➤ Have brought a child into this world
> ➤ Have received lavish praise for something you did at work
> ➤ Have received a healthy promotion
> ➤ Maintain a nice home
> ➤ Are a volunteer for worthy groups
> ➤ Have started your own business
> ➤ Have attained financial security
> ➤ Care for your aging parents
> ➤ Have become involved in local politics

Word Power
Self-talk is the internal dialogue—the little voice, deep inside of you—that pretty much chatters all day long. It largely influences the degree of your self-confidence and, hence, the degree of assertiveness you're able to generate.

Handle with Care
Your mission, should you choose to accept it, is to develop the mindset of people who have a healthy degree of self-confidence.

The point of this exercise is to illustrate that you have many victories in your life, things that you have accomplished, and honors that others have bestowed on you. People who maintain self-confidence seemingly have greater perspective, or simply better memories, than those who don't.

All that you've learned in this chapter thus far will help lead you to a physical manifestation of one who appears self-confident, hence outwardly projecting confidence. This is no small feat. Kinesthetics don't lie. If you walk and talk with confidence; stand more erect; throw your chest out; take deep, measured breaths; and, in general, appear to be confident, guess what? You tend to be more confident.

By acting the part, you increase the frequency of proceeding with confidence. There are a variety of techniques, which we'll discuss in the next three chapters, that will enhance and accelerate your progress toward being a more self-confident person.

The Least You Need to Know

➤ When faced with rapid change and unique challenges, many people lose confidence on a professional or personal level.

➤ Some people find wonderful opportunities in the face of uncertainty; others are able to be confident despite rapid change.

➤ Determining where you shine and where you don't is a fundamental step toward increasing your ability to be self-confident more often.

➤ How you talk to yourself largely dictates how confident you'll feel.

➤ The more self-confident a person is, all other things being equal, the more attractive that person is to others.

Increasing Your Vocal Self-Confidence

James Cameron, director of the movie *True Lies,* an Arnold Schwarzenegger blockbuster, was asked why he chose Charlton Heston to serve as CIA Director, Schwarzenegger's boss in the movie. Cameron replied that Charlton Heston was the "only person who can plausibly intimidate Arnold."

In Hollywood and in Republican circles, Charlton Heston is considered the epitome of the self-assured, self-confident individual. He has an unmistakable presence that men and women, actors and directors, politicians, and pundits can't ignore. More specifically, he has vocal self-confidence. When he speaks, it's like Moses, one of the characters he's famous for portraying, handing down the law.

In this chapter, I'm going to discuss how to increase your vocal self-confidence, offering strategies you can adopt and steps you can take to learn and practice conveying to others through your voice that you're in command.

What Is Vocal Self-Confidence?

There are people in my life, and undoubtedly in yours, who, when they say something, prompt you to act. My father was one such person. I had several teachers and professors, a coach or two, and even a high school buddy who had vocal self-confidence. It's something in the way they speak—their measured tones, often speaking in a deeper bass voice, but not necessarily so—that summons something within me to take notice.

If you've never regarded your voice as a tool for being more confident and assertive in this life, you're in for some revelations. I'm not going to ask you to change your voice. (Unless you have already repeatedly received feedback to the contrary, chances are, you don't need to make it lower or higher.)

By practicing what you learn in this chapter, you'll make the best of the voice God gave you. As with all change, you can't expect a miracle overnight. It's about setting some reasonable expectations for yourself. Although not everything presented here may be your cup of tea, by following most of what's recommended one step at a time, you'll rack up small achievements that spur you on to even greater confidence.

Using Technology to Hide

Have you noticed a curious development in this age of rapid technological advancement? All the communication technology that surrounds you can be, and often is, used as a shield, a way of not having to deal directly with people, as I discussed in Chapter 2.

Literally millions of people are getting online every evening, "cruising" the Internet, CompuServe, and America Online chat rooms rather than bars.

These online conversationalists, pick-up artists, and bon vivants are keeping company with others they've never seen, never met, and are never likely to meet. Technology has offered them a world where they can be whoever they want to be within certain bounds. They conjure up images in the minds of their online conversation partners through the typewritten word. Therefore, not only are they not seen, but they are not physically heard.

Because of the relative novelty of this form of communication, there are no longitudinal studies indicating the effects of such communication on the individual with regard to their ability to grow and change in the work-a-day world.

You don't develop real-world self-confidence in cyberspace, and you don't develop vocal self-confidence using a keyboard. People who have vocal self-confidence quite naturally are out there speaking in front of others. Happily, you have opportunities to do this all day long, day in and day out.

Talk Totals

Do you realize that every half hour you speak to someone, you're producing an amount of text equivalent to 20 transcribed pages? If you were to take such transcription, clean it up, and eliminate the redundancies, you'd end up with about 14 to 16 pages of material. This equals the amount of information presented, say, in each chapter of this book.

In other words, for every two minutes that you're speaking to someone, you are creating the equivalent of one complete manuscript page. So, there can be no more discussion about a lack of opportunity to get in some practice.

Who Has Vocal Self-Confidence?

To understand who has vocal self-confidence, you need to pay attention to people who talk to you. Let's start with those who apparently do not have it. These are people who:

➤ Don't speak in clear, resonant tones.

➤ Stumble over their words.

➤ Use sentences punctuated by "um," "er," and "ah."

➤ Inject "you know," "it's like," and other verbal asides that only distract from a listener's ability to gain meaning.

Effective speaking increasingly is becoming a highly demanded attribute of rising career professionals. Nearly every organization wants technologically competent professionals who can reasonably articulate their thoughts.

I'm not saying you have to become an orator of the same caliber as William Jennings Bryan, develop the elocution skills of Winston Churchill, or make deliveries with the drama and emotion of Jesse Jackson; far from it. Indeed, some of the most persuasive people you may know, those who have oodles of vocal self-confidence, may be relatively unskilled as public speakers.

On a one-to-one basis, in a small group setting, or, when the situation merits, in a larger group setting, some people are able to convey their thoughts and ideas, wishes or demands to others so that everyone in the room understands the first time. Those with vocal self-confidence don't necessarily have the best grammar or diction, but it helps.

Just the Facts

Some people, by virtue of their size or physical appearance, well-developed muscles, or other distinguishing physical characteristics, seem naturally to catch the attention of others. Most of the rest of us have to work a little more on it.

While there are all kinds of techniques you can use to strengthen your voice and improve your delivery (and I'll touch on some of them in this chapter), in the end, the fastest and easiest way to become more vocally self-confident is simply to practice speaking to others in a more confident way. You wanted to hear that, didn't you? I mean, it's a lot easier than having to undergo hours of instruction!

Be Kind to Your Vocal Chords

There are simple techniques you can practice right now, especially if no one else is nearby, to give your vocal cords a good workout. In the last chapter, I discussed how self-confident people ultimately appear more attractive to others than people who lack confidence. Concurrently, studies show that rather average-looking people with clean, crisp articulation and melodious voices are rated as more attractive than objectively attractive people with poor speaking voices or voices that are scratchy, or these who lack articulation, or are otherwise weak.

Practice Makes Perfect

When you get up in the morning, do you practice using your voice just as you'd practice using any of your other muscles? Probably not. I suggest running through the vowels in a harmonic way. Say out loud, Aaaaay, Eeeee, Iiiii, Ooooo, Uuuuu. Then, do it almost as if you're singing them.

Next, try some long words. Out loud, say:

➤ Discombobulate

➤ Prestidigitation

➤ Clavicle

➤ Philanthropical

➤ Aphrodisiac

When you've said those a couple times, try some geography:

➤ Monongahela River

➤ Mount Kilimanjaro

➤ Tahiti

➤ The Susquehanna River

➤ The Tigris and the Euphrates

➤ The Mekong Delta

By giving yourself a vocal workout you'll be potentially more expressive all day.

A Warm Drink in the Morning

Have a warm drink early in the morning. Your vocal chords will thank you. Cold drinks contract the vocal chords, making it harder for you to use them.

Strengthen Your Throat

If you have a sore or weak voice or throat, try holding your jaw with your hands. Put one hand under each side of your jaw so that your fingers touch your ears and your palms are under your chin. This brings immediate warmth to the area and helps to loosen you up.

Also, yawn frequently, especially if you're alone where you can let out a big, loud yawn. Lions yawn all the time, and you don't see anyone ignoring their roar.

It also helps to rotate your shoulders around and around in one direction, then in the alternate direction. Stretches, particularly those where your arms are above your head, can also help.

Orchestra conductors live longer than the average person. Perhaps it's because they keep their hands above their heart; that is, their circulatory systems are strengthened while they work.

An Occasional Sigh

Breathing plays an important role in your ability to convey authority in your voice. Don't be afraid to talk breathily on occasion, but don't make it your standard mode of delivery. Sigh when you need to and even hum. The following exercises all help to unlock energy:

➤ Make gentle out-breaths.

➤ Hold your breath for a moment, and then suddenly release it.

➤ Yell. (This one works best when you're alone.)

What part do your lungs play in establishing vocal authority? Strong lungs help achieve more effective breathing. If you're born with strong lungs, thank your lucky stars.

Just the Facts

The only thing you can do to potentially improve your lung capacity is swim. Researchers think that this is because of the increased pressure on your lungs when you are in the water. The way to make your lungs weaker is clear: Exercise in polluted air near carbon monoxide, or in cities where the smog level is high. Also smoke heavily until regular wheezing and coughing become natural for you.

Diaphragmatic Breathing

You've probably heard this before, but it warrants repeating because it's so true, and so few people pay any homage to it. The most effective and efficient breathing is done by

Make It So
The fastest way to understand diaphragmatic breathing is to lie down on the floor, place your hands over your midsection, and breathe normally. Do you feel your stomach going up and down? That's diaphragmatic breathing, and you can do it while you're standing or sitting.

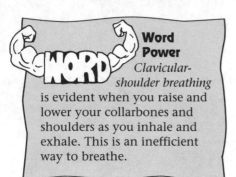

Word Power
Clavicular-shoulder breathing is evident when you raise and lower your collarbones and shoulders as you inhale and exhale. This is an inefficient way to breathe.

using the abdominal muscles rather than the rib cage. Whenever you use your diaphragm (located on the inside of your stomach roughly where your navel is) to do the work instead of your rib muscles, you're far more efficient.

If you've been speaking for a while and you notice that your breathing is shallow, try to bounce a little. Let your knees unlock and go up and down just an inch or so. A mild bounce actually helps you engage your diaphragm while you breathe. Hence, you breathe more efficiently, and are able to summon your resources and maintain vocal strength.

Too many highly athletic types, myself among them, make the mistake of raising their shoulders as well as expanding their rib cages to draw a strong, deep breath. During the heat of battle, such as when you've been racing up and down a basketball court, it makes perfect sense to breathe this way. In fact, you probably have little choice. At a resting pulse rate, athletes would be better off breathing using the diaphragm only.

Sit-ups and crunches are helpful for abdominal conditioning, but you also need to give these muscles aerobic conditioning on a regular basis. What is the single best aerobic exercise? Walking.

The Music of Your Voice

Have you ever received a phone call from someone you haven't heard from in years? Even though he or she didn't announce who it was for a few moments, you knew instantly, and you only needed to hear a word or two. Perhaps they only said hello and your name.

Like your fingerprints, your voice is unique. Yes, some people sound quite a bit like others, just like some fingerprints are close to others, but they are all different.

Your voice has a "music" to it. This is defined by how loudly or softly you speak, how quickly or slowly you speak, whether your pitch rises or falls at the end of sentences, and other characteristics such as richness, texture, and timbre.

What about lower tones? What you may have heard is true. Those who use the lower end of their voice range tend to appear more assertive. Why?

➤ Low pitch equates to being in control of your emotions and the situation you face.

➤ High pitch conveys excitement and possibly fear, insecurity, or nervousness.

Experts say that vocal variety is the key to being an interesting conversationalist and someone to whom others will pay attention. If you want to convey high energy, you can actually tone down your pitch a notch or two. Contrary to Hollywood movies and most TV sitcoms, loud booming voices and ranting and raving behavior grate on your listeners' nerves after a while.

It's Never Too Late to Articulate

Your degree of articulation also helps define the music of your voice. How many times have you made a phone call and been greeted with something like "Joce Smitken Sultin," when the other party was really saying, "Joe Smith Consulting," or "Marilyn Pierce Fennerinsmith," when the other party was saying "Merrill Lynch, Pierce, Fenner, and Smith"?

When I encounter such receptionists, I help them out all I can! My standard response is, "I'm sorry, I didn't catch a word of that." It's just my gentle, understanding way of getting them to repeat the greeting so that callers have a fighting chance of knowing they've reached the right organization.

A Little Practice

There are hundreds of books on how to speak with greater precision. Go get them if you want, but you can improve dramatically on your own if you simply tape yourself with a camcorder or an audiocassette recorder.

Are you among the masses who mess up on "t" sounds? Many people don't say them with crispness and clarity. Try saying butter with "t's" in the middle of the word, not "d's." Probably the majority of English-speaking peoples shortchange the common ending "ing." They say "goin'," "doin'," "comin'," and everything but "going," "doing," and "coming."

When evaluating yourself, listen as if someone else is speaking. Be critical. Indeed, is this person enunciating his words, clearly making "ing" endings and delivering crisp "t's," "th's," "sh's," and "ch's"? Is the speech pattern punctuated by "ers," "ahs," "ums," and other detractors, or is it clean and unfettered? Following are some quick but effective tips for improving your speech:

> **Make It So**
> I suggest using an audiocassette recorder to practice your speech, because then you won't have to deal with visual cues as well. Simply listen to how you talk, whether on the phone, in a conversation with someone across the dinner table, or speaking in a small group.

➤ Use vocal variety for a more interesting presentation.

➤ To convey more energy, tone down your pitch a notch.

➤ Use broad sweeping gestures and a booming voice in moderation. These begin to wear on the audience.

➤ Tape yourself while practicing your presentation. Then play it back and critique yourself.

➤ Eliminate "um," "uh," and "er." They add nothing to your communications.

➤ When you need vocal strength, a mild bounce right where you're standing will summon your resources.

➤ Keep your jaw relaxed as you speak.

With Real-Life Subjects

The proof is in the pudding, or, if you're a *Fried Green Tomatoes* fan, the secret is in the sauce. You'll know you've achieved a notable level of vocal self-confidence when you get in front of others and they:

1. Tell you that you're a new and improved you.

2. Do what you say with a lot less resistance.

In Chapter 12, I'll talk about the four key groups and venues you can use to practice speaking before others. For now, let's cover a few fundamentals of how to be more effective every time you open your mouth.

It's Not What Is Said, It's How It's Said

Any audience you're speaking to, whether it's a party of one or one thousand, assesses you on many different levels, not only on what you say, but how you say it. Hence, you want to open your part of the conversation or presentation with authority. Communicate with your eyes that you're in control.

Let your audience know that you're speaking to them, not to your notes, the back of the room, the microphone, or the ceiling. Try to be as relaxed and comfortable as you can in front of any group. The vocally self-confident have the magical ability to be themselves, whether speaking with one or many. They know that there's no need to change.

Certainly, in front of a large group, any gestures you use need to be larger. The pauses between your sentences need to be a tad longer. Convey your message with your eyes, mouth, body, and heart. To be at your influential best, stand erect with your best posture. A stiff body, clenched fist, or unanimated expression makes it tough for your listeners to be on your side as they follow along with you.

Appeal to your audience's emotions and intellect, but primarily to their emotions. If you're not naturally animated, work on your facial expressions, gestures, and movement about the podium. If you are naturally animated, thank your lucky stars, but keep trying to improve on how you use your speaking gift.

Start with small groups, perhaps speaking to a neighbor, co-worker, staff member, or even a spouse. On each occasion, try to master one new element of advancing your vocal authority. The first time, perhaps, fully pronounce the "ing" at the end of words.

Another time, work on becoming comfortable with pausing between sentences, and, perhaps another time, use some dramatic hand gestures that are outside of your normal repertoire. No one is likely to know what you're doing, but they may begin to notice the difference in your effectiveness.

When I first started in the speaking business, I developed the habit of speaking to three smaller, local groups for free before taking a speech on the road and delivering it to a company or association at their convention or conference for a fee. Your assignment is to use three situations in the next day or so to visibly display some new measure of vocal self-confidence.

Advanced Exercises

Here are some advanced exercises to improve your speech:

➤ To improve your diction, practice speaking with marbles in your mouth, or with a pencil sideways. Also practice intentionally over-enunciating.

➤ Use exercises to elongate your speaking channel. For example, stick your tongue all the way out, all the way up, left, right, on your back molars as if you're trying to swallow peanut butter, and roll forward.

➤ Try tongue-twisters to get good at handling lots of words. You know, the old "Peter Piper picked a peck of pickled peppers."

➤ Practice speaking while dribbling a basketball or engaging in some other physical activity.

➤ Practice speaking loudly and softly.

➤ Practice giving certain words emphasis.

Finding a Speech Pattern You Can Live With

In his classic book, *You Are the Message*, author Roger Ailes, former media advisor to George Bush during Bush's successful 1988 presidential campaign, says that "Once you can 'play yourself' successfully, you'll never have to worry again."

What he means is that once you find what represents for you a comfortable speech pattern, one that you can offer consistently and to which others respond, you don't have to tinker with it. You'll know that you're coming across okay. This speech pattern will serve you day in and day out for the rest of your days. This sounds like a good deal to me.

The Least You Need to Know

➤ Vocal self-confidence tells others that you are confident and in control.

➤ To improve your level of vocal self-confidence, practice in front of the mirror, with the camcorder rolling, or with an audiocassette recorder.

➤ You can strengthen your vocal chords much as you can strengthen muscles in your body. Practice saying long words, melodious words, vowel sounds, and consonant combinations such as "st," "ch," "sp," and "sh."

➤ Practice in front of real-life subjects as well, starting with one-on-one situations and small groups.

➤ Find a speech pattern you can live with and which is influential to others, and you can stay with it for a lifetime.

Chapter 7

Self-Confidence Tips You Can Practice Today

In This Chapter

➤ Confidence building

➤ Having reasonable expectations

➤ Capitalizing on what you do well

➤ Looking for small wins

➤ Imitation and experimentation

So far, you've seen that it's normal to be a little concerned about your future; hundreds of millions of people are concerned about their futures! Yet, there are people who find opportunity in adversity and are confident in the face of uncertainty. Recognizing where you shine and where you don't is a major step in increasing the rate and frequency of feeling self-confident.

You've also learned that vocal self-confidence can help you have a greater impact on others. Also, people who have self-confidence and/or vocal self-confidence are regarded by others as more attractive.

Now we turn our attention to neat stuff you can do to increase your self-confidence—and live to try some more.

Read 'Em and Reap

Let's jump right into some specific strategies you can use to build your self-confidence unfailingly, naturally, and easily.

Maintain Reasonable Expectations

Rome wasn't built in a day. You've heard that before? How about this: The Chicago Bulls didn't win a championship in the first six seasons that Michael Jordan played with them. Happily, it won't take you seven years to develop more self-confidence. You actually can see results in as little as seven days, even more in 21 days, and magnificent results within a few months.

Add an Ounce of Preparation

Suppose you're a salesperson and have a territory that you cover by car. How much better would each of your presentations be if you spent a few minutes in the car carefully collecting your thoughts, perhaps reviewing or rearranging your notes, taking a few deep breaths, and contemplating how you would like the encounter to unfold? Do you realize that many of the world's top income earners, even years into professional selling, still spend significant amounts of time preparing before each sales call? In many respects, what these top producers are doing is simply going over the basics. They know that preparation, even a few minutes worth, is worth its weight in gold in terms of boosting self-confidence.

> **JUST THE FACTS MA'AM.** **Just the Facts**
>
> The basics are what propel top performers all over the world. Olympic athletes, major league baseball players, chess masters, you name it. All spend time at the beginning of each season or each contest reviewing the fundamentals. It's the mediocre performers who think they can skip vital steps. They get bored, or they assume that they're naturally doing everything okay.

While practice doesn't always make perfect, practice does help you increase performance in every endeavor.

Find Peace Within

You may have noticed that self-confident people seem to resonate an inner calm. Even in a crisis situation, they appear to have a sense of equanimity that impacts every aspect of their lives.

The best athletes play with fire and intensity, while maintaining an air of relaxation. By staying focused and relaxed, you can empty your mind of distractions and, hence, increase your ability to perform, regardless of the task at hand.

Word Power
Equanimity is the ability to maintain balance and perspective, even in the face of turmoil.

Give Yourself a Pep Talk

This may sound like a small gesture in terms of building your overall self-confidence. Consider, however, that a verbal, private, self-elevating pep talk helps you to overcome negative self-talk, which you learned about in Chapter 5.

I sometimes say to myself:

> "Okay Jeff, you know you can handle this."

Or

> "I'm going to ace this."

Use whatever lingo is appropriate for you. I know one person who says, "All right, I've tackled bigger fish than this one." And someone else who says, "Hit me with your best shot." If you've never tried this approach before, you're in for a treat.

Use Empowering Language

Suppose you're in a phone conversation with someone and he or she makes a request of you. What if, instead of saying, "I'll have to get that file, make copies, and fax them to you," you were to say, "I'll be happy to get that file…" What would you imagine the impact would be on your psyche, your inner being? Would you feel better about your job, the request that's been made of you, and your ability to fulfill it? Chances are you would. In fact, in one study, office workers who used self-empowering language such as:

➤ "I'll be happy to."

➤ "I certainly can."

➤ "I'll take care of that for you."

instead of:

➤ "I'll have to."

➤ "I don't know if…"

➤ "That's not my job."

…actually felt better about themselves and had more energy, not to mention how their attitude put other people at ease!

It's funny how such a small change in word use can create a change in disposition and confidence. Yet, as we've seen, these little things sink in and infiltrate profound levels of your inner being.

Suppose your spouse asks you to take out the garbage. Normally you give a reluctant, "Okay." What if you were to say, "I'd be happy to," and mean it? After all, you're likely to be asked to do this repeatedly in the future. Since the task isn't going to go away, it's not that big a deal, it's at least partially your responsibility, you intend to live with this person for more than a few days, and your psyche could use a positive stimulus, you have more than enough compelling reasons to say, "I'll be happy to take out the garbage," and mean it!

The same principle can be put into chart form, then posted in a highly visible location:

Upbeat Language

➤ "Can do."

➤ "The buck stops here."

➤ "We try harder, and succeed more often!"

➤ "Make miracles an everyday occurrence."

➤ "Deadlines? Love 'em!"

➤ "Ask and ye shall receive."

➤ "We're the 'A' team."

➤ "Enthusiasm spoken here."

➤ "Smiles at no extra charge."

➤ "Your problem is our problem."

➤ "Leading men (or women) take leading roles."

➤ "The journey of a thousand miles begins with one step."

➤ "I came, I saw, I pitched in."

➤ "There is no time like the present."

➤ "When all else fails, try a different approach."

➤ "You've come to the right place."

When You're Smilin'...

"Okay, you told me to give myself a pep talk, to use more upbeat language, and now you're saying to smile. What's next? Sprinkling fairy dust over my shoes?" Before you work yourself into a tizzy of skepticism, consider that I'm talking *science* here. When you're able to impart a sincere smile, even if there's no one else around, a whole host of factors inside of you are put into gear.

Your physiology literally changes when you smile. The serotonin level in your brain increases, your blood circulates more freely, your respiratory system operates with greater efficiency, and a variety of organs and glands are engaged, each of which increases your overall well-being. The long-standing phrase "Laughter is the best medicine" contains a megadose of truth.

Whether you're married or single, think back to the last time you approached someone you thought was attractive. Odds are, if you were smiling, you had a much better chance of having a successful encounter with that person. A smile imparts to others messages such as:

➤ "I'm glad to be here."

➤ "I want to be your friend."

➤ "I feel at ease."

➤ "I can help."

➤ "I'd like to learn about you."

➤ "I know what I'm doing."

➤ "Let's have some fun."

➤ "We're going to make a good team."

➤ "I'm okay, you're okay!"

Please Yourself

One of the last hit songs from the late Ricky Nelson was called "Garden Party," and it contained the memorable line, "You can't please everyone, so you've got to please yourself." I'm not suggesting that self-confident people are egotistical, conceited, or selfish. Rather, they inherently understand the need to engage in activities that are rewarding to them.

Extending yourself for the express purpose of impressing others runs counter to the notion of self-confidence. You end up spending more time and energy doing things simply because you want to impress others.

In the grand mix of activities in which you engage in life, there's certainly nothing wrong with doing things to please or occasionally impress others. The issue is, do you have a choice?

The self-confident person engages in such activities, or does not, at will. He recognizes that he's most likely to succeed at those things that he enjoys doing, and as the situation dictates, he looks for ways to include others.

Trust Others

Few individuals make it in society without the help and support of others. Even if you're an entrepreneur, there are frequent times throughout the day and week when you need to rely on others. The self-confident person in a work setting delegates freely and easily, but also carefully and methodically. He or she knows that the confidence placed in others helps create a victorious circle, wherein both parties bolster each other's confidence.

Perhaps the saddest, most pitiful people you're likely to know are those who cannot place trust in others. They vehemently cling to whatever projects, information, or good fortune may come their way. They neither share nor benefit from the synergy that could occur from letting others into their "private" domain.

The great leaders of the world, some of the most self-confident people among us, are able to engender a loyal following because they trust people. The greater the trust, the greater the following.

Getting the Best of Yourself

Years ago, I used to display on my wall laminated copies of each of my book covers, awards and plaques I received, and citations and honors given to me by the groups to whom I spoke. Later, I thought that these were all history and wouldn't adequately motivate me for what I wanted to achieve in the future, so I took them down.

As a result of writing this book and researching what makes the highly self-confident people among us stay highly self-confident, I brought out all the book covers (24 of them), and all the plaques and awards (18 of them), and have nary a space left on any of my walls for what's next. However, I will find space, because more is coming.

Look for Victories, Large and Small

Make It So
If you win small victories all day long and acknowledge them as such, your subconscious will begin to believe that you are indeed a winner. After all, you rack up victories every day.

Research has shown that your subconscious, that inner sanctum of your being, can't differentiate between a large issue and a small one. If you're promoted to the division vice-president or simply gain kudos for an excellent report you turned in, the subconscious "records" both events as "wins."

Before you discount this as some type of self-congratulatory system, consider that since the subconscious makes no assessment about the magnitude of your victories but earnestly works to support you in garnering more of the same, each time you acknowledge yourself, whether the accomplishment is large or small, you set in motion the internal apparatus that will increase the probability of you achieving even more.

Reward Yourself

When you do something wonderful, take time out of your day to not only acknowledge yourself, but to do something nice for yourself. Stop off and get an ice-cream cone. Go to that movie you want to see.

If you treat each day and each event as just part of the job or one of many responsibilities, all days begin to look the same. What are some good activities and events for which you can have at least a mini-celebration? The list is very long. Try these for openers. When you:

> ➤ Complete a report prior to the deadline
> ➤ Are under budget this quarter
> ➤ Finish three strokes under your handicap
> ➤ Have an article accepted for publication
> ➤ Get your Web site up and running
> ➤ Complete your taxes
> ➤ Clean out and organize your garage
> ➤ Reorganize the company library
> ➤ Drop those six pounds you've been seeking to shed
> ➤ Finally decide to book that vacation in Martinique

Make It So
Self-confident people understand the vital importance of enjoying their successes.

Learn from Your Mistakes and Then Move On

Ah, if life were nothing but victories! Everyone makes mistakes by the boatload, but confident people somehow learn along the way that mistakes need not drag them down. They don't dwell on them. They regard them as life lessons that give them insights that perhaps they did not have before.

Life repeats itself until you learn the lesson, and then you move on. If you were to never make any mistakes or make only tiny ones, that would be a sign that you probably weren't attempting enough in life. After all, if you play it safe, hardly taking your foot off first base, you'll never get picked off, but you won't score many runs either.

Make It So
Cut yourself some slack. Give yourself some leeway to make mistakes on occasion and be far less than perfect, especially when it comes to being assertive.

Conjure up the image of someone you know who is self-confident. Does she go to pieces when she makes a mistake? Does she get bogged down in what didn't go right, or does she learn from it and move on?

Handle Criticism Adroitly

No matter what you do in this life, there will always be somebody out there sometime (if not daily!) who will offer well- or ill-constructed criticism of what you've done. Self-confident people don't fear criticism; indeed, some actually seek it. Even harsh criticism often contains some nuggets of truth that are worth hearing, despite the otherwise painful encounter.

If you're frequently criticized by the same person, such as a boss or spouse, you might conclude that what they say has less relevance because they've been down this path with you before. Yet, whether it's a frequent criticizer or not, there are ways to handle criticism so that you glean the best from the situation without inciting any antagonism:

1. Let the other party finish what he's saying before you respond.

2. Indicate that you've understood what you just heard, whether or not you're in agreement, by summarizing the criticism using your own words.

3. Don't attempt to justify your behavior or actions, belittle the criticizer, make light of what he says, or offer rebuttal criticism.

4. Remain open to and address the criticism about what you have done or allegedly done. Do not be open to criticism about who or what you are.

Stay focused on the activity or issue in question, and things will turn out okay.

Going a Step Beyond

Self-confident people are not afraid to use their imaginations. They've come to draw upon imagination as a creative, visual, internal rehearsal of what can be. Consider this—how often does stuff just fall into your lap? How often does good fortune smile on you, when you've had no hand in it at all? I'm guessing far less than you'd like it to happen.

Conversely, how often do things work out for the best, when you at least contemplated the possibilities? A bit more often, I'll wager. Those who lack confidence are afraid to engage their imagination, as if there will be some kind of penalty for having the temerity to wish for more.

Unbottle Your Imagination

A philosopher once said, "The imagination is the workshop of the mind." Visualization, a tool discussed in Chapter 5, is one of the many tools of imagination. Here are some ideas to imagine your way to greater self-confidence:

➤ Imagine yourself giving an effective presentation to your team on Wednesday.

➤ Imagine yourself going up to someone you're attracted to and easily initiating a conversation.

➤ Imagine marching into your boss's office and, in a relaxed and confident manner, discussing why it's time for you to receive a raise.

➤ Imagine yourself being chosen to lead the local chapter of some national civic organization.

➤ Imagine the press eagerly writing down what you have to say.

➤ Imagine being assertive whenever you choose to be.

Experiment with Roles

Earlier I discussed the importance of acting the part. Experimenting with roles expands somewhat on that notion.

I once heard of someone who wore several different hats—literally! Depending on the type of challenge he likely would face that day, he put on the most appropriate hat. He wore a Texas ten-gallon hat when he faced tough negotiations. He wore an English sleuth hat like that of Sherlock Holmes when he had to resolve puzzling situations. He wore a top hat like that worn by President Lincoln when he was going to make proclamations to his staff, customers, or constituents.

Hey, if this sounds a little crazy, then don't do it. Do whatever works for you. In many respects, increasing your self-confidence is simply a matter of finding out what makes you feel good about yourself and then engaging in the relevant behavior patterns.

Imitate Self-Confident People

The most potent suggestion comes last. All around you—at work, on television, on the streets, and in your neighborhood—you have the opportunity to observe self-confident people. Undoubtedly, you already know several. Have you ever taken the time to stop and observe what they do?

➤ How do they work?

➤ What do they say?

➤ How do they dress?

➤ How do they carry themselves?

➤ When do they pause?

➤ How do they interact with others?

Yogi Berra, a former baseball great for the New York Yankees and then a manager of the Yankees for several years, once remarked, "You can observe a lot just by watching."

After you've watched for a while, question as well. Ask self-confident people why they do what they do. Most will be happy to tell you.

If you find yourself attracted to the self-confidence in others, it's likely that you have the capacity for greater self-confidence yourself. Imitation is a fundamental mode of learning. The qualities you admire in other people quite often indicate what's undeveloped but fully attainable within you.

If you could arrange your life so that you were surrounded by self-confident people, human nature being what it is, eventually you'd become more like them. Unfortunately, it's not likely you can structure your life to be around self-confident people all the time. You've got to interact with people from all parts of the behavioral spectrum. Hereafter, though, if you remain cognizant of who's self-confident and the distinctions between his or her behavior and that of others, you may just be among the lucky few who awake one bright morning and find that they, too, are highly self-confident people.

The Least You Need to Know

➤ Practice nearly every day the many simple strategies for increasing your self-confidence.

➤ Prepare, prepare, prepare. The most accomplished among us keep returning to the basics.

➤ Look for the small victories as well as the large in everything you do, and reward yourself often.

➤ Don't dwell on your mistakes, but learn from them and then move on.

➤ Use your imagination to devise scenarios in which you act in ways that you normally don't allow yourself.

➤ Hang around, observe, and imitate self-confident people. Self-confidence leaves clues.

Self-Confidence Every Day

How would you like to put into practice what you've learned in Chapters 5, 6, and 7, so you can become self-confident nearly all the time and assertive whenever you need or want to be? Of course, no one is 100 percent self-confident around the clock, in every situation. We're talking degrees here!

This chapter expands upon what you learned in the previous chapters and gives you a framework for being more self-confident in every aspect of your life.

Self-Confident People Are Not Paragons

Too many people erroneously believe they have to be some type of exalted being to be assertive because, after all, assertive people never blow their tops. Au contraire! Anybody can get angry, even the most highly self-confident, assertive people. However, the self-confident, assertive person expresses his anger in a constructive manner as opposed to a destructive way (such as by shouting, threatening, insulting, or otherwise abusing others).

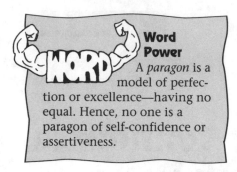

Word Power
A *paragon* is a model of perfection or excellence—having no equal. Hence, no one is a paragon of self-confidence or assertiveness.

When angry, the self-confident, assertive person resorts to first-person communication, highlighting how they feel and what they want instead of acting hostile to others. For example:

> "Ed, I am extremely upset about this situation and need to have you get on this right away, so we can wrap up the project by 4:30 p.m. today and maintain our commitment to the client. Then, tomorrow morning we need to have a one-on-one session to review our overall game plan and how we can more effectively tackle the forthcoming challenges."

Likewise, the self-confident, assertive person handles other challenges in a similar manner. More specifically, they:

➤ Identify what's needed.

➤ Express how they feel.

➤ Indicate what needs to be done.

➤ Refer to the bigger picture.

➤ Elicit agreement or cooperation.

➤ Close the discussion cordially.

There are people, and you may know some, who are self-confident most of the time. Sure, they face challenges that stymie them, and, like anybody, they can "lose it" on occasion. Generally, though, they approach each day and most situations with relative grace and ease. You can almost feel the calmness disseminating from the center of their being.

Paradoxically, self-confident people don't strive to be self-confident. It's almost as if they just allow themselves to "be." They seem to tap into internal resources that have, perhaps, been there all along, or—and this is exciting—are within each of us.

Self-Confident People Know Who They Are

Self-confident people let vital qualities rise to the surface. They're not at war with themselves. Think of it—how would it feel if you were so self-assured that no one could shake your view of yourself?

Certainly, self-confident people have doubts about themselves, their work, and their lives in general. However, rather than try to force themselves to think and see everything as positive, they allow their doubts to be part of the total mix of their experiences. They don't allow their doubts to rule them. They maintain a level of honesty with themselves that draws on all of what they think and feel, sorts it out, and almost automatically redirects them toward the most appropriate thinking, behavior, and action.

A successful high school basketball coach was once asked by one of his mentors to join the college ranks as an assistant coach. This would mean an increase in salary and, perhaps, a chance to work as a head coach of a college team someday. The high school coach thought about it and said, "I'm flattered, but I have to decline. I know what I am; I'm a high school coach."

Did he show a lack of ambition, or was he simply being true to himself?

> **Make It So**
> "This above all: to thy own self be true…"
> —Hamlet, Act 1, Scene 3

Some Well-Chosen Rules

Many people regard General Colin Powell, retired head of the U.S. Joint Chiefs of Staff, as a highly self-confident person. In his autobiography *My American Journey*, Powell remarks that people were always asking him about where society should be heading. Powell would respond that he didn't have all of the answers, but he did have a few "rules that he tried to live by." Following are a couple of his rules. What's remarkable to me is how well entrenched and evident his sense of self-confidence is:

➤ It ain't as bad as you think. It will look better in the morning.

➤ Get mad; then get over it.

➤ Avoid placing your ego so close to your position that when your position falls, your ego falls with it.

➤ It can be done!

➤ Don't let adversity stand in the way of a good decision.

➤ You can't make someone else's choices. You shouldn't let someone else make yours.

➤ Share credit.

➤ Remain calm. Be kind.

➤ Perpetual optimism is a force multiplier.

Is Optimism Necessary for Self-Confidence?

Powell's inherent optimism leads to the question of whether or not optimism is necessary for self-confidence. After exploring the issue, I believe that it is not. Optimism certainly doesn't hurt, however, and it well may help.

Surprisingly little research exists about what makes people optimistic. In his book *Learned Optimism*, Martin Seligman contends that optimists see tough situations as temporary, while pessimists see them as permanent. Optimists also tend to be specific: "Professor Sandler is tough"; whereas pessimists tend to generalize: "All professors are tough."

Seligman believes that optimism is mandatory for those embarking on a career in sales, brokering, public relations, speaking, acting, or fund raising, as well as those involved in creative, highly competitive, or high-burnout jobs.

> **Just the Facts**
>
> Data from Optimists International reveal that optimists catch fewer infectious diseases than pessimists, have better health habits and better functioning immune systems, and generally live longer than pessimists. Optimists are also less likely to miss work, be tardy, or leave early because of sickness.

Optimism doesn't necessarily equate with high self-confidence. You can be pessimistic but self-confident. But if you are naturally optimistic, your ability to develop or maintain self-confidence is probably enhanced. If not, you still have a variety of everyday situations where you can "flex" your self-confidence muscle. Let's look at some of these situations, starting with self-confidence at work.

Self-Confidence on the Job

Of all the people who will accompany you through each job, no boss, co-worker, peer, spouse, parent, relative, or friend will be with you every step of your career journey; you're it! Similarly, you're the only one who can significantly increase the self-confidence you experience and convey to others. Once you accept that, you're practically halfway there. The seven factors that follow, in combination with what you've learned in the previous three chapters, will take you the rest of the way.

1. Work with a Coach

I was fortunate early in my career to recognize the need to retain a career coach. A career coach is not another term for mentor. This is a person you pay to help you.

In a nutshell, a career coach can:

➤ Help diagnose and sort out your situation and opportunities.

➤ Offer new strategies for coping with office politics and competition from other firms.

➤ Show you vital stress management skills.

➤ Help you discover or capitalize on new opportunities.

A good coach provides new tools for improving communication and helps chart your goals and career path. Your career coach can also be your personal, behind-the-scenes confidant, consultant, and resource. For more on career coaching, visit http://www.coachu.com on the Internet where you'll find information about career coaching as a profession, discussion topics, what career coaching can provide you, and contact information for individuals who can answer your questions.

If you have a lack of self-confidence or if you're faced with any of the following, then it's likely you need a career coach:

➤ Organizational changes within your company, especially if they have a direct impact on you

➤ Acquisitions or mergers

➤ Expansion into new markets

➤ Diversification into new products or services

➤ Increased competition to your firm from other firms trying to take over your market share

➤ Increased management or supervisory responsibility

➤ Increased leadership opportunities

➤ A recent or soon-to-be available promotion

➤ A new boss or a leadership shake-up above you

➤ Changes in your role or assignments within your company

➤ In-company competition and power plays, corporate intrigue, jockeying for position, or turf protection

➤ Blockades of your progress by internal feuds or informal political processes

➤ Increased media exposure or public-speaking requirements

➤ Increased production or sales quotas

➤ A new project you must lead or participate in developing

➤ Being a woman, a member of an ethnic or racial minority, or someone with disabilities

For several years I used the career-coaching service of Penny Garner in Alexandria, Virginia. We met only once quarterly for two hours, but I would leave supercharged!

2. Work with an Employment Contract!

An employment contract is a document that spells out your relationship with your employer and your compensation, benefits, job responsibilities, length of employment, and special incentives. The concept of generating an employment contract has been around for at least three decades. Unfortunately, most career professionals have no idea what it is, how to draw one up, or how to ensure that they only work with a contract.

Penny (my career coach) advised me on the importance of establishing a contract. When I first heard this, I was amazed. "You mean that I, a 28-year-old neophyte, am supposed to march into my boss's office and suggest that we develop a contract that defines both the company's and my responsibilities over the next 12 months?" Yes! Exactly!

Why address the notion of an employment contract in the middle of a chapter on everyday self-confidence in a book about assertiveness? Having an employment contract is a great confidence booster. Essentially, it defines your working conditions for the length of a specified term. It establishes your compensation rate. It practically secures your employment.

The kicker is, the contract enhances your confidence while you're writing it and gives you practice in acting assertively, both when you first broach the subject with your prospective or current employer, and when you actually conduct the session to consummate the contract negotiation.

JUST THE FACTS MA'AM.

Just the Facts

In all industries, the most valuable people work with a contract. This is true in Fortune 500 companies; Major League Baseball; the highest levels of government; philanthropic organizations; and civic, social, and charitable organizations. The top talent works with employment contracts. In fact, the inability of management and an agent, representing some top performer, to agree on contract terms is often front page news.

3. Become Indispensable on the Job

In my earlier book, *The Complete Idiot's Guide to Managing Stress* (Macmillan Publishing, 1997), I discuss at length how you can distinguish yourself from the rest of the pack at work by becoming indispensable. Here's a summary of the many strategies you can employ to become the kind of employee your company can't live without:

➤ Take the job no one else wants.

➤ Go the extra mile.

➤ Work harder when the cat's away.

➤ Get credit for your group.

➤ Make your boss look good.

➤ Become a mentor (ad hoc advisor or counselor) to junior or new members of your company.

➤ Figure out what's needed, not what's expected.

4. Know Your Product or Service Line Cold

In state legislatures, the senator who knows the most about the specifics of the legislation that has passed, is pending, or is about to be signed has an advantage over his peers. The sales professional who knows his product or service line cold is more confident in front of prospective buyers and customers and with peers, bosses, and top company management. The health care professional who learns about the latest equipment, diagnostic procedures, and patient care techniques automatically becomes a more valuable and more confident employee.

Right now, I challenge you to learn everything about the products or services that your organization provides.

When you know as much or more about your products and services than anyone in the organization:

➤ Your self-confidence automatically increases.

➤ Co-workers and staff members naturally turn to you.

➤ Bosses and those higher up consider you a valuable resource.

➤ You're more confident in front of clients, customers, constituents, and other business contacts.

➤ Your oral and written communication abilities naturally grow stronger.

> **Make It So**
> I suggest that you engage in such intensive learning that you become the organizational authority on the products or services that your organization provides. You'll know you've achieved this when people who outrank you in the organization come to you for answers.

Now, if you're an attentive reader, you may remember that in Chapter 2 I told you that there's more information produced in every profession than anyone can possibly keep pace with. I advised you not to whip yourself into a frenzy, attempting to keep up with every shred of knowledge concerning your profession. Am I contradicting myself? No.

You don't need to know *everything*. Rather, you want to identify the critical information that will keep you at the forefront of your profession. This requires far less time and energy than you would think. Watch one less television show per day, for example, and you will probably have more than enough time to do this.

5. Increase Your Professionalism at Work

Every organization has its weak points.

Every boss has his or her shortcomings.

Every job has its drudgery.

It would be easy for you to compose a list of all that's wrong at your place of work. Perhaps you can write an article about it, or even a full-length book! Rather than travel that road, increase your level of professionalism a notch or two.

Straighten up your desk and office. Rearrange the pictures, posters, and plaques on the wall. Acquire the support items that will make you more productive. Consolidate material in files, on shelves, and in supply cabinets. Consolidate reminder notes, pads, and slips of paper, so your office is no longer covered with them.

Beyond improving the overall organization and appearance of your office, how about creating a more professional you? Do you need to get your hair trimmed or have your fingernails manicured? Do you need to dry-clean some of your suits? What can you do to improve your overall appearance?

I'd like you to take a personal image inventory. Review the following list and for each item, ask yourself how you currently rate. In what areas do you need improvement?

Wardrobe	Cosmetic	Personal
suits	hairstyle	posture
shirts/blouses	eyebrows	bearing
pants/dresses	beard/mustache	expressions
ties/scarves	fingernails	demeanor
shoes	makeup	gestures
belts	other	eye contact
coats		
glasses		
jewelry		
briefcase		
other		

Most importantly, how is your professional attitude? Are you a smoldering fire or a beacon of light? Adopt the attitude of focusing on your own job and helping others where and when you can.

When your office and appearance improve and you consciously choose to approach each day with a higher level of professionalism, your self-confidence automatically gets a boost. Others notice. You begin accruing the psychological strokes that propel you further. Once again, you benefit from the victorious circle.

6. Act with Greater Decisiveness

As you saw in previous chapters, effective executives tend to make decisions more quickly, and they don't retreat from them. This doesn't mean that they're bold and impetuous, but rather, they have learned to trust their instincts. Instinctive decisions aren't made out of the blue, but are based on a complex set of decision-making guidelines that have been developing inside of you for years.

General Colin Powell said that one of the reasons he was able to make effective decisions in his military career was that he would wait until he had about 60 percent of the data that he could amass for a decision and then make his choice, rather than wait for all the information. More data is not always the answer, and too much data can lead to too many answers, which clearly gets in the way of acting decisively.

Make It So
If morale is currently low where you work, take it upon yourself to be the one person, or the one among a few, who remains cheerful and positive in the face of tough challenges.

Make It So
When your gut and your head come up with the same decision, it's a lock. That is, when your intuitive or internal feeling along with any rational decision-making process that you've undergone are in agreement, don't have any qualms regarding making the decision. When your gut and your head disagree, go with the gut.

7. Volunteer at Work

Volunteering to take on new challenges at work is a way of engaging yourself at a higher level. One of my mentors once told me that "leading men and women take leading parts."

It's okay to be a bit player for awhile. However, if you stay in the bit player role too long, it will become a habit that's tough to break. Miraculously, the mere act of stepping forward—volunteering—often summons within you that which is necessary to be successful. In other words, on some deep level, you volunteer only for those things in which you know you have a good chance of succeeding.

Volunteer to head up a task force, committee or subcommittee, team, or work group, where you normally would not have volunteered. You'll gain greater visibility, respect, and perhaps an enhanced understanding of how your organization works.

Volunteer to help someone rehearse a presentation. Serve as an audience, sounding board, and/or a critic. Volunteer to review someone's report, key letter, or strategy paper.

Handle with Care

If you worry that people will start coming to you for all kinds of things, take heart. They will. As a result, their confidence in you, your self-confidence, and your pro-motability will all rise.

Volunteer to assume some responsibility for a task your boss is currently trying to juggle. Let her know that you're willing to relieve some of the pressure she feels. Naturally, in all cases, you don't want to volunteer to do something that commits too much of your time and energy. Volunteer only for that which seems within your pool of physical and mental resources.

As you're asked to take on new challenges, some of your other responsibilities may be reassigned or reallocated. After all, as your perceived value in your organization grows, the wisest within your organization will find others to handle the lower-level projects. They don't want the star player carrying the water cooler!

Self-Confidence in Social Situations

For every opportunity you have at work to stretch yourself and increase your self-confidence, at least three exist in the rest of the world. Happily, the measures you take away from work to increase your self-confidence greatly add to what your peers see back in the workplace.

I'm going to set a quota for you that you can easily achieve. I'd like you to engage in a minimum of one confidence-building activity a day away from the workplace. Here's a list of ideas to get you started, some of which may be right for you right now, and some of which you may want to try another time:

➤ Smile as you pass someone in a hallway or on the street. Make sure this is someone you don't know and to whom you're not necessarily attracted. In other words, you're randomly smiling at someone who does not seek or expect it. You're smiling at another human being just because you choose to.

➤ Focus intently on what another person is saying. This could be the teller at your bank, the clerk at the fast-food counter (although I hope you're not still eating fast food), the attendant at your health club, or your racquetball partner. For at least a few minutes, give this person your complete and undivided attention. Indeed, make listening to them your reason for being.

➤ Put yourself in a position where you're likely to get rejected. Make a legitimate request of someone for something that has a low probability of engendering a favorable response. For example, ask a friend or spouse to attend some function, when you know in advance that he or she is not likely to say yes. If you receive a favorable response, wonderful. If you don't, your goal is then to accept the response graciously.

➤ Volunteer for something away from work. It could be helping out someplace on a temporary basis. Perhaps you could stand by a door and collect tickets to an event or greet people as they enter. Maybe a little old lady, or a little old man for that matter, does need help crossing the street.

➤ Make a minor request of someone whom you barely know or have recently met. For example, if you're at a party, ask someone to help you straighten your tie, hand you a plate at the buffet table, or get some other minor item for you. Make a sincere and, of course, friendly request. The more easily you're able to make minor requests of strangers, the more naturally you'll begin to make more significant requests of anyone, when the situation merits it.

> **Make It So**
> The more you're able to graciously accept rejection and see it for what it is—usually a rejection of your *offer*, not of *you*—the more you'll be able to confidently ask for something.

➤ In conversation with another person, when appropriate, tell him:

"I'm not sure."

"I don't know."

"I'm not the right party to ask."

"I wish I could say."

"I don't have much information about that."

"Sorry, I can't help you there."

Legitimately pleading ignorance helps free you from any potential feelings of always needing to have informative responses. Self-confident people have little trouble saying, "I don't know," when that is so.

> JUST THE FACTS MA'AM.
>
> **Just the Facts**
> When handling question-and-answer sessions, speakers are often advised to respond truthfully with "I don't know," and then add, "But I'll be happy to find the answer to that for you." This assures the audience that you're fully able to admit when you don't know the answer to something, and at the same time have the professionalism to seek out the answer.

➤ Strike up a conversation with a complete stranger over a common activity. For example, if you're heading out of the movie theater, briefly ask someone you don't know, "Did you like that?" Similarly, at the supermarket checkout counter, ask the clerk, "Have you ever tried this?"

Self-confident people feel free to engage in conversation with others. Their conversation powers are not limited. They live in a bigger and more often brighter world because they can reach out to others.

➤ Make a difficult phone call—you know, the one you've been avoiding. The call could be to someone who owes you money or to whom you owe money. You could call a relative you haven't talked to in a while or someone who's been avoiding you. The call could be to air a grievance or to purchase something you've been postponing.

Automatic Self-Confidence

Like many things in life, developing self-confidence is a habit, similar to generating wealth or staying in shape. If you keep working at it, one fine morning you'll wake up and, whether you notice it or not, you'll be among the ranks of the self-confident.

On that bright morning, you still may not be a master at dealing with others, able to give a virtuoso performance when making a presentation to a group, be the perfect parent, or be a totally wonderful spouse. You will, however, more completely accept who and what you are in life, and recognize where you're highly capable and not so capable.

While no one is ever free from self-doubt, you'll be able to more accurately assess it, almost with curious self-detachment, without allowing it to immobilize you. You'll be thankful for the confidence that you feel in your profession and life—not arrogant, elitist, or smug. You'll face less resistance to embracing appropriate change because you'll be less attached to much of what doesn't matter.

From Self-Confidence to Assertiveness

When you're self-confident, you're naturally assertive. You speak up for yourself when the situation merits it. You're able to express yourself to others in various ways so that they understand and accept your message.

Being self-confident doesn't automatically qualify you for the assertiveness hall of fame. A variety of situations, techniques, and approaches still require discussion, and we've got the whole rest of this book to do that. If you were to do nothing else, however, but work on increasing your self-confidence, your assertiveness would predictably increase as a result.

The Least You Need to Know

➤ You have what it takes to be more self-confident in your life.

➤ At work you can practice increasing your self-confidence a little bit at a time by volunteering to head up projects, pitching in when you weren't asked, relieving some of your boss's burden, reorganizing your office, and cultivating a more professional appearance.

➤ Away from work, look for opportunities to help others, smile more often, approach someone you're attracted to, and start up a conversation with someone you don't know.

➤ You know you have self-confidence when it comes to you automatically—you don't have to think about it or practice it.

➤ To have self-confidence is to be assertive.

Part 3
I Assert, Therefore I Am

This pivotal section will offer five chapters that you won't want to miss. In Chapter 9, we'll look at the array of items and issues that you deem are worth asserting yourself. In Chapter 10, I'll explore the many levels of assertiveness at your disposal, depending on the situation you face (digressing to simply getting what's yours).

In Chapter 11, I'll look at the issues of birth order, cultural heritage, and social status and how they affect your ability to develop effective assertiveness skills. In Chapter 12, I'll highlight key organizations that give you the opportunity to actually throw yourself into situations where you have to speak up (yup, you're going to do it!).

To round out the section, I'll discuss physical assertiveness in Chapter 13—standing tall, walking with a purpose, being more aware, being more alert, and projecting greater strength and authority to others. With all this in mind, I'll bet you're eager to begin!

Must Haves, Wants, and Nice Ifs

In Chapter 3, I discussed the importance of establishing priorities and supporting goals and of being a more effective decision maker. In this chapter, I'll explore what's important to you on a day-to-day basis, at home, as you proceed to work, and as a variety of daily situations unfold.

Sorting Out What You Want

What are the "must haves" for you as you proceed throughout the work day? Respect? The latitude to air your views? The corner office?

These "must haves" are separated from the "wants"—those things you'd like to have, but which are not crucial for making your day go better, adding to your peace of mind, or keeping you in balance. Your "wants" list could be as long as you like. Some of them you'll go for, some of them you won't. Still, it's important to identify them.

Make It So
By using this three-point classification system—the "must haves," "wants," and "nice ifs"—you will be in a far better position intuitively to assert yourself when the situa-tion or issue calls for it, and to lay back when it doesn't.

Finally, you'll look at the "wouldn't-it-be-nice-if…" aspects of your life. These are things that, if they fell into your lap, would certainly be pleasant to have, but which, if they never materialized, wouldn't necessarily be missed. I'll call these the "nice ifs."

Life's Little Menu

On the following pages, I list most of what you could want in this world at work, much of what you might seek at home, and lots of stuff in between. As you review each item on these lists, please mark it as one of the following:

➤ M for "must have"

➤ W for "want"

➤ N for "nice if"

Remember, the Ms represent things you must have: Your day, your week, or your life would be rotten without them. The Ws represent things that you want to have: You could go on without them, but it is far better to have them. The Ns represent things that would be nice to have: If they fall into your lap you'll take them, but they're not anything for which you'd extend yourself.

Before you start, here are a few potentially helpful hints and observations:

➤ You may need to go through the lists several times, and you may find yourself changing around Ms, Ws, and Ns. That's okay.

➤ If you're not sure in what category to assess something, leave it blank for now. Perhaps the answer will become clear later.

➤ If something doesn't apply to you at all, that is, you have no interest in it, try rewording it to make it fit into one of the categories. If you've tried rewording it and it still is of no interest to you whatsoever, feel free to cross it out.

➤ You might want to copy these lists on a copier. I give you permission.

➤ Use different-colored writing instruments if that inspires you.

All About Your Workplace

Now, whip through this list, or slowly and carefully consider each item, and decide where you rate each one in the "must have," "want," or "nice if" categories.

Item	Must Have	Want	Nice If
A corner office	_____	_____	_____
An office with a view	_____	_____	_____
An office of strategic location	_____	_____	_____
A swivel chair	_____	_____	_____
A bigger desk	_____	_____	_____
A private phone line	_____	_____	_____
Your own fax machine	_____	_____	_____
Your own fax line	_____	_____	_____
An administrative assistant	_____	_____	_____
A personal assistant	_____	_____	_____
Nightly cleaning	_____	_____	_____
Biweekly cleaning	_____	_____	_____
Weekly cleaning	_____	_____	_____
Your name on the door	_____	_____	_____
A name placard for your desk	_____	_____	_____
An "in" basket	_____	_____	_____
An "out" basket	_____	_____	_____
Shelves	_____	_____	_____
More shelves	_____	_____	_____
A filing cabinet	_____	_____	_____
Another filing cabinet	_____	_____	_____
A credenza	_____	_____	_____
A sound screen	_____	_____	_____
A bulletin board	_____	_____	_____
A wall clock	_____	_____	_____
Plants	_____	_____	_____
An extra chair	_____	_____	_____
A couch	_____	_____	_____
A closet	_____	_____	_____
Artwork	_____	_____	_____
Posters	_____	_____	_____
A printer	_____	_____	_____
A color laserjet printer	_____	_____	_____
A door that locks	_____	_____	_____
Drawers that lock	_____	_____	_____

continues

continued

Item	Must Have	Want	Nice If
A mini-refrigerator	_____	_____	_____
A microwave	_____	_____	_____
An extra table	_____	_____	_____
Drapery	_____	_____	_____
New carpeting	_____	_____	_____
A desk lamp	_____	_____	_____
A second phone line	_____	_____	_____
A third phone line	_____	_____	_____
Additional office supplies	_____	_____	_____
Space for photos of your family and friends	_____	_____	_____
The most modern versions of software	_____	_____	_____
State-of-the-art computer equipment	_____	_____	_____
DirecTV	_____	_____	_____
Other _____			
Other _____			
Other _____			

Online Capabilities

Suddenly the cyberworld is another vital dimension of the workplace. Accordingly, a whole host of "must haves," "wants," and "nice ifs" follow.

Item	Must Have	Want	Nice If
Internet access	_____	_____	_____
Unlimited Internet access	_____	_____	_____
An e-mail account	_____	_____	_____
A private e-mail account	_____	_____	_____
A fax modem	_____	_____	_____
A fax/modem connected to a fiberoptic network	_____	_____	_____
A bigger hard drive	_____	_____	_____
A faster operating system	_____	_____	_____
More RAM	_____	_____	_____

Item	Must Have	Want	Nice If
Enhanced intranet access	_____	_____	_____
Newsgroup access	_____	_____	_____
Enhanced newsgroup access	_____	_____	_____
A personal Web page	_____	_____	_____
A personal Web page designer	_____	_____	_____
Web page maintenance	_____	_____	_____
An enhanced mail program	_____	_____	_____
Mailing list access	_____	_____	_____
Web access at home	_____	_____	_____
Home e-mail access	_____	_____	_____
Home intranet access	_____	_____	_____
Security protection	_____	_____	_____
Software access	_____	_____	_____
An FTP account	_____	_____	_____
Access to other nets	_____	_____	_____
Other _____			
Other _____			
Other _____			

Office Perks

The variety and nature of items offered in benefit packages have witnessed dramatic shifts since the early 1980s, as organizations scramble to remain solvent and still keep employees happy. For which of the following would you assert yourself?

Item	Must Have	Want	Nice If
One week of vacation annually	_____	_____	_____
Two weeks of vacation annually	_____	_____	_____
Three weeks of vacation annually	_____	_____	_____
Four weeks of vacation annually	_____	_____	_____
Liberal leave policy	_____	_____	_____
Flexible hours	_____	_____	_____
Generous personal leave time	_____	_____	_____
Generous sick leave time	_____	_____	_____
Major medical coverage	_____	_____	_____

continues

continued

Item	Must Have	Want	Nice If
Health care insurance	___	___	___
Dental care insurance	___	___	___
Optical care insurance	___	___	___
Pension fund	___	___	___
Annuity fund	___	___	___
Profit-sharing plan	___	___	___
Stock-option plan	___	___	___
Option plans with employer contributions	___	___	___
Compensation for accumulated sick leave	___	___	___
Compensation for accumulated vacation time	___	___	___
Year-end bonus	___	___	___
Semiannual bonus	___	___	___
Quarterly bonus	___	___	___
Automatic percentage increases	___	___	___
Health club membership	___	___	___
Golf club membership	___	___	___
Tennis club membership	___	___	___
Swim club membership	___	___	___
First-class air travel	___	___	___
Business-class air travel	___	___	___
Airport limo	___	___	___
Airport van	___	___	___
Golden parachute	___	___	___
Severance plan	___	___	___
Replacement counseling	___	___	___
Letter of recommendation	___	___	___
Employee credit union	___	___	___
Loan program	___	___	___
Advanced pay	___	___	___
Tuition credits	___	___	___
Tuition reimbursement	___	___	___
Spouse travel	___	___	___
Family travel	___	___	___

Item	Must Have	Want	Nice If
Corporate relocation	____	____	____
Corporate home purchase	____	____	____
Financial planning assistance	____	____	____
Tax planning	____	____	____
Career counseling	____	____	____
Stress management counseling	____	____	____
Automatic salary renegotiation	____	____	____
Choice of assignments	____	____	____
The right to refuse to relocate	____	____	____
Advanced commission rate	____	____	____
Choice of territory	____	____	____
Company car	____	____	____
Garage parking	____	____	____
Permanent parking space	____	____	____
Parking reimbursed	____	____	____
Company equipment	____	____	____
Company supplies	____	____	____
Telecommuting privileges	____	____	____
MBA enrollment	____	____	____
Work/study program	____	____	____
Travel abroad	____	____	____
Other _____			
Other _____			
Other _____			

Resources and Support

As you well know, the level or amount of resources and support you receive in the execution of your responsibilities can make a huge difference in how much you accomplish and how much energy you expend personally. Which of the following would make your work life oh-so-much better?

Item	Must Have	Want	Nice If
Staff size increase	____	____	____
Staff budget increase	____	____	____
Staff specialties	____	____	____
Temporary help	____	____	____

continues

continued

Item	Must Have	Want	Nice If
Department budget increase	_____	_____	_____
Freedom to select team members	_____	_____	_____
Freedom to select own staff	_____	_____	_____
Administrative help	_____	_____	_____
Research help	_____	_____	_____
Technical help	_____	_____	_____
Management training seminars	_____	_____	_____
Management training courses	_____	_____	_____
Personal instruction	_____	_____	_____
Private tutoring	_____	_____	_____
Designated mentor	_____	_____	_____
Cross-functional training	_____	_____	_____
Interdepartmental training	_____	_____	_____
Reduced work load	_____	_____	_____
Enhanced resources	_____	_____	_____
Upgraded equipment	_____	_____	_____
Expanded facilities	_____	_____	_____
Other _____			
Other _____			
Other _____			

Home Life

The list of identifiable items in your work life that you must have, want to have, or think would be nice to have is relatively finite. Of course, if I added interpersonal elements, such as more respect, more attention, or more credit, the list could go on forever.

With Your Spouse or Significant Other

The same dilemma crops up when assessing what you must have, want to have, and think would be nice to have in your home life. There simply isn't room to list all the dynamics of interpersonal relations—respect, more tenderness, time alone, more attention, and so on—so I've confined the next list to a few more readily observable aspects of your home life. I strongly invite you to more fully develop the rosters so that, once and for all, you have a framework for standing up or speaking up for yourself.

Item	Must Have	Want	Nice If
More time together	_____	_____	_____
More time at specific events	_____	_____	_____
More time at your events	_____	_____	_____
More sex	_____	_____	_____
More time at dinner	_____	_____	_____
More help with meals	_____	_____	_____
Less time in front of the television	_____	_____	_____
Time to exercise together	_____	_____	_____
Help with household tasks	_____	_____	_____
Help with the children	_____	_____	_____
To be heard	_____	_____	_____
Respect	_____	_____	_____
More tenderness	_____	___	_____
Time alone	_____	_____	_____
To not have the toothpaste tube squeezed in the middle	_____	_____	_____
To have the toilet seat put back down after use	_____	_____	_____
Other	_____
Other	_____
Other	_____

You may, perhaps, decide to share this chart with your spouse, as opposed to keeping it to yourself. After all, if you're interested in knowing what your spouse considers important, this will help.

As you can quickly surmise, you could then create the same type of grid for others in your household, then in-laws, friends, neighbors; working your way to even clerks, cashiers, receptionists, attendants; and so forth.

So, What Must You Have?

Your goal now is to consolidate by topic area all the things you indicated earlier as "must haves." If you truthfully must have these things, you now have the complete roster of everything for which you will assert yourself in the coming weeks, months, and years.

Make It So
In a sense, the items you identify as "must haves," once you assign specific time horizons, become goals that support your chosen priorities.

It might also help to allocate these "must haves" in accordance with your priorities from Chapter 3.

If you find something in your "must" list that, on closer inspection, doesn't support one of your priorities in any way, perhaps you can redirect it to your "want" list.

What Do You Want to Have?

Now, proceed through the master list again to create a consolidated list of the things that you want to have but that are not absolutely crucial to you. For these items, you'll assert yourself on occasion and when appropriate, but you won't go out of your way.

Many of these items may be important to you, but their absence does not impede your progress for peace of mind in work or in life. You can continue to support your priorities, regardless of the wants you're able to attain.

Nice Ifs

Review the list one more time and consolidate those items you indicated as "nice ifs"— that is, nice if they fell into your lap. Once again, these are items you'll accept if they come your way, but you won't extend yourself to obtain them. Sometimes, however, something that once made your "nice if" list might later grow in importance.

How Much Energy Do You Choose to Allocate?

Now you're at the turning point, perhaps, when you recognize the truth of that old saying, "If it is to be, it's up to me." If you intend to have the "musts haves" that you've identified, you'll have to generate the necessary energy to make them a reality in your life.

Even the most skilled or assertive individual has to expend some energy, along with timing, language use, persistence, and follow-through.

After that, it's likely that some "must haves" will still continue to elude you. After all, who gets everything, even among the "must haves" of life?

Merely drawing up the list is valuable in itself, however. If you have firmly resolved that each item on your "must haves" list will be yours one fine day, your progress will be astounding.

Keeping Your Chin Up Even if Nothing Is Going Right

When you're making your way through rough terrain, be aware of this odd phenomenon. Suppose you're trekking over a series of mountains. You're on top of one mountain, and you look over to see the next peak. It doesn't look that far away.

You start making your way down the first mountain to the valley below. Halfway down, you look up to see the next peak. Suddenly, it seems much farther away, despite the progress you've made since you first saw it.

The same phenomenon is at work when you first identify all of your "musts" and go about attaining them. When you first generate the list, you feel good because, unlike 99.9 percent of the population, you've identified what's vital to you in your career and personal life. This is much further than most people ever get. In a sense, you're on one mountain peak.

As you descend into the valley, where the task of appropriately requesting these items takes place, you may feel as if you've got an even longer way to go. Yet, you're already en route and farther along the trail than when you started.

It's economical from a personal energy standpoint to have identified what you must have in life. Now, at least you won't expend energy on things that didn't make the list.

Perhaps the biggest obstacle to being assertive is knowing what to be assertive about. So, take a deep breath, throw your shoulders back, and smile. You're way ahead of the rest of the class.

The Least You Need to Know

➤ By identifying the "must haves," "wants," and "nice ifs" in your career and life, you can allocate your energies more efficiently.

➤ Hopefully, the majority of your "musts" can readily be converted to goals that support the priorities you chose earlier.

➤ Assert yourself for the "wants" as opportunities present themselves, but don't extend yourself. Don't try for the "nice ifs" at all.

➤ From peak to peak, the journey doesn't look so difficult. Down in the valley, though, the next peak looks much farther away, as will attaining what you've identified as "musts."

➤ Keep your chin up; merely by identifying what you must have, you're way ahead of most people.

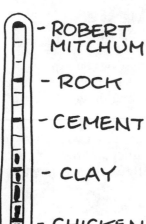

- ROBERT MITCHUM
- ROCK
- CEMENT
- CLAY
- CHICKEN
- JELL-O

Chapter 10

The Aggressiveness/ Assertiveness Grid

In This Chapter

➤ When it pays to burn your bridges

➤ Taking no prisoners

➤ Deciding to come to the peace table

➤ Establishing smooth relations

➤ When to ignore an "offense" all together

We move now from identifying your "must haves" in Chapter 9 to a different gear wherein you are faced with an array of, perhaps less important, semi-nagging issues. It would be wonderful if you could always be your fine, upstanding, balanced self.

Still, there are some situations in life and in business where it makes sense to get totally aggressive yourself, even to the point of burning bridges, if that's what it takes. Perhaps somebody owes you a small fortune, for example, and you never care if you see this despicable person again; you just want your money.

This chapter represents a departure from what's come before, in that I'm going to lay out a strategy for you as to how you might care to vigorously pursue an issue given varying circumstances. Let's face reality—if you're never going to see the other party again, you don't care what they think of you, and you have been rightfully denied what is owed you, burning bridges can make sense. The strategy you choose will depend on your situation.

A Measuring Tool for How and When to Be Aggressive

Suppose you're confronted by a situation initiated by someone else or you experience outright transgression by someone else such that you feel compelled to vociferously speak up for yourself. The following grid shows potential responses to four different types of situations associated with four categories of individuals.

Although the instances when you feel you may need to vigorously assert yourself do not always directly result from an offense or transgression on the part of another, for purposes of shorthand I'll use the word "offense" to connote something you feel merits redress.

The four categories are across the top of the grid:

➤ A one-time minor offense

➤ A repeated minor offense

➤ A one-time major offense

➤ A repeated major offense

The second dimension of the grid relates to the other party with whom you'll be dealing. Reading down, these categories include:

➤ Someone close to you who you see every day, such as a spouse, family member, boss, or coworker

➤ Someone you see on occasion, perhaps once a week or less, but it is known that you'll see this party many more times

➤ Someone you see rarely, or perhaps see less frequently than once every few months, or even once a year

➤ Someone you'll likely never see again or choose to never see again

The Aggressiveness Grid

	One-Time Minor Offense	Repeat Minor Offense	One-Time Major Offense	Repeat Major Offense
You see the other party frequently (may be someone close to you)	40°	50°	60°	70°
You see the other party occasionally	50°	60°	70°	80°
You see the other party rarely	60°	70°	80°	90°
You'll never see the other party again	70°	80°	90°	100°

This approach provides guidelines for what techniques you may choose to use in particular situations. Now, let's explore each of the sixteen cells, starting from the lower right-hand corner (which rates 100° on the "response" meter) weaving our way through to the top left-hand corner (which rates 40°).

A Repeat Major Offense from a Party You're Not Likely to See Again (100°)

Suppose you brought your car in for repair at a service center you had not tried before. Rather than repair your car, the center makes the problem worse. You return to the shop several more times, and every time you get your car back, there's something else wrong. Perhaps you've been assertive all along, even diplomatic, patiently working with the manager and focusing on the single goal of having your car in top condition.

You pay a fairly significant repair bill after the first time you pick up your car. After all, you hadn't expected to make return visits. After X number of visits, you conclude that you're wasting your time, you're certainly not going to pay, the center is incompetent, and you want to have nothing further to do with this organization.

You ask for a credit voucher to offset the credit card payment you made following your first visit. The service manager is reluctant. He claims his mechanics have already spent many hours on your car, and they intend to make it "right for you." From your perspective, this service center is highly incompetent and deserves none of your money; you'll never come back.

In this case, it makes sense for you to either get the credit voucher or call your credit card company and cancel the charges.

On the Aggressiveness Grid, a repeat major offense by a party you're never likely to see again equals 100°.

When to Burn Your Bridges

The second set of circumstances calls for a milder form of assertion (90 degrees on the Aggressiveness Grid) but a vigorous response nevertheless.

A One-Time Major Offense by a Party You're Not Likely to See Again (90°)

You're standing in line for tickets to a special event. You heard from a reliable source that it's going to be a sellout, and there are not many tickets left. Suddenly, someone cuts in front of you, and no one else seems to notice. This jostles your sense of fairness. You're hot, tired, have waited for quite a while, and can't even be assured that any tickets will be left when you get to the front of the line. Also, you made some sacrifices to get here to pick up these tickets today.

This is an example of a one-time major offense from a party you're not likely to see again. Your appropriate options include suggesting to this person that he move to the back of the line, or if that doesn't work, asking someone else to hold your place in line while you go get an official.

Although the odds are probably slight that this one person will cause you to miss getting a ticket to the performance, most people would agree it's your right to induce this person to go to the back of the line.

A Repeat Major Offense by a Party You'll See Rarely (90°)

Suppose you have small children who frequently play in your yard. One day, someone from your local power company comes barreling into your driveway at a speed that you consider unsafe. He reads your meter and then leaves.

You recall this happened once before, when no one was in the yard and you happened to be looking out the window. Now you decide the situation clearly merits action. You walk over to the attendant and politely suggest he enter your driveway at a much slower speed, reminding him that safety is the first rule of any job that involves a motor vehicle. He accepts your suggestion and promises to drive more slowly in the future.

Next month, he again comes barreling into your driveway. It is now time to burn the bridges. This is a repeat and major offense (a 90° rating) by someone you'll see once a month, at best, for five minutes. Yet, the stakes are too high.

In addition to admonishing this person for his driving, you choose to also tell him you'll be reporting him to the utility and will ask that another driver be placed on this route.

Taking No Prisoners Has Its Place

The next three situations each rate an 80° on the Aggressiveness Grid. In these situations your response doesn't need to be as strong as when you burn your bridges; nevertheless, due to the nature of these situations you will respond with vigor.

A Repeat Minor Offense by a Party You're Not Likely to See Again (80°)

Suppose you live alone in an apartment complex, and you travel a lot for work. You don't like to have newspapers stack up while you're away because it's an indication to crooks that your apartment would be an easy one to burglarize. You notice, repeatedly, that one free circulation newspaper is delivered to your door every Wednesday. You call the circulation manager and ask that they stop delivering this paper since you're frequently away and don't want any telltale signs that you're not home. On top of that, you never read the paper.

The manager promises to stop delivery. Upon returning from your next trip, you find that the paper is still being delivered. You call or perhaps visit the office of the circulation manager. You explain how you've asked before, put notes on your door, and nothing seems to work. The circulation manager promises that it won't happen again.

It happens again. The Aggressiveness Grid shows 80 degrees. Now is the time to take no prisoners.

Go over the head of the circulation manager to the publisher. Explain the situation and say if it happens even once more, you will begin to explore your legal rights.

Yes, papers stacking up at your door is relatively minor, but one burglary of your apartment can ruin your whole day, week, month, and potentially year, depending on whether or not the place gets ransacked.

A One-Time Major Offense by a Party You'll See Rarely (80°)

You're a home-business entrepreneur and occasionally receive overnight packages via express delivery services. One time, a package is left a few feet from the usual drop-off spot. As it turns out, you're away for most of that day, and there is a torrential rain. When you return, you see that the package is water-logged. You go inside and open it. Its contents are completely drenched, ruined! The Aggressiveness Grid says 80°.

This has only happened once, from a service you encounter once a month or less. Unfortunately, you consequently miss an important deadline and need to call the original party to have the package resubmitted. Not a happy situation.

It's important for you to call this delivery firm to establish precisely where the drop-off point is, credit the sender's account for the ruined package, and ensure that this situation will not happen again.

A Repeat Major Offense by a Party You'll See Occasionally (80°)

You live in a high-rise condominium complete with a doorman. Usually, you enter from the parking garage and take the elevator up to your apartment. Once a week or so, you enter from the front door, returning from some trip or errand on foot.

You don't really know the doorman, and he certainly doesn't know you, but for some reason, he makes a remark about your appearance every time he opens the door for you:

➤ "Mm..., Mm..., you're lookin' good!"

➤ "You're certainly a sight for sore eyes!"

➤ "My, my..."

109

At first, it's tolerable. Then it becomes a little irritating, until finally, it's offensive. What's more, he's made his comments when you've been with others, or when others not accompanying you have been within earshot. This, too, rates an 80° on the Aggressiveness Grid.

You only see this person about once a week or so, and his running commentary only lasts for about 15 seconds.

Why make a big deal of things? You have the right to because it's where you live, it's the front door you have to go through, and you don't need to be repeatedly subjected to this person's running diatribe about your appearance.

You indicated to him via gestures that you don't appreciate the remarks. Another time, you said to him directly in a low voice, "Okay, that's enough." Finally, you came right out and said, "Please refrain from making such comments." The next couple of times you see him, surprise, no remarks!

Then it starts again. You assert yourself, saying, "I've asked you before to please refrain from making such comments." If that doesn't do it—if you hear even one more remark on subsequent trips through the front door—it's time to burn your bridges.

Your next message to the doorman needs to be on the level of, "I think it's time that you, I, and the condominium association manager had a long chat."

Deciding to Come to the Peace Table

You have now reached the midpoint of the Aggressiveness Grid, where the temperature registers 70°. There are four cells in this category.

A One-Time Minor Offense by a Person You're Likely to See Again (70°)

You ask a question during a lecture. The presenter comments that your question would take too long to discuss. You feel a little put off. You wish to speak up, but you decide to wait until after the lecture. It would be too vigorous to speak up during the meeting.

As the session ends and everyone files out, you make your way to the front of the lecture hall to converse with the presenter. Rather than leave that evening feeling hurt or offended, you decide to come to the peace table and air your views regarding the validity of your question and the manner in which he handled it.

If you gain satisfaction from his response, then all is well; there is no need to dwell on the issue any further. If you don't gain satisfaction, then perhaps you want to restate your position another way and end the encounter. That's all you can do. In the grand scope of things, it's only a minor offense and you gave it your best shot.

A Repeat Minor Offense by a Party You'll Rarely See Again (70°)

In their effort to do a good job, you surmise, the nightly cleaning crew rearranges things on your desk so when you begin work in the morning, you're thrown off-course. You only encounter the crew members every few weeks or so, and they come in very late. Nevertheless, you don't wish to spend several minutes every morning reorganizing the materials on your desk.

Your options are clear; you can leave a note explaining the situation. In it you'll need to state that you will take responsibility for cleaning your own desk. Otherwise you can stay late the very next evening, so you can explain to the crew in person the importance of not rearranging items on your desk.

Suppose that the cleaning contractor rotates its crews, or that hired help is consistently turning over? From week to week or month to month, different people are cleaning your office. This case calls for at least two measures:

➤ One, put a sign or placard on your desk as you depart each evening. In it, request that your desktop contents not be touched.

➤ Two, call the supervisor or foreman responsible for the company's offices and explain the situation. Perhaps you could provide an actual map indicating where your office is, or if the offices are numbered, you can simply refer to the number.

A One-Time Major Offense by a Party You'll See Rarely (70°)

You don't go into the post office often—you can't stand the wait. You order stamps by mail, send others to make pickups and deliveries, and, in general, minimize your actual trips.

One time, after ordering $60 worth of stamps by mail, you receive only $48 worth of stamps. You call and present your case to a variety of post office personnel, but get no satisfaction. You decide it's time to make a trip to personally meet the window clerk supervisor, someone you've seen occasionally, who may recognize you.

You explain the situation. Then, the supervisor explains how stamp-by-mail orders are carefully filled out and accounted for before the stamps are sent to the customer. That's all fine and dandy, you say, but, nevertheless, you're still missing $12 worth of stamps.

You intend to get the number of stamps you know you're missing, but you haven't come to make war. After all, you haven't been shortchanged before. What's more, it was probably an honest mistake. Additionally, this is the only post office in your small town. *You have to deal with these people.*

Considerable time passes; meanwhile, the supervisor keeps re-articulating his point. You mention that you could take this grievance to the postmaster, the highest authority in town, or fill out a grievance card and send it to Washington, D.C., but you choose not to because you've come here to achieve an effective resolution and keep the peace.

Stand your ground and do not leave until you're given the requisite number of stamps.

A Repeat Major Offense by a Party You'll See Regularly (70°)

You live with your significant other. Practically every time your S.O. takes a shower, he or she ends up flooding the bathroom floor. This really irritates you. What does it take to fix the shower curtain and re-aim the shower head so no water leaks out of the tub area? What's far worse, you also notice that moisture is seeping through into the basement. If your S.O. keeps this up, very costly structural damage could result, possibly requiring thousands of dollars worth of repairs and a grueling clean-up.

If you were never to see the offending party again, the Aggressiveness Grid would show 100, but we're talking about your significant other. This is someone you live with and sleep with. Therefore, it only registers as 70 on the grid.

Lovingly, but emphatically, state that it's time to stop drenching the bathroom floor. Without being condescending, show your partner how to solve the leakage problem.

If the situation resolves itself, fine. If it happens again, you'll need to be more demonstrative, because water seeping through to the basement, causing structural damage, is cumulative, costly, and avoidable, not to mention hazardous, messy, and *stinky!* After a repeated number of occurrences, you'll have to be the judge; maybe it's time to consider a different partner. Or, go to a home center and investigate glassed-in bath areas or other options that automatically will diminish any incidents of shower water hitting the bathroom floor.

On Being More Diplomatic

You're in the home stretch, and now, with three 60 degree examples, you'll be a master of the entire grid. If all the previous situations benefit from a touch of diplomacy, for the next three it's more or less mandatory.

A One-Time Minor Offense by a Party You'll See Occasionally (60°)

A different utility company representative comes monthly to check your meter. In fact, this situation comes directly from my personal experience. I happened to be home one morning when a power company representative parked her vehicle in my driveway. She left the motor running, went and read my meter, and then returned to her vehicle. Upon her return, she saw someone she knew in the next yard and walked directly over to her.

Then, for the next 12 minutes, she engaged in conversation with her vehicle's motor still running. I was aware of the situation from the first few minutes because I heard the vehicle approach and looked out the window. I don't think it is a great practice to leave the motor running while checking the meter, but I figured it would only take a minute or so, and this was not a big deal.

After a few minutes, I could still hear the motor running, so I looked out the window, and saw that the representative was engaged in conversation. I waited another four or five minutes, equaling about nine minutes total, and began to get irritated. I waited three more minutes and made for my front door. Just as I passed through the front door and began walking down the sidewalk steps, the representative came back to her still idling vehicle.

At this point, I confronted her. I told her I thought it was neither professional nor very safe to leave a car idling for as long as she had. She was taken aback. She saw nothing wrong in what she had done. I explained to her the large gap between a parked car and one with the motor running. After all, things can happen to an unattended, idling vehicle.

To her credit, she had a change of heart (perhaps she feared I would report her). She conceded that maybe she was in error, and she wouldn't let it happen again. We parted amicably.

A Repeat Minor Offense by a Party You'll See Regularly (60°)

Ever have a coworker who opens the door to your office, comes in, and then leaves with the door open? How about the reverse? Someone comes in when your door is open, speaks to you for a few moments, and then leaves closing the door?

This is obviously a minor offense; after all, we're not talking nuclear armaments here! Nevertheless, wouldn't most people assume that how you had your door before they entered is how you'd like to have it upon their exit? At the least, if they're unsure, they could ask how you'd like to have your door.

If they retreat slowly enough upon leaving your door open after first finding it closed, you could always say, "Please close the door." If they retreat closing the door when you originally had left it open, you might be able to say through the door, "Could you leave the door open, please?"

It's probably overkill to post a note saying *please leave the door as you found it.*

You could rush after the person and politely implore them to leave the door as they found it in the future, or you could bring up the topic later on when you see them in the halls or around the office.

Handle with Care
One of dozens of problems with a passive/aggressive behavioral approach is the other party frequently doesn't get the lesson. They may not be aware that they aggravate you. What is an issue for you may not be an issue for them, so how could your actions possibly "teach" them anything?

Either way, you've got to be judicious about this; otherwise you're likely to offend them by admonishing them over what they perceive as a piddling affair. Indeed, they may be more offended for being told how to leave your door than you were when they made the unrequested change in the position of your door.

In any case, keep the situation light. Say something like, "When I decide to apply for sainthood, I'll probably overlook such matters. But for now, I'd appreciate it if you'd leave my door the way you find it."

You could try turning around the situation, but it won't work. Suppose you go into your coworker's office, and if you find the door open, leave closing it, or vice versa. This is a form of passive/aggressive behavior, which I discussed in Chapter 1. Presumably, through your actions you attempt to teach the other party how to treat you.

A One-Time Major Offense by a Party You'll See Regularly (60°)

You made a major contribution to a report that your team recently turned in. The report had profound ramifications for the entire organization. Yet, yours was the only name that did *not* appear anyplace within the report. You're steamed, and normally, the Aggressiveness Grid would show 100°.

Since this is a group you see every day and need to work with closely, you regain your composure. You diplomatically approach the report's final editor and air your grievance. He or she offers apologies, possible remedies, such as circulating a memo stating that your name was inadvertently left out of the report, and you move on.

You have no need for creating a campaign out of this—the transgression is obvious. Assuming your team members individually and collectively maintain a sense of justice, they're as likely to remedy the situation as you are. Therefore, let them do it.

Establishing Smooth Relations

Now you're getting way down on the Aggressiveness Grid, around the 50 degree mark. When someone you encounter on a regular basis commits a one-time minor offense, if possible, adroitly address the situation directly after it happens.

If time has passed, perhaps it's better to not bring it up. If you feel the situation does merit mention, however, give it the air time it deserves and nothing more. Keep your observations brief and light. Then, in the same paragraph, or the next, turn to something else. In other words, direct the other party away from the issue you raised.

Here are some ideas for establishing smooth relations at those times when someone you know or see regularly does something which offends you a little.

➤ Meet with the other party on their turf.

➤ Be convincing, but highly tactful.

➤ Listen earnestly to what the other party has to say.

➤ Maintain perspective; keep the situation as light as possible.

➤ Work to obtain a common understanding.

➤ Propose a solution.

➤ Allow the other party to save face.

➤ Acknowledge any responsibility you have for the issue.

➤ Keep the issue private.

➤ Avoid using your authority or position.

➤ Use the other party's name(s) frequently.

➤ Lightly touch the shoulder of the other party.

➤ Smile when appropriate.

A second situation that calls for establishing smooth relations is when someone close to you commits a repeat minor offense. While this normally might register higher on the grid, you're going to contain yourself and keep it at 50 degrees because the person is close to you.

For example, if your spouse squeezes the toothpaste in the middle and this drives you crazy, bring up the topic in casual conversation now and then, but if it continues to happen, let it go. You have so many other solutions that this isn't worth the energy.

What are the solutions if your spouse squeezes the toothpaste in the middle? I'm glad you asked! I never met a tube of toothpaste that no matter how badly squeezed in the middle, couldn't be fixed. Close the cap tightly. Then, using the handle of your toothbrush, squeeze up all the toothpaste from the bottom toward the top of the tube like you normally would if you were using only your hands.

Next, open the cap and put the excess that has risen to the top on your toothbrush and brush your teeth.

You can also buy one of those metallic devices that you attach at the end of your toothpaste tube, which you use to roll up the tube as the toothpaste is dispensed. This effectively shortens the tube as you proceed, hence minimizing the effects of your spouse squeezing the tube in the middle.

As a last resort, go buy your own tube.

The Final Jeopardy Category (40°)

The final category on the grid is the situation in which someone close to you commits a one-time minor transgression. In this case, your path is clear—FORGET IT!

The Least You Need to Know

➤ When you've paid good money and the product and/or service you acquired repeatedly doesn't give you the results you rightfully expected it to, you deserve complete and swift restitution.

➤ One-time or repeat major offenses from parties you'll rarely or never see again may require swift, forceful action on your part.

➤ Your goal is to stand up for yourself, as often as you can, while maintaining the peace.

➤ There are many tools you can employ for smooth relations, including meeting with the other party on his or her turf, being convincing but highly tactful, listening earnestly to what the other party has to say, maintaining perspective, keeping the situation as light as possible, and working to obtain a common understanding.

➤ When someone close to you commits a one-time minor offense, forget about it.

Separating Myth From Reality

If you're the eldest child in your family, supposedly you are inclined to be more assertive. True sometimes, but not across the board. I've even heard it said that if you are from an affluent family you tend to be more assertive than someone from less well-to-do origins.

Let's take a brief tour to see if these notions hold water.

Born on the Right Side of the Tracks?

From Little Orphan Annie to Richie Rich, an age-old question persists: What advantages are there to being raised in an affluent environment? More specifically, is there a link between wealth and assertiveness? Are the wealthy wealthy because they're assertive? Does someone raised in affluence tend to become assertive?

Assertiveness May Lead to Wealth

It appears that assertiveness does indeed lead to wealth. Denis Waitely, who from the early 1970s to the early 1990s studied wealthy, successful, high achievers from all walks of life, found *a strong correlation between a strong vocabulary and greater income-producing potential.* This doesn't mean that merely having an extensive vocabulary or being verbose adds up to assertiveness or wealth. Brilliant Ph.D.s may speak poetically on one topic and give an extended philosophical discourse on another, but may not be assertive. Perhaps you had a professor in college like that. Perhaps you are a professor like that. A good vocabulary, however, certainly helps.

As you learned in Chapters 7 and 8, the natural ability to speak up is a valuable skill. In addition, the assertive tend to rise faster in their careers and, yes, earn more money.

Within professional service firms, the "finders," people who go out and get new business, earn much more than the "minders" who manage the projects, and the "grinders" who actually do the work. In large organizations, the people who make themselves heard rise to the top.

"Can I Say Something?"

Some of the very wealthy asserted themselves at a young age. Whatever else you may think of him, Henry Ross Perot is an excellent example of someone from humble origins and short of stature, who, by virtue of his assertiveness, generated nearly incalculable wealth.

Perot grew up in the Depression era. At age 12, he approached the circulation manager of his town newspaper, the *Gazette*, and offered to deliver newspapers to people's homes in the poverty-stricken area of town. No one had ever conceived of this idea—the prevailing assumption was that poor people could not afford, let alone read, a newspaper. Perot felt otherwise.

Within a short period Perot was making so much money by delivering newspapers that his commission was in jeopardy of being reduced. Never one to sit back and let others control his destiny, Perot wrote to the publisher and complained about how he was being treated by the paper's management after making so much money for the paper. The publisher agreed with him and he was able to continue the lucrative arrangement he had set up.

While working for IBM and becoming their top sales representative, Perot conceived of initiating a service branch within IBM which would help client companies learn how to use and apply office technology to improve their business operations. IBM declined to follow through on his idea, and Perot, at age 31, decided to leave his high-commission-earning job to start his own company, EDS. In 1984, he sold EDS to General Motors for $2.5 billion, and in 1986 sold his remaining stock in the company for $700 million. In one move after another, Perot asserted himself on the way to his ultimate prosperity.

Neither Gender Nor Language Barriers

Consider Kavelle R. Bajaj, who came to the United States from India in 1974 and faced cultural and gender barriers. In her conservative Indian upbringing, Bajaj was expected to place family affairs over a career. She opened a small business selling imported goods, but almost immediately became dissatisfied and disappointed in this venture.

Eventually she opted to try again. In the early 1980s, following the breakup of American Telephone and Telegraph, Bajaj borrowed $5,000 and took computer and database management classes at a nearby college. She then started a company called I-Net, which provided telecommunication contracting services primarily to the Department of Defense.

The company developed a solid reputation and grew quickly, if not evenly, over the next several years. In 1990, Bajaj landed a $100-million long-term contract from the Air Force for computer systems engineering and software. Bajaj attributes her success to initiative, assertiveness, and commitment to ideals. "There is opportunity in the United States for the person who wants to make it," she says. "There is no reason to make excuses."

The Ways and the Means

If assertiveness leads to wealth, does wealth lead to assertiveness? Those who are wealthy have the means to make their wishes more readily known than those who are not as wealthy. If you're wealthy, perhaps you have more time to be in organizations and take leadership positions. Certainly, someone who is wealthy has more options in life than someone who is not.

Make It So
When it comes to assertiveness, there doesn't seem to be a right or wrong side of the track. Your ability to be assertive is there for the taking.

Gauging if children *born into affluent environments* tend to be assertive is a more reliable indicator of whether wealth enhances assertiveness. We have to be careful here because the nature versus nurture elements need to be acknowledged. That is, children born to parents of wealth may inherit assertive characteristics. Nevertheless, from my observations and the studies I have encountered, there seems to be a reverse effect. *Children born into affluent environments generally seem to be less assertive than expected.*

Perhaps the parents' assertiveness and possible domineering qualities, which aided them in their accumulation of wealth, detrimentally affected their children's assertiveness. It's been well documented that wealth in families is often dissipated between the first and second generations, and certainly the second and third generations.

Are Men More or Less Assertive than Women?

In Chapter 17, I dwell specifically on special assertiveness situations for women. For now, suffice it to say that because of historical and social developments, it appears that men as a population group tend to be more assertive than women, at least in situations outside of the family.

While the number of women in the workforce and in higher corporate positions has increased dramatically in the last few decades, a great deal of balancing still needs to be done in those areas in the next millennium. And women can improve the odds through assertiveness.

> JUST THE FACTS MA'AM.
>
> ## Just the Facts
>
> Historically, men have been heads of nations, leaders of governments, generals, warriors, orators, debaters, professors, and scholars. They were more likely to be published, broadcast, and celebrated. Male children emulated their fathers, while female children emulated their mothers. Once again, however, your ability to be assertive, whether you're a man or a woman, is dependent mostly on the unique and particular aspects of your own situation.

More Alike Than Different?

Professor Julia Wood of the University of North Carolina disagrees with the otherwise popular notion that most men are alike and most women are alike. Professor Wood says that too many popular psychologists and authors maximize the differences and minimize the similarities between the sexes. She contends that although there are differences between men and women, *the similarities far outweigh those differences.*

Dr. Wood finds that much of the gender communications lore "overemphasizes the differences while eclipsing important similarities, and discourages the quality perceptions of individuals." In other words, you have to consider each person on a case-by-case basis. Just because someone is this sex or that doesn't mean you can assume they are assertive or not.

Is it really true today that men are more assertive than women? Probably not! Are men and women assertive in different circumstances? Probably so. If women are still the primary caretakers of children, how is it that they produce more assertive sons and less assertive daughters? Do parents treat boy and girl children differently and reward them for different behaviors? Most studies say yes. These and other burning questions of the day are not easily answered because of rapid and recent shifts in the family structure.

Are Men Less Sensitive Than Women?

In her book *Communication and the Sexes*, published by Harper and Row in 1988, Barbara Bate concluded that, in general, women tend to be more sympathetic, compassionate, gentle, and warm than men. Other studies and books before and after this one confirm these findings. Obviously, this doesn't mean that all women exhibit these characteristics more than all men; it means that in the aggregate, women tend to exhibit these qualities more frequently than men.

If men are more assertive and women are more responsive, then men are heard, and perhaps understood and heeded. If women are assertive and men are perhaps unresponsive, then women might understandably be frustrated.

All of this leads to the conclusion that women face special challenges to being assertive. Tune in to Chapter 17 for the compelling conclusion.

You Can Learn to Be More Assertive

Everything that you've encountered in this book, including this chapter, shows that you can learn to be more assertive, regardless of whatever potential disadvantages, impediments, or obstacles may be in your path. In fact, you can look for small victories in everyday life that will enhance your ability to be assertive.

The Least You Need to Know

➤ The more assertive you are, the more likely you are to generate wealth, although the converse is probably not true.

➤ Women have special challenges to being assertive.

Speak Now or Forever Hold Your Peace...

Do you realize that there are groups right in your own community or region that will let you practice being assertive, and on top of that, invite you back again and again? You may think that such opportunities are too good to be true, but this is true! Toastmasters International and other speaking, training, performance, consulting, and instruction-based societies can be found in every major metropolitan area, many suburban areas, and probably right near you.

These groups are not in existence specifically so that members can become more assertive. As a by-product of your participation, however, you can achieve spectacular results.

In this chapter, I will elaborate on four major professional societies that you can contact and join if you choose, so that you can begin to become more assertive and more effective in ways you may never have imagined.

All About Toastmasters International

Toastmasters International (TI) asserts that whatever your goals may be, your success in life will mostly depend on your ability to speak. People who have the ability to effectively communicate possess one of the skills necessary to achieve their goals.

> **Just the Facts**
>
> Dr. Ralph C. Smedley founded Toastmasters International (TI) in 1924 in Santa Anna, California, to help people develop their communications skills. In 1932, Toastmasters International was incorporated under California law, and now administers business and services through its world headquarters, located in Rancho Santa Margarita, California. Toastmasters employs neither paid promoters nor instructors, and no salaried staff except the executive director and world headquarters staff, which provides services to the clubs and districts.

Members of Toastmasters International learn by doing; each member presents short speeches and impromptu presentations in front of other group members. TI contends (with lots of supporting evidence) that at membership fees of less than $50 per year, the program is cost-effective, especially when compared to seminars charging hundreds of dollars per day. The program must be working very well, as it has members from all over the world!

A Little Toastmasters Philosophy

To understand and appreciate Toastmasters and how it can help you to achieve dramatic breakthroughs in assertiveness and leadership, you have to understand a little about the Toastmasters philosophy. They believe that a person's success, at least in business, is based on how effectively one communicates—hard to find fault with that! In Toastmasters, people learn to effectively communicate, conduct a meeting, manage a department or business, lead, delegate, and motivate.

"As your improved communication skills become obvious within the workplace," says TI, "increased visibility, recognition, and promotion will follow." While these may sound like high fallutin' claims, I personally find them to be more true than not. As I emphasized in my book *Blow Your Horn: How to Get Noticed and Get Ahead* (Berkley), once you improve your presentation skills, you begin to attain the respect and sometimes the admiration of your peers.

A Few Good Men and Women

The leadership skills you can acquire in Toastmasters can increase your potential as an executive or manager. As with most organizations, however, you must have the initiative! By serving as club officer, you learn to use parliamentary procedure, accept and delegate responsibility, and implement the basics of planning and leadership.

Resources Galore

Each Toastmasters club has access to many educational materials, including books, audio- and videotapes, and seminar programs. Most of these come from the Toastmasters International Supply Catalog, but really, they're a good deal. Toastmasters offers several self-paced programs you can use to meet your own goals at your own speed. For example, there are programs on:

➤ Prepared speeches

➤ Impromptu speaking

➤ Using visual aids

➤ Using voice inflection

➤ Giving a persuasive speech

➤ Introducing others

➤ Improving your grammar

Make It So
Many Toastmasters clubs change officers every six months or so. Hence, you can obtain leadership training and experience in short order by becoming an officer. As a Toastmaster, you can also increase your ability to persuade or inspire others.

Each new member receives several educational materials, including the "Toastmasters Basic Communication and Leadership Program" manual. The manual contains speech assignments for the meetings that follow (don't worry, we're not talking drudgery here). The probability is that by the time you finish the manual, you'll organize and present an invigorating and effective speech.

From there, you can become part of Toastmasters' Advanced Communication and Leadership Program, which consists of more challenging assignments that you complete in pursuit of your own career objectives. In other words, what you do in Toastmasters has immediate, real-world applications.

Each member also receives *The Toastmaster*, a monthly magazine that offers the latest insights into speaking and leadership techniques. I've read it and been published in it several times—this is a highly worthwhile magazine that you'll want to receive.

Scouting Out These Guys

With thousands of Toastmasters clubs around the world, there is undoubtedly one near you, and you don't need a personal invitation to join. Some clubs are listed with their local Chamber of Commerce; some are listed under "Clubs" in the Yellow Pages; and some list their meetings in the weekly calendar section of the local newspaper. Once you find the club that is convenient for you, attend one of their meetings. You will be made to feel welcome—no one will ask you to "speak up," although you can if you want to. Don't be surprised to find members from such diverse backgrounds as executives, auto mechanics, teachers, attorneys, homemakers, artists, college students, doctors, supervisors, engineers, and salespersons. In the highly unlikely event that there is no club near you, you can even form your own with permission and assistance from Toastmasters International.

> **Just the Facts**
>
> About half of the new Toastmasters clubs since 1990 have been organized as in-house company clubs. In other words, many companies choose to sponsor a Toastmasters club as a way to provide high-quality, cost-effective communication training for their employees.

If you want to increase your assertiveness, speech power, or leadership potential, put down this book right now and contact Toastmasters International at:

Toastmasters International
P.O. Box 9052
Mission Viejo, CA 92690
(714) 858-8255
Fax: (714) 858-1207

American Society for Training and Development

The American Society for Training and Development (ASTD) asserts that the most consistent advantage for individual employees and businesses is the ability to learn faster and perform more efficiently than the competition.

> **Just the Facts**
>
> Founded in 1944, ASTD is a leader in the field of workplace learning and performance. ASTD's membership includes more than 58,000 individuals and organizations from every level of the field of workplace performance in more than 100 countries. The leaders and members of ASTD work in multinational corporations, small- and medium-size businesses, government agencies, colleges, and universities worldwide.

ASTD serves as a resource provider on topics related to workplace learning and performance. The organization sees itself as worldwide leader in this field.

What Can It Do for Me?

One of ASTD's goals is to find, create, and disseminate the world's most successful practices for achieving better performance at work. Attending and possibly joining ASTD programs either at the national or local level can give you insights and tools for being more effective in training, managing, and leading others.

While enhancing one's assertiveness is just one benefit of the many programs ASTD chapters offer, there are more than enough resources on the topic and opportunities for growth in this area to justify your joining, particularly if you have some responsibility for the performance of others.

Each year ASTD identifies high-priority issues for members and the human resource development field in general. It then develops and promotes national public policies that support workplace training and performance. If you work for a large organization, it's a safe bet that there are several ASTD members within your company.

At ASTD meetings, trainers and human resource professionals listen to a fellow presenter and exchange ideas. At any given meeting you're likely to hear about methods for:

➤ Enhancing learning and performance in the American workplace

➤ Increasing workers' ability to learn and adapt in a changing environment

➤ Sustaining competitive advantages, personally and organizationally

➤ Reinventing, reengineering, or revitalizing a department or organization

➤ Operating in a diverse workplace

➤ Being more assertive in the face of challenging situations

A Little ASTD Philosophy

ASTD contends in its literature that "performance is a precious commodity sought by every business. In the United States and around the globe, companies are responding to new demands. They have introduced technology, focused on recruiting a qualified workforce, downsized, restructured, and trained. All of these activities have been undertaken to achieve and sustain higher performance."

As companies, particularly those that are small and medium-size, undertake change, they often find it difficult to develop a skilled workforce and maintain a modernized workplace. So, the more than 158 local ASTD chapters offer opportunities for those who supervise or train others to get involved through regular meetings, newsletters, conferences and workshops, position referral services, community outreach programs, and social activities.

Some Key Resources

ASTD's *Training & Development* monthly magazine investigates the latest trends and topics in training, performance, human resource management, and learning new technologies. It is sent to the nearly 31,000 members and 6,000 non-member subscribers.

Technical & Skills Training magazine is dedicated to serving the specific needs of technical trainers. Each issue is targeted to help people who plan technical programs, purchase products and services, and train workers.

Another key resource is ASTD Online, a software database of learning, training, and performance literature. Using its electronic-mail and bulletin-board features, you can contact performance specialists around the world to discuss issues.

> JUST THE FACTS MA'AM.
>
> ### Just the Facts
>
> ASTD produces several conferences each year, such as the "International Conference and Exposition" and the "Technical and Skills Conference and Exposition." Training and development professionals from around the world attend.

Like Toastmasters, membership dues for ASTD are surprisingly affordable. Here's how to get in touch with them:

> American Society for Training and Development
> 1640 King Street
> P.O. Box 1443
> Alexandria, VA 22313-2043
> (703) 683-8100
> Fax: (703) 683-8103

National Speakers Association

The National Speakers Association (NSA) is a professional speakers' association of members from the United States, Canada, and around the world. NSA offers workshops, seminars, conventions, support materials, and other learning opportunities. Like TI and ASTD, NSA is a membership organization and charges a first time fee as well as an annual membership fee. Unlike TI and ASTD, to join NSA, you must meet certain criteria as outlined on the membership application, such as having spoken to a certain number of groups in the past year. In this way, it's a somewhat more exclusive organization, although new members are openly welcomed and encouraged to stay from the start.

Some people erroneously think that NSA is a speakers' bureau and that it "books" speakers. It does not. NSA is, however, a place where you can be a part of a like-minded community of speaking professionals where the pursuit of knowledge and the sharing of ideas is a way of life. Members fall into three distinct categories:

➤ Experienced professional speakers

➤ Developing professional speakers

➤ Individuals who serve the profession with products and services, such as speakers' agents and bureaus, seminar producers, presentation skills coaches, cassette producers, and other industry professionals

Handle with Care

Once they get your address, ASTD inundates you with its literature. To remove your name from the mailing list, call the office of the chief executive and speak to an assistant. This way the request comes from the top down.

Just the Facts

NSA was founded in 1973 in Phoenix, Arizona, by veteran speaker Cavett Robert. Most of the 3,700 members seek to pursue a greater capacity to influence others through the spoken word. NSA regards itself as "a vast universe of learning opportunities, friendship, participation, and growth."

Broadly defined, NSA membership offers you opportunities for professional development, networking, and leadership, plus platform competencies, business development strategies, and professional recognition.

As with many such professional organizations, the benefits you can derive by joining are directly related to your level of participation in activities and commitment to greater personal effectiveness.

Make It So

In NSA you will encounter some of the most exquisitely assertive people in the world. If you seek to be more effective in communicating, influencing and, indeed, inspiring others, NSA can dramatically shorten your learning curve.

Membership Bennies

NSA's programs, meetings, publications, and resources are structured around what they call eight "Professional Competencies," with each of the Competencies having numerous subtopics. The big eight include: *Authorship and Product Development, Managing the Business, Platform Mechanics, Presenting and Performing, Professional Awareness, Professional Relationships, Sales and Marketing,* and *Topic Development.*

Meet and Greet

Most new or prospective members start off at the chapter level. NSA has 37 chapters, with more being developed each year. Chapters offer members networking opportunities with individuals who share similar goals. The typical chapter offers keynote and seminar-type presentations, mentor programs, speakers' schools, leadership sessions, and showcase presentations.

Each July, NSA holds its National Convention, where you can be a spectator, a participator, and/or a presenter.

As with TI and ASTD, you get to learn from some of the best and brightest members; in this case, top-level speakers who command high fees for their presentations. Members often build lifelong relationships with one another. I'm a member of NSA and have been to ten of the last 12 annual conventions. I can tell you firsthand that for at least the first couple of years that you attend them, NSA conventions are on the order of life-changing experiences.

It just doesn't seem possible that so many positive, assertive, supercharged people could exist in one association. NSA's Educational Workshops are held twice each year. Here, members meet in a more intimate setting for specific nuts-and-bolts sessions. Single-Focus Labs are educational sessions that focus on one of the eight competencies. These sessions are held at NSA's International Center for Professional Speaking, in Tempe, Arizona.

Professional Emphasis Groups (PEGs) provide another opportunity for members with particular interests to share ideas and experiences. Thus far, 11 PEGs serve the NSA membership: *Bureaus, Consultants, Sales Trainers, International Speakers, Humor, Health and Wellness, Technology, Educators, Motivational/Keynote, Writers & Publishers,* and *Seminar/ Workshop Leaders.*

Other Membership Bennies

Among many other benefits of membership, ten times each year NSA offers a sterling audiocassette program called "Voices of Experience." The tapes include top achievers who share their experiences with the other members. NSA's magazine, *Professional Speaker*, is published ten times a year and offers features about what's happening in the speaking profession and meetings industry.

> JUST THE FACTS MA'AM.

Just the Facts

Every NSA member is featured in the *Meeting Planner's Guide to Professional Speakers*. This 450-page guidebook contains each member's photograph and professional description. The book is mailed free to meeting professionals throughout the country.

Here is contact information for NSA:

National Speakers Association
1500 South Priest Drive
Tempe, AZ 85281
(602) 968-2552
Fax: (602) 968-0911

International Society for Performance Improvement

The last of the four key professional societies where you will find ample opportunity to increase your assertiveness skills is the International Society for Performance Improvement (ISPI). ISPI regards itself as the "leading association dedicated to increasing productivity in the workplace through the application of performance and instructional technologies."

> JUST THE FACTS MA'AM.
>
> ### Just the Facts
>
> Founded in 1962, ISPI's approximately 10,000 international and chapter members are located throughout the United States, Canada, and 40 other countries. ISPI is populated by performance technologists, training directors, human resource managers, instructional technologists, and organizational development consultants. These professionals work in business, industry, universities, governmental agencies, health services, banks, and the armed forces.

To Join, to Grow

You can join ISPI to help yourself and others to grow professionally and personally, to meet and know leaders in the field of performance and instruction, and to stay on its leading edge. ISPI's *Performance & Instruction Journal*, published ten times a year, offers approaches and methodologies that can improve your skills and effectiveness in helping to improve human performance through incentives and feedback, performance aids, organizational development, job design, and instruction. A second publication, *Performance Improvement Quarterly*, offers articles on research and theory in performance technology.

ISPI's annual conference draws the largest gathering of performance and instruction professionals in the country. It offers nearly 200 different sessions, touching almost every aspect of improving human performance. At a recent conference, for example, nearly 2,200 members from 20 countries attended for the opportunity to network with peers and learn the latest developments in human performance improvement.

To learn more about ISPI, contact:

> International Society for Performance Improvement
> 1300 L Street NW #1250
> Washington, DC 20005
> (202) 408-7969
> Fax: (202) 408-7972

What Else Is Available?

Beyond these big four, there are opportunities on the local level for you to participate as a member, presenter, or leader. Every other club, professional society, and civic group in town represents potentially fertile ground for you.

It's a Privilege

Even if you are only speaking to a group of three at work, the opportunity to assert yourself is there. Naomi Rhode, a successful entrepreneur in partnership with her husband, Jim, and a talented platform speaker, refers to what she calls the "privilege of the platform"—the honor of being able to speak to others and to have them be willing to listen to you. You can join TI, ASTD, NSA, ISPI, or go local—you have dozens of opportunities awaiting you in the forthcoming year.

The Least You Need to Know

➤ There are groups in your community that will let you practice being assertive and even invite you back for more.

➤ Your mission is to join and become an active member of an organization such as TI, ASTD, NSA, or ISPI.

➤ The benefits you derive by joining are directly related to your level of participation.

➤ Speaking to a group gives you the chance to assert yourself in grand fashion.

Chapter 13

Physical Assertiveness

In This Chapter

➤ Projecting authority

➤ Unleashing the dynamic you

➤ The link between physical assertiveness and vocal assertiveness

➤ How to summon and focus your energy

I once had a five-foot-five, 110-pound girlfriend who feared going out after dark, even in suburban or rural neighborhoods.

At another time in my life I had a girlfriend who was five-foot-two and weighed 98 pounds. She boldly went anywhere, anytime. There was something about her, a physical assertiveness, that projected to others. Even at a distance, it was evident that she walked with purpose, stood tall, and was aware and alert. She projected authority and yes, even strength. This greatly diminished her chance of being a target for crime and gave her a higher level of freedom than others of her physical stature.

In this chapter, we'll explore what physical assertiveness is all about and how you can project it. You don't necessarily need to run to the gym and pick up the barbells. Instead, you'll merely learn how to project that you're in control.

Walking Tall—Will the Dynamic You Please Step Forward?

As a six-foot-three, 180-pound athletic male, I probably appear to be physically assertive. Indeed, I've been fortunate that no matter how late at night I've taken a walk in any city, I've never even been jostled. Don't get me wrong; I'm not going to push my luck. I look tougher than I am. (Actually, I'm probably a pushover.)

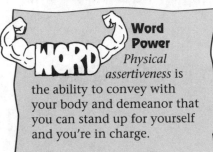

Word Power

Physical assertiveness is the ability to convey with your body and demeanor that you can stand up for yourself and you're in charge.

You may have observed, however, that size and bulk in and of themselves do not necessarily equal physical assertiveness.

If you speak to the police in your community, you'll find that they have at least a loose profile of the typical victim of a mugging. Independent of sex and age, those most prone to be attacked:

➤ Walk with shoulders slumped forward.

➤ Look down.

➤ Have poor posture.

➤ Do not swing their arms.

➤ Seem unaware of the larger surroundings.

Conversely, independent of sex and age, those less likely to be targets of muggings exhibit at least a few if not all of the following characteristics:

➤ Walk with an even stride.

➤ Swing their arms a little.

➤ Keep their heads up.

➤ Take in much if not all of their surroundings.

➤ Have good posture.

➤ Glance carefully at the people they pass.

➤ Look alert.

➤ Walk briskly.

Whether you're walking down the street or in the office, think back to the times when you were your most dynamic self. How do those times differ from those when you were a shrinking violet?

Among the many behaviors and gestures you might exhibit, here are some that convey, physically, that you are a assertive person:

- ➤ Look the other party right in the eye.
- ➤ Speak with authority.
- ➤ Confidently enter a room.
- ➤ Take the seat of your choice.
- ➤ Maintain good posture.
- ➤ Dress well.
- ➤ Prepare.
- ➤ Smile.
- ➤ Maintain a pleasant demeanor.
- ➤ Speak at an even and unhurried pace.
- ➤ Firmly shake hands.
- ➤ Take the initiative to heartily greet the other party.
- ➤ Remain in control during the meeting.
- ➤ Deliver your points with gusto.
- ➤ Leave at the appropriate time.
- ➤ Stride out with vigor.

What about those times when you were a shrinking violet, not at your best? What can you recall about the messages that you imparted, either verbal or nonverbal?

Now, think back to some time when you were more of a shrinking violet. Do you recall that you:

- ➤ Didn't look the other party right in the eye?
- ➤ Didn't speak with authority?
- ➤ Weren't confident entering the room?
- ➤ Didn't take the seat of your choice?
- ➤ Didn't maintain good posture?
- ➤ Weren't dressed well?
- ➤ Weren't well prepared?
- ➤ Didn't smile?
- ➤ Didn't maintain a pleasant demeanor?
- ➤ Didn't speak at an even and unhurried pace?
- ➤ Didn't firmly shake hands?
- ➤ Didn't take the initiative to heartily greet the other party?
- ➤ Didn't remain in control during the meeting?

➤ Didn't deliver your points with gusto?

➤ Didn't leave at the appropriate time?

➤ Didn't stride out with vigor?

Now, for the Illinois Lotto Jackpot, here's your question: What was the difference between the times you were your dynamic self, projecting physical assertiveness, and those when you were your shrinking-violet self, projecting wimpiness? Chances are, you felt confident in those situations in which you projected well, and experienced a lack of confidence in those situations where you came off as a dishrag.

Noted interpersonal communications specialist Dr. Janet Elsea says that you cannot *not* communicate. Body language is critical in establishing a positive image.

Body language certainly accounts for a sizable chunk of the message you impart to others. My five-foot-five, 110-pound girlfriend imparted to others that she was fearful. My five-foot-two, 98-pound girlfriend imparted that she was confident. The simple key to projecting an aura of greater physical assertiveness is self-awareness. When you're aware of what your body imparts to others, the changes you need to make come naturally and easily.

Meeting Yourself for the First Time

I once had a rare encounter with my physical image that few people have the opportunity to experience. I was in Worcester, Massachusetts, (for those not from New England, that's pronounced "Wuhster") on my way to an appointment. As I turned a corner, walking away from one building, much to my surprise, I encountered someone roughly my height walking directly toward me.

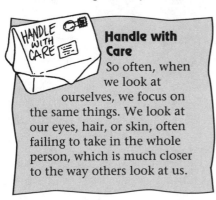

Handle with Care
So often, when we look at ourselves, we focus on the same things. We look at our eyes, hair, or skin, often failing to take in the whole person, which is much closer to the way others look at us.

It took a few seconds for the realization to register. I was looking at myself in a huge mirror. This particular building I was approaching had one side that was covered completely with mirrors. For a few seconds, I saw myself as others do because, indeed, I did not realize it was me.

Although slightly but not overly critical of myself when looking in the bathroom mirror, I curiously was somewhat pleased when seeing myself, unexpectedly, in the middle of a large metropolitan area. I could stand up a little straighter—my mother always told me to do this. Overall, however, it was okay. My quick and unscientific assessment was that I projected well.

Simulating a Surprise Viewing

Since you're not likely to stumble upon a mirror unexpectedly, here's how you can assess how you come across in general and, in particular, whether you're physically assertive:

➤ When you leave your house or office for 30 minutes or less, set up a video camcorder to capture yourself on videotape as you return through the door.

➤ If you enter the first time having completely forgotten that you put the camcorder in place, you'll capture on tape the "true you" for at least a couple of seconds.

➤ If you remember that you have the camcorder in place before opening the door, the experiment will be skewed. In that case, leave the camcorder in place, and tape yourself the next couple of times you run a short errand.

➤ It's likely you'll forget you put the camcorder in place one of those times, and, hence, will be able to capture the valuable data.

➤ You could also ask a friend or someone at home to capture you on videotape when you're not aware of it. Perhaps he or she can film you through a window without you noticing. Yes, I know this recommendation sounds a little funny, but it's hard for you to get this critical data about yourself any other way.

You could ask people to describe you in terms of your physical presence, but it's just not the same. A snapshot can help, but it's static. Only videotape will give you the motion and dynamism that are most revealing.

Working Out, a Little

It's not mandatory for you to hit the gym, but you don't see many couch potatoes who are that physically assertive. Even the mildest exercise will help you stay in reasonable physical shape and, hence, help you to project to others. If you belong to a health club or a gym, undoubtedly you know that a variety of weight machines are available today that can help you work out virtually any muscle group in your body.

Make It So
Health professionals say that working out for as little as 30 minutes three times a week is sufficient to give you vim and vigor.

Free weights and various pulley machines are available in most health clubs or gyms. Many of the exercises you can do with weights help strengthen your upper body, which in turn helps your posture. When you're able to throw your chest out and your shoulders back naturally as you walk, you breathe more efficiently, stand up straighter, tire less easily, and appear more physically assertive.

As I discuss in Chapter 6, while lung capacity is largely hereditary, swimming above all sports helps keep your lungs in their best possible "shape."

Just the Facts

With the preponderance of exercise equipment offered via infomercials on TV practically every hour of the day, you might be inclined to order a piece, enabling you to work out at home. For too many people, unfortunately, the exercise equipment becomes a white elephant they end up stashing in some corner of their home or apartment, or offer for sale in those classified ads, along with dozens of other people trying to sell *their* equipment. The reason people quickly abandon their home exercise equipment? You tend to work out more often and more vigorously if you're surrounded by others who are also working out. If you're that one in 25 or 50 who has the fortitude and discipline to work out at home, go ahead and get exercise equipment for your home.

Projecting Alertness and Awareness

Why do some people command your respect, even when they say nothing to you or do nothing in particular? Beyond how you carry yourself, and how your body moves, many other factors contribute to your physical assertiveness. Let's review each of these briefly, keeping an eye on ways you can convey the kind of message to others that you want to.

Facial Expression

Make It So
If you're the person with the blank expression, this may explain why it often appears that no one is listening to you. Use your face to express meaning!

Do you go around smiling all day? Do you frown or scowl? Those facial expressions convey messages; a blank expression conveys little. If you have a blank expression on your face, no matter what you're saying, the other party will have a hard time "hearing you" and look for other clues, such as your body language and voice, to get your overall message.

The blank of face are not giving you enough of the cues you are accustomed to receiving in conversation with others. Hence, you have to pay attention even more closely to get their meaning.

Voice Strength and Quality

Are you among the masses who ramble, mumble, or otherwise truncate words? Are you normally soft spoken, particularly when you need more vocal power to convey your message? Many people have particular problems with using their voices when it comes to meeting a stranger, speaking to others over the telephone, or speaking to a group.

We'll focus on the link between physical assertiveness and vocal assertiveness a little later in the chapter. For now, get in the habit of taping yourself with an audio cassette recorder. Unlike the recommendation to videotape offered previously, you have many opportunities all day long each day to tape your voice.

You can tape meetings conducted in your office or elsewhere, or simply read a few pages and play back the recording for feedback. Of course, when taping yourself, you'll be aware of what you're doing and may change your voice somewhat. After a few minutes, however, you'll most likely revert back to something closer to your normal speaking pattern. In any case, you'll gain much more feedback than you originally had.

Posture

I've touched on this before in the section, "Walking Tall—Will the Dynamic You Please Step Forward?" Regarding posture, mentally review how you go about your day. Do you sit up straight in your chair, or are you frequently slumped over? Is your chair at the proper height for you to use your desk, computer, telephone, and other equipment? When conversing with others, say, in the hallway, do you frequently lean on the wall or a table, or do you stand erect but relaxed?

While there are a few exceptions in life, for most people, sitting up straight projects more authority.

Eye Contact

Whether you're speaking to someone or listening, your use of eye contact says a lot about you. Looking at someone only intermittently, looking past him, or looking down at the floor is a much less effective means of keeping him in the conversation and having him heed what you say.

Instead, maintain more extended eye contact. I'm not talking about staring somebody down, fixating on him to the point where you don't ever turn away. That can be considered rude and disconcerting, among other things. I'm talking about holding your eye contact for at least three to five seconds at some points, and as long as 20 to 25 seconds at others.

You can break this up by nodding occasionally, briefly looking up at the ceiling or down at the floor when you're trying to recall something or come up with a point, pointing to a chalkboard or document between you, or simply glancing away for a moment in any direction.

> **Handle with Care**
> If you know someone who frequently speaks to you with a blank expression, you now know why you find yourself consistently drifting off when this person speaks to you. You'll have to engage all of your listening skills to gain a fuller meaning of their message.

> **Make It So**
> Once you get the equipment in place, you can tape your phone conversations, play them back, and have a better idea of how you come across, your ability to listen, the pace of your speech, whether your voice is loud or soft, and how expressive you are.

Think about the times when you had a conversation with someone who avoided eye contact with you at all costs:

➤ Was this person influential?

➤ Did their words have the most impact possible?

➤ Did you feel comfortable about the conversation?

Chances are, you answered no in all three cases. Others may feel the same if they're in conversation with you and your eyes are everywhere except on them.

Use of Gestures

Gestures help those around you more fully understand what you're trying to convey.

If you're like most people, you're probably unaware of the gestures you use when speaking to others. Videotaping can again help you learn a great deal about how you come across to others. Some gestures help you make your point and win the attention and respect of others.

Other gestures, including those you probably impart unconsciously, can actually detract from your message and say, "I don't really intend to follow up on this," or "I don't intend to hold you accountable." Gestures in this category might include:

➤ Inattentive facial expressions

➤ Withdrawing from the other party, even moving away from them

➤ Putting up your arms or hands as if to shield oneself

➤ Physically stepping back

➤ Short, rapid hand or arm movements

➤ Craning of the neck

People most commonly gesture with their hands or arms. They use these body parts as tools to make a point. Generally, it pays to keep such movements restricted within the area of about two feet to your left or right.

Stuff that Just Ain't So

Handle with Care
Excessive gestures can actually impart the notion to your listeners that you are not in control.

A lot of misinformation about what some gestures mean has been handed down over the years. For example, dozens if not hundreds of books suggest that if someone's arms are folded across his chest, he's conveying defensiveness and appearing closed to the information being presented. This could be true on occasion, but it is largely hogwash. A person might fold his arms across his chest for a number of reasons, including the following:

➤ He might be cold, and crosses his arms and hands across his chest for warmth.

➤ He might be bored but still not defensive.

➤ He might simply feel comfortable with his hands in that position.

Certainly, any fidgeting, nervous tapping, or other involuntary gestures you display repeatedly may distract the other party and diminish the impact of your message. We've all been in conversation with someone who taps their foot, fidgets with a pen or pencil, or frequently scratches their ear. Most likely, these types of gestures do not add to that person's interpersonal effectiveness, but detract from it.

Here are some vocal detractors, the presence of which will diminish the impact of your message, followed by the antidotes:

➤ Stiff or formal speech

Antidote: Spice up your language, use contractions, put down your notes.

➤ Gross mispronunciation of words, particularly common words

Antidote: Use a dictionary to look up words and practice enunciating them before uttering them to others.

➤ Overuse of clichés, slang, and hackneyed expressions

Antidote: Listen to yourself on tape and pick out overused expressions. Also ask others if you overuse some phrases.

➤ Use of non-sequiturs

Antidote: Stick to the main point; don't ramble.

➤ Overuse of filler language, such as "um," "er," "ah," "you see," and "you know"

Antidote: Give yourself more time between sentences. Get comfortable with pausing in silence between phrases or thoughts instead of relying on "um," "er," "ah," and "you know" types of unnecessary connectors.

➤ Lack of clarity

Antidote: Think about the point of your message in advance. Lead to it all along.

➤ Failure to come to a coherent point

Antidote: Have your strong point ready. Mentally rehearse it before speaking.

> **Handle with Care**
> Moving in too close to someone can be as ineffective as pulling away from them. Many people don't like to have someone, "in their face," and may get defensive or feel threatened. This will detract from their ability to actually hear you, and they may capitulate in the short run, not adding to a climate of respect or trust.

Physical and Vocal Assertiveness

We all know people who are vocally assertive but not physically assertive. These are people who, by virtue of their positions, demand you pay attention to them. One of these people may be your boss, or some bureaucrat who speaks with authority but never gets out of his chair.

It's possible as well to have physical assertiveness without vocal assertiveness. Generally, however, the two go hand in hand. Someone who has good posture, stands tall, uses gestures appropriately, and has sufficient eye contact has the best chance of being heard, understood, and heeded.

When you can combine physical assertiveness with vocal assertiveness, also known as vocal authority, you're cooking with gas heat! It helps if you have a rich, deep, bass voice, but if you don't, take heart. Millions of people all over the planet with far less than rich, melodious voices still manage to have vocal authority. It's all a matter of how you use your voice.

As you learned in Chapter 6, you want to employ vocal variety and engage your listeners— let them know that you're speaking to them, not to your notes, the back of the room, the microphone, or the ceiling.

Talking Your Walk!

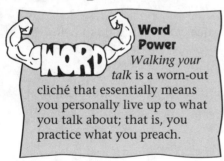

Word Power
Walking your talk is a worn-out cliché that essentially means you personally live up to what you talk about; that is, you practice what you preach.

Over the years, much has been written about walking your talk. I'd like to introduce, for the first time in this universe, the importance of *talking your walk*—using your voice in a manner that connotes vocal assertiveness and is consistent with the physical assertiveness you may also display.

If you are able to talk your walk, you have the best of both worlds. Everything about you says, "When I speak, there's a good chance it's worth listening to."

The Least You Need to Know

➤ Conveying physical assertiveness is based less on your size, weight, or muscles and more on how you carry and project yourself.

➤ You convey alertness and awareness to others mainly through your eyes.

➤ You don't have to exercise to convey strength or authority. However, it can't hurt, and it certainly can help.

➤ Effective use of gestures helps the other party stay attuned to what you're saying.

➤ Being both physically and vocally assertive gets others to listen and respond to you.

Part 4
Assertiveness in Your Home Life

Every darn day, you have the opportunity to practice being assertive with others, whether you're married, married with children, unmarried, unmarried with children, living with in-laws, or living with outlaws.

Regardless of how assertive you are in most cases, you may have noticed that sometimes you have difficulty being heard, understood, and heeded among those who are closest to you.

When you're speaking and have everyone's rapt attention or are generating big laughs and standing ovations, it feels wonderful. While most people report in surveys that their number one social fear is speaking to groups, it's a natural high for people like myself who look forward to it. You have the opportunity to assert yourself in a grand way with hundreds, if not thousands, of followers! Then, perhaps you fly to another city and do it again.

Eventually, you need to return home. Once you step into your own house, your powers of assertiveness seem to diminish rapidly. *After the initial embraces, your spouse can barely give you a few moments. You can't get your kids' attention. The same situation might occur with relatives, neighbors, or other acquaintances. From leaders of nations to John or Jane Doe, nearly everyone has experienced this phenomenon at one time or another.*

The chapters in this part address most of the domestic situations in which you may find that assertiveness is not only necessary, it's vital!

MOM, GET OFF MY BACK!!

Chapter 14

Being Assertive Within Your Immediate Family

In This Chapter

➤ The rigors of being assertive within your immediate family

➤ But my spouse won't listen to me!

➤ Getting your children to listen and respond

➤ Getting anyone to listen and respond!

Sometimes the hardest place to be assertive is within your immediate family. Perhaps your spouse won't listen to you. Maybe you have trouble getting your kids to respond. This chapter focuses on how to make some headway in your family!

Being Assertive with Family Members

In his book, *Care of the Soul*, Thomas Moore says that human beings are "infinitely complicated and profound." He observes that our family relationships might be good or not so good, but in either case, we could understand them better if we more often acknowledged just how complicated and profound other members of our family can be. Many of our family members have a history that we'll never know; that is, a history that they've created during the time they're away from us.

Moore also suggests that instead of trying to diagnose or predict the behavior of our spouse, parents, or children, we could better spend our time appreciating them for who and what they are. That in itself undoubtedly would improve family relations.

Same Old, Same Old

Undoubtedly, you've experienced firsthand the rigors of attempting to be assertive within your immediate family. Do you find yourself falling into familiar communication patterns when interacting with members of your family to try to get someone to do something or drive a point home?

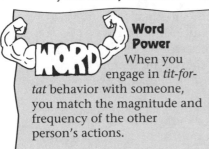

Handle with Care

Perhaps a major impediment to being assertive within your immediate family is the sheer proximity of your family members. It's easy to fall into the mindset that you know all about them because you see them so frequently—what their views are, how they'll respond, what sets them off, and how you are set off by them.

You tell your child to straighten up his room and you notice he barely lifts a finger. You raise your voice, and he moves a little faster.

You come back in a few minutes, and perhaps he is dawdling again. You reemphasize what you want him to do. Now, however, you sound like your parents when they talked that way to you 28 years ago.

Perhaps you're having a discussion with your spouse about where you want to go on your next vacation. Your spouse says the mountains, and you say the shore. You present your case; your spouse presents his case. Neither side really listens, and the conversation degenerates into a spat.

You may realize you've been down this trail before. Once you become a little heated, the argument takes on a life of its own. The net effect is *you are anything but assertive*.

Hey, I'm on Your Side

A growing body of evidence suggests that to be effective with members of your immediate family, or anyone else for that matter, you need to connect with that other person so that she actually thinks you're on her side. In other words, achieving the outcome you seek often involves helping the other person achieve the outcome they seek.

There's no need to think that every interpersonal encounter you have with members of your family hereafter means you have to go out of your way to help them achieve something in a *tit-for-tat* manner. Sometimes the other party needs only to gain a sense of respect, attention, caring, or some other feeling that you can impart while asserting yourself.

Word Power

When you engage in *tit-for-tat* behavior with someone, you match the magnitude and frequency of the other person's actions.

If you're like many people, you may need to let your internal engine rev down after work before interacting with your family. After all, you're not talking to Joe in accounting, Sally in marketing, Hal in logistics, or Jennifer in the Springfield division anymore.

Here's a quick quiz to help remind you that professional assertiveness (the focus of Chapter 21) is not the same as assertiveness in your family. Before making your wishes known at home…

➤ Have you taken three deep breaths?

➤ Do you exchange pleasantries?

➤ Do you ask your spouse or children how their day went?

➤ Do you make eye contact and speak face-to-face?

➤ Do you give your complete and undivided attention?

➤ Do you use polite and complimentary language?

➤ Do you offer praise or acknowledgment for something other family members have done?

➤ Have you pitched in on some household task or chore?

> **Handle with Care**
> If you are a gung-ho, career-climbing world-beater, arriving home still mentally immersed in the affairs of the workday and revving at the pace of business, members of your family may have difficulty relating to you, let alone heeding you.

Here's how to score your answers. If you answered "yes" to seven or more of the above, you're probably fooling yourself. If you answered "yes" four to six times, your family will probably be responsive to you. If you answered "yes" three times or less, you need to take immediate action. Review the list again and decide which five gestures you'll employ tomorrow after work.

But My Spouse Won't Listen to Me!

Is it harder today to be in a marriage or a relationship than in previous eras? It's an issue I won't explore in detail, but undoubtedly you have some opinions about this. In an era in which divorce rates are high and some domestic quarrels make the evening news, it's safe to say that it's difficult for many spouses to interact effectively with one another these days.

Open any of a number of women's or men's magazines, and you'll find that communicating with one's partner is at the top of the list in articles on relationship problems.

Thomas Moore says that each marriage has its own identity, direction, and movement. It takes on a life beyond the original intentions of either spouse. Because the roots of any spousal interaction (including any argument) may go back to the very start of the relationship, marriages or other intimate relationships may well be the toughest relationships to keep vibrant and on an even keel.

> **Just the Facts**
>
> In the book *The Day America Told the Truth* by James Patterson and Peter Kim (Prentice Hall Press, 1990), "communication problems" were most frequently cited by survey respondents as the top reason for divorces in America. Spousal infidelity, constant fighting, emotional abuse, falling out of love, unsatisfactory sex, not enough money, physical abuse, falling in love with somebody else, and boredom all trailed.

We're in This Thing Together

When you know your spouse is willing to really listen to you, and vice versa, you both can be more effective at resolving differences of perspective or opinion. Besides drawing on everything you've learned up to this point, here's an extensive checklist of behaviors and communication techniques you may wish to use on your next encounter:

➤ Minimize any negative feelings you have before speaking.

➤ Eliminate the notion that your partner "should have done this" or "could have done that."

➤ Contemplate how he/she might view the issue you're about to discuss.

➤ Let go of feelings of omniscience or superiority.

➤ Realize that your way may be the way this time, but it's not always so.

➤ Look for the good in your partner.

➤ Consider things to appreciate rather than issues to analyze.

Once you engage in conversation, especially if there is a chance that the conversation might get heated, your challenge to remain assertive becomes even greater. If you recall and employ even a few of the following interpersonal communication techniques, you're bound to have more favorable results:

➤ Start your sentences with the following phrases:

"I would enjoy having…"

"I would prefer if…"

"I would appreciate it if…"

"I like it when you…"

"Could you please…"

"I need your help in…"

"I'm hoping you'll…"

"Would you join me in…"

"Could you get me…"

"It would really be helpful if…"

➤ Use feeling words more often than thinking words: "I feel as if we…" rather than "I think we…"

➤ Make requests; don't issue orders:

"Could you…"

"Would you…"

"Will you…"

"My request is that you…"

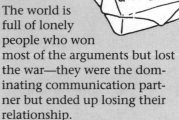

Handle with Care
The world is full of lonely people who won most of the arguments but lost the war—they were the dominating communication partner but ended up losing their relationship.

Often, a brief statement of empathy before making a request helps soften any assertion you might make. For example:

"I need to request something of you…"

"I can see you've been working hard…"

"I know you wanted to relax today…"

"There's something I need to ask you…"

"I need your attention for three minutes…"

"Could I steal you away for a moment?"

"Let's sit down for a moment…"

Language to Avoid

Here are some gestures and statements to avoid because they'll *reduce* your chances of being assertive. For example:

➤ Any of the unassertive phrases contained in the list in Chapter 1, such as, "Let me repeat myself."

➤ Blaming language, such as, "It's your fault that…" or judgmental language, such as, "I think it was a bad idea for you to…"

➤ Demanding language, such as, "Pay attention…"

➤ Accusatory language, such as, "What's going on here…"

➤ Abrasive language, such as, "Look, I only have a minute…"

➤ Domineering language, such as, "I already told you…"

Also, when asking a question, avoid language in which you apologize, such as, "I'm sorry to bother you with this, but…," or ask for permission, such as, "May I ask you a quick question?" People often believe they are softening their request, but it makes a person sound unsure or timid.

Supporting Tones

As you engage in give-and-take dialog, depending on the situation and where the conversation is heading, use one or more of the following modes of conversation:

➤ Support the others' viewpoint, with phrases such as, "I think I understand where you're coming from…"

➤ Acknowledge the other person's non-vocal response by saying, "I know what I'm saying may come as a surprise…"

➤ Allow for other possibilities, such as, "I know you may see this differently…"

➤ Offer periodic praise, such as, "You've been good about this, bear with me for one more minute…

➤ Offer links between points, such as, "So you see, adding A to B, I figure…"

Obviously, in a print medium such as this book, I can't give you the vocal nuances that would make each of these phrases work as intended. Even if you used any one of them magnificently, that would not guarantee success. Still, using this kind of language in an engaging interpersonal manner will help enormously in many situations.

If Only that Were Enough

Because being assertive with a spouse or significant other is *special*, you may have to extend yourself even further than what I've just covered. I mean, hey, you're going to have endless conversations that involve some form of give-and-take. So, periodically try some approaches that help grease the skids.

Admit When You're Wrong

I don't know anyone who really likes to do this, but doing it on occasion creates an environment in which you keep your credibility at a nice, high level. If you've ever known anyone who always insists they're right, you know how infuriating it is when such a person approaches you with yet another issue, especially when their position is once again questionable.

By freely acknowledging your own *fallibility*, you project yourself as a more balanced, rational, reasonable person.

Who would be more influential with you: Someone who always maintains his correctness, or someone who asserts himself for what he wants, but acknowledges he might make mistakes along the way?

Keep it Light

Sometimes, when making a request of a stern nature, your body language, posture, and demeanor don't need to be stern. If you play the heavy all the time, especially when making requests of others who regularly comply with your requests, they will regard being around you as burdensome.

Getting Your Children to Listen and Respond

What's the matter with kids today? Probably nothing more than what was the matter with kids of the previous generation.

I'm not a child psychologist, and chances are you aren't either. Neither of us needs to be one, however, when it comes to being assertive with our children. One secret I can impart to you, also one that other parents have confirmed for me time and time again, is that if you treat your children as full-fledged human beings from the time they are small, they'll respond to you in ways only previously imagined.

Make It So
You can be much more assertive when you say some things with a smile or a twinkle in your eye, because the other party finds your approach so much more palatable.

Lording over someone, even if that someone happens to be your child, is rarely as effective as being assertive with them in the short run, and it never is in the long run. You can, however, employ all of the ideas about assertiveness that you learn in this book with your children.

What Kids Don't Need to Hear From You

When you speak to another person in your office or around town, do you use language that is similar to the following:

➤ "Because I know what's best for you…"

➤ "Because I said so…"

➤ "I don't want to say it again…"

Handle with Care
Treating your children like full-fledged human beings doesn't mean treating them like adults. They are, however, individuals with their own sets of likes and dislikes, perceptions, and notions about the world.

151

➤ "If I have to ask you one more time…"

➤ "If I have to tell you one more time…"

➤ "Never mind what I do…"

Hopefully, the answer to my question above is that you never use such language with other adults. Why? It simply wouldn't work. They'd look at you, roll their eyes, and tell you to get off it, and that's the most polite language they might use.

Why, pray tell, would you believe that using such language would be effective with your children? Is it because you:

➤ Heard it from your own parents?

➤ Saw it on television?

➤ Believe your children are unintelligent?

➤ Heard something somewhere about something called tough love and think you're dispensing it?

➤ Don't know how else to make a request?

Make It So
Your assignment is to forever banish unassertive communication patterns with your children to the far corner of the universe.

The statements above use unassertive language and de-motivate people. They do not prompt action, inspire others, or leave the other party feeling good about the interaction.

Don't let any minor or temporary "success" you think you achieve by using these statements cloud your view. You might be winning battles, but you'll be losing the war. Anyone who is confronted with such language may concede and bow to your demands, but they do so begrudgingly. The last thing you need to create is a rebel in your own family. You have enough problems already!

What Makes Children Listen and Respond?

Okay, you ask, how do I get little Justin or Kristen to respond to my requests?

Here, in order and without adornment, is composite advice from leading child psychologists and authors on what your child wants and needs. Receiving these items on a regular basis will make your child more than willing to capitulate to most of your requests most of the time—by golly, the first time you ask!

➤ *Love your children and demonstrate it.* Love may not conquer all, but it conquers a lot. Do you go out of your way to do things for the people you love? When you love your children, they tend to love you back and honor much more of what you request.

➤ *Spend some time with your children each day.* I don't care how hectic it gets at work, what your responsibilities are, or what your life is like in general.

A lot of rubbish has been written in the last two decades about the importance of spending "quality" time with your children. What exactly is the *lack* of quality time—junk time? Given the choice between spending an hour with you in less than the best circumstances and five minutes of "quality" time with you, I assure you most children will choose the hour. To them, quantity equals quality in many regards.

If you simply bop in and out of their rooms or in and out of their lives, however, the likelihood that you can be assertive with them logically diminishes.

Make It So

All the time you spend with your children can be quality time, even if you're only watching an inane television show. There are always things you can explain, conversation you can initiate during the commercials, and little tidbits of communication that go back and forth all show long.

➤ *Constantly reinforce your children's behavior.* Kids are approval and attention machines; at least they start out that way. Nine-tenths or more of what they do is either to get your approval or your attention. If you withhold your approval, they try even harder to get it. If you continue to withhold it, they give up in time and settle for getting your attention. The problem is that they may get your attention in ways you might not enjoy.

When my little girl was a toddler, her mother and I used some of the Psychology 101 we learned in college. Whenever our little girl did anything even remotely personally or socially acceptable, we applauded. Yes, we clapped when Valerie stood up, said something, held a fork in her own hand, walked across the rug without falling, you name it. We applauded Valerie so often that by the time she was three or four, anyone could see the reasonable odds of her growing up happy and well balanced.

Just the Facts

Every shred of wisdom I have read on the topic of influencing another person essentially boils down to the maxim, "Behavior that is rewarded is repeated." In terms of getting your children to listen and respond to you, this means that you can begin right now, today, even if your relationship with your children is somewhat strained. You can get them to listen and respond by "rewarding them" when they do things you want them to do.

Do you want your child to clean his room? The next time he cleans his room as well as every other time, offer responses such as the following:

"You've done a wonderful job here. Congratulations."

"Your room looks sparkling. You've done well."

"What a pleasure to walk into such a clean bedroom."

"I'm pleased to see the fine job you've done here."

"I love it when you clean your room."

"Excellent, excellent job!"

Handle with Care

It's of no avail to comment three days later on the wonderful job your child did cleaning his room. Why? If your verbal, gestural, or material reward trails the performance over too great a time interval, the mental and emotional connection is lost.

In addition to your words, let your body language express your glee as well. Widen your eyes. Perk up. Smile. Convey your joy, pleasure, and rapture for your child's efforts in cleaning his room. You practically cannot overdo this. Even if you think it's not working, your support has a cumulative effect.

Each time you reward a child through gestures or verbal acknowledgment, you add to the probability that he'll clean his room again, more readily after your request. You may even reach the point where he cleans his room without you asking at all; the response he receives is so personally rewarding he cleans his room simply to receive it again.

Can You Assert Yourself Using Rewards?

What about giving rewards such as money, a trip to the ice cream shop, or staying up late? These items can work. However, the situation is different for everyone. Dr. Aubrey Daniels, in his book *Bringing out the Best in People,* says that what motivates one person may not motivate another. You have to explore.

You have to specifically find out what works best for your child. However, this much is clear: Regardless of the reward you offer, it must closely follow the performance.

What kind of language can you use to reach the point when your child looks forward to cleaning his or her room or honoring any other request that you make? Try some of these on for size, noting that none of this is parent-to-child language; that is, "Because I told you to do it." Rather, this is person-to-person language. You're treating your child as a fully functioning human being, albeit a younger, smaller, less knowledgeable, or less-experienced version of an adult.

➤ "I'd like you to clean up your room now."

➤ "It's important that you finish your homework by seven. Please get started on it in the next couple of minutes."

➤ "It's okay if you don't want to finish all your vegetables, but I'd like you to eat at least half of them."

➤ "Would you prefer to take out the garbage or dry the dishes?"

➤ "You can stay out until 9:30 p.m., but no later. This is a school night, so I look forward to seeing you at 9:30, or before."

Are Eldest Children More Inclined to Be Assertive?

The eldest child in the family has different characteristics than those of succeeding children. For example, among many, the eldest child tends to be more adventurous. She may be inclined to travel more; live further from her original, nuclear home; and take more risks personally and socially.

In cases where the eldest child is put in charge of the other children, the child might have had a head start in becoming assertive. If the eldest child is a female, she, in particular, may have had to practice parental, or more specifically, "mommy" skills at an early age. Some women I know who were placed in this situation later resented it. Others simply viewed it as a head start to a role they later would fulfill.

As I've emphasized throughout, your ability to be assertive is largely optional. Eldest child or not, you always have the choice to engage in assertive behavior. Even if you are the youngest in your family, the opportunity to assert yourself is there for the taking.

My friend Jim tells a story about his younger son Jason. Before age four, Jason's assertiveness was clear.

"We spent our summer vacation at a one-week summer institute," Jim says. "My wife Glenda and I took classes, while our sons Zack, age eight, and Jason, three years and ten months, were taken care of all day by their teenage counselors. One of the requirements to attend the summer institute was that Jason had to be totally toilet trained, a skill he had only recently mastered.

"Each night, adults and children ate dinner together in a big dining hall. On the third evening, Jason spontaneously got up on our table and made this startling announcement to the 200 adults and 35 children present: 'Ladies and gentlemen, I want everyone's attention. I have a very important announcement to make.' His voice was so loud and firm he commanded everyone's attention. 'I want you all to know that today is the first day that I wiped myself—all by myself!'

"Jason received a standing ovation from everyone in the dining room except for Glenda and me. While Jason smiled from ear to ear, and Zack giggled uncontrollably, we hid behind one of the columns near our table."

Make It So
Rejoice in the little ways that your children assert themselves. They'll need such skills when they get older.

155

Teaching Your Children the Difference Between Bossiness and Assertiveness

Sometimes it's difficult for children to learn assertiveness. Often, assertiveness in making requests and standing or speaking up for yourself in a way that makes the other person feel good about the interaction slips into the realm of bossiness.

Children are perfect mirrors of our own behavior. All studies show that the habits you engage in are likely to be picked up by your children, whether it's smoking, swearing, driving too fast, or abusing your spouse.

If you boss your children around, not treating them as full-fledged human beings but as your property or chattel, don't be surprised to find them bossing around their siblings or other children. After all, they imitate you, and they're probably doing a good job of it.

Lucy in the "Peanuts" comic strip is the epitome of the bossy personality. Lucy calls people names. She doesn't make requests; she issues demands. There are times when the other kids barely tolerate her. She is the one who causes Charlie Brown to say, "Good grief!" more often than anyone else. If you want your kids to act like Lucy, keep yelling at them, bossing them around, and haranguing them for what they did not accomplish.

The Least You Need to Know

➤ To be effective with members of your immediate family, you need to connect with them so that they feel you're on their side.

➤ Because being assertive with a spouse or significant other is special, you may have to extend yourself even further.

➤ "Communication problems" is most frequently cited by survey respondents as the top reason for divorces in America.

➤ Rejoice in the little ways that your children assert themselves. They'll need such skills when they get older.

➤ Children are perfect mirrors of our own behavior.

UNCLE JERRY, PLEASE.

Chapter 15

Assertiveness Among Relatives

In This Chapter

➤ Being assertive with your parents

➤ Being assertive with your spouse's parents

➤ Being assertive with all other relations, near and far

Are you among the many people who have longstanding miscommunications with your relatives? By relatives I mean parents, mothers-in-law, fathers-in-law, uncles, cousins, nieces, and nephews, whether they are of the first, second, or once-removed variety. Vast numbers of people have problems in this area. If they didn't, Hollywood movies and endless TV sitcoms wouldn't profit from milking "mother-in-law" scenarios and jokes decade after decade.

In this chapter, I'll take a look at your ability to be assertive with different categories of relatives, including your parents, your spouse's parents, uncles and aunts, nieces and nephews, cousins, and other relations, both near and far.

Getting Your Parents to Listen and Respond

If you've ever stayed at your parents' home after years of living on your own, undoubtedly you found yourself falling back into familiar communication patterns. Perhaps your

Make It So
With all the exclamation in the world, you can say, "MOTHER!" or "FATHER!" and your mother or father will give you rapt attention. If your parents are like most parents, tell them that you really have to talk to them, and you've got their attention.

parents have house rules that you don't fully agree with. Perhaps they criticize you or nag you, and you respond. Perhaps your communication pattern even reverts back to when you lived there as a child, a teenager, or young adult.

Nevertheless, for many people, being assertive with their parents is among the easier tasks when it comes to assertiveness. Why? They cut you more slack. They give you more latitude.

The way to get your parents to listen and respond is much the same as you'd proceed with your spouse, children, or anyone else you're close to. You can go back to Chapter 14 and reapply what you've already learned to situations with your parents.

Steer Clear, Paul Revere

There are a few nuances to asserting yourself with your parents. If you can steer clear of some of these pitfalls, then you greatly enhance your ability to get your parents to listen and respond.

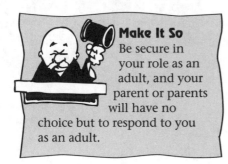

Make It So
Be secure in your role as an adult, and your parent or parents will have no choice but to respond to you as an adult.

➤ *Speak to your parent adult-to-adult.* Don't fall into any role you might have played when you were six, 11, or 19. If you revert back to childlike communication with your parents, chances are it will evoke responses from your parents similar to those of the past.

➤ *Avoid being manipulated by guilt.* You call your mother. She answers and says, "Oh, hi. I was so surprised. You hardly ever call anymore!" This is the part where you don't fall for it.

If your mother (or father, just as well) wants you to call more often, she needs to buy this book, practice assertive behavior, and pay homage to the principle that rewarded behavior tends to be repeated. If she wants you to call more often, each time you call she should say something like:

"It's wonderful to hear from you."

"I'm so happy when you call."

"The sound of your voice is comforting to me."

"How are you doing; I've been thinking about you!"

If you're face-to-face with your parents and they attempt to make you feel guilty, don't respond to it. Suppose your father says, "Is it too much to ask you to blank

blank blank." If you say yes, you contribute to a climate of potential hostility and hurt feelings. If you say no, you capitulate to his wishes and set yourself up for further manipulation and feelings of guilt another time. What would be a more appropriate response? How about:

"What's the real issue behind all this?"

➤ *Don't allow your parents to offer prolonged criticism.* Because they're your parents, they may feel entitled to criticize you, and some criticisms can actually be objective, valid, and even helpful.

It's much too easy to fly off the handle in the face of criticism from your parents, especially when you're an adult. "You never approved of anything that I..." Don't reciprocate with anger or criticize in return. Instead, assert yourself! The more balanced and even-toned you remain, the more your parents get the message that you're not willing to engage in the same old unproductive behavior patterns anymore.

> **Make It So**
> Tired of being criticized by your parents? Try making a request about how you'd like to discuss the issue. Tell them how you'd like them to offer recommendations that they think might be helpful for you in the future.

Dealing with In-Laws

You'd think the more you get to know your spouse's parents and vice versa, the less potential there is for any misunderstanding. But I have not encountered a study correlating the length of time you know your in-laws with your ability to communicate effectively with them. Indeed, some people naturally hit it off in a matter of seconds, while others don't seem to connect effectively, even after years of knowing one another.

The possible causes for the difficulty you may have communicating effectively and/or being assertive with your in-laws are as numerous and diverse as personality characteristics among human beings. Here are a few of the possibilities. Perhaps your in-laws:

➤ Regard you as an outsider, someone who has invaded their nuclear family (even if their son or daughter is a full-fledged adult in society, left their household more than a decade ago, and chose a partner wisely).

➤ Are insecure about their relationship with their son or daughter and feel you may represent some type of threat to that relationship.

➤ Never warm up to anybody, and you just happened to marry into their family.

➤ Have unrealistic expectations about the kind of partner their son or daughter would find in life, and try as you might, you'll never live up to those expectations.

➤ Can't concede that you had a life before you met their son or daughter and hence, regard you as something less than a fully functioning human being.

➤ Have always had trouble communicating with their son or daughter and now are extending that inability to include you.

➤ Subconsciously never wanted their child to marry. After all, that's a signal that they're aging.

➤ Liked someone else their child dated before you and wanted that person to be part of their family. Thus, anyone who comes after, in their minds, will never completely live up to their expectations.

➤ Are prejudiced about your background, education, religion, social status, ethnic origin, or some other personal characteristic. There are Archie Bunkers in the world, even though, miraculously, their children sometimes grow up to be nice people.

➤ Connect you with someone else who made them feel uncomfortable, or they simply don't like your looks.

➤ Resent compromises their child has made to be in a marital relationship with you. For example, you may have ended up moving far from the in-laws' home, or you're in a profession that demands odd hours or prolonged travel.

➤ Feel they never see their child enough, and now they will see him or her even less with you in the picture.

➤ Feel their ability to communicate with their child was unique and special and that anyone else in the "channel" is a distracting or disruptive element.

➤ Have not had a happy marriage, and they project onto your marriage the same misery and misfortune. Thus, without knowing you or attempting to get to know you, they surmise that you will be the cause of such misery for their child.

➤ Vigorously disapprove of some aspect of your life; for example, you have been married before, have children, smoke, drink, have a large dog, or drive a pickup truck, and they have let this single factor cloud their perception of you.

You can see from this extensive list above—and it could have been much longer—that many of the reasons why you may have communication and/or assertiveness problems with your in-laws have little to do with you.

Of course, there are things *you* could be doing to create the difficult situation—perhaps you expect them to be more like your parents, or blame them for difficulties their child has, and so on. Getting along is a two-way street!

Don't Push Here

In their book *How to Keep People From Pushing Your Buttons*, Dr. Albert Ellis and Dr. Arthur Lang note that the first step in not letting others upset you is to accept the fact that they can behave like "real creeps." This statement doesn't mean that they actually are creeps, but rather that they can behave that way. Moreover, there's nothing particularly wrong in feeling nervous, angry, concerned, guilty, upset, flustered, embarrassed, grief-stricken, displeased, or edgy on occasion, even in the proximity of your in-laws.

The key, say Drs. Ellis and Lang, is to realize that other people don't really control these emotions within us. We're in charge of the emotional control room of our lives, and we need to remember that. "When we worry too much about what others think of us or about getting respect, failing, or making fools of ourselves," say the authors, "we forget we're really the ones in charge of ourselves."

Just the Facts

Abraham Lincoln once said, "It is difficult to make a man miserable while he feels he's worthy of himself." He also said, "Act well your part; there all the honour lies." Sage observations and advice from more than 130 years ago.

Being Assertive with Your Spouse's Parents

Let's look at a variety of encounters you may have with your in-laws, keeping an eye on how you can assert yourself when you need to and still have a life and a wife or husband.

First, I need to lay down a couple of ground rules. You might want to examine this list closely because these are non-negotiable:

1. You don't have to earn the right to be your spouse's husband or wife. You already did on the day you married.

2. You're going to have to be forgiving and forgiving and forgiving. As the late Dr. Norman Cousins once said, "Life is an adventure in forgiveness."

3. Relax. If you are calm and relaxed, you'll be perceived as being more emotionally intelligent, regardless of what else you do. In addition, if you intend to be married for a long time, you'll need this capability.

4. Give up the notion of trying to become what you think your in-laws want you to be.

Okay, now that you've fully absorbed these ground rules, here are some scenarios in which you can be assertive with your spouse's parents, and still live to eat at their dinner table another day.

The Polite Decline

You'll undoubtedly be asked to do many things, such as have another helping of some food you cannot stand, spend another two hours with "Dad" tinkering with his car in the garage, or stay far longer at a family function than you can possibly stand.

Assuming that you've talked with your spouse in advance about your parameters for the endurance tests posed by your in-laws, offer a brief apology and excuse yourself. For example:

➤ "It's been great, but it's getting kind of late."

➤ "I'm sorry, I didn't realize the day was passing so quickly."

➤ "As much as I'd like to, I simply couldn't force down even another bite."

➤ "Thanks, I'll take a raincheck on that one."

Don't start apologizing left and right for things over which you are not sorry, or over choices you've made about your time or level of participation. Do not compromise yourself. Remember the essence of assertiveness conveyed in Chapter 1:

➤ Conveying appropriate self-interest

➤ Maintaining integrity

➤ Upholding your rights as a person

You Can Leave Me Out of This One

Suppose you're drawn into an argument between your spouse and his or her parents or into an argument between the parents themselves. If you don't choose to be part of the encounter, you have a variety of options for bowing out gracefully:

➤ "I don't have a well-developed opinion in this area and, so, won't offer one."

➤ (Said while smiling) "Sorry folks, I'm just not going to be drawn into this."

➤ "In all honesty, I don't see a part for myself in this particular discussion."

➤ "I'm going to bow out." (Then physically retreat from the scene by stepping out or simply walking away.)

➤ "I'm *positive* that I can't be helpful here."

➤ "I wish I had something worthwhile to contribute here, but I don't."

These kinds of statements enable you to withdraw from an argument probably as gracefully as can be done.

Don't Tread on My Spouse

Suppose you encounter a situation where one or both of your in-laws dump on your spouse. Perhaps they tell you anecdotes about what your spouse did when he or she was younger. Perhaps they reveal some "deep, dark secrets" they feel you ought to know. If this is within earshot of your spouse and you want to have a long, happy marriage, you probably need to quash this mode of communication as quickly and courteously as possible.

Parents and relatives sometimes feel they have the right to dispense such information because, after all, they're talking about their daughter, son, brother, or their sister. They feel that they know this person best and have observations that are long-term and seemingly helpful. Don't fall prey to this maneuver.

Handle with Care

If insights about your spouse are offered outside of his or her earshot, you need to quash this as soon as possible, no matter how juicy or enticing the anecdote is. Why? Turn the tables. Suppose your parents said the same to your spouse when you were not present. How would you feel if you found out later?

You may ask one of your in-laws for help in a particular area in relation to dealing with your spouse, but a major issue arises when they open up the broadcast channel and dispense whatever information they want to about your spouse and you willingly listen.

Here are a variety of potential responses:

➤ Ask, "Why are you telling me this?" (Wait for their response.) If the response is that your in-law thinks it will help you in your relationship, tell them something along the lines of "I'm already aware of this," "I prefer to find these things out for myself," or "I appreciate your concern but I prefer not to hear this."

➤ Change the subject. If this works, fine; if it doesn't, change the subject again. If your in-law still doesn't allow you to do this, try excusing yourself and leaving, using the restroom, or going for a walk.

Here, actions indeed speak louder than words. You send a clear message to your in-laws that this is not the kind of conversation in which you intend to engage. If they don't understand this time, they will the next time you leave.

Are You Talking to Me?

Suppose your in-laws have a nickname or pet name for you of which you don't approve. Or, suppose they label you in some way behind your back that is less than flattering. In

Handle with Care

If you know your in-laws call you something behind your back or refer to you in some derogatory manner, going out of your way to convince them that you're just the opposite won't work. You'll then mute your own personality and capitulate to their erroneous notions.

the former case, simply saying, "I prefer to be called Bob" should be sufficient. If it's not, try suggesting, "Please, call me _____."

As for labels your in-laws may use to refer to you (behind your back or told to you by your spouse), the best advice in terms of standing up for yourself is to ignore it. Such labels might include egghead, dizzy, fashionable, homeboy, and so on.

You need to be yourself, with them and away from them. Hopefully, their labels will drop off as they learn more about you, but if they don't, you're better off ignoring the issue. If you challenge or question the image your in-laws have of you, you may never live it down.

Leave Me Out of This

I wouldn't wish this on you, but suppose one or both of your in-laws are non-stop complainers. Almost every time you encounter them, they yap about the government, economy, media, neighbors, or something else. Suppose they feel the need to place blame on everything large and small for the things that are not going right with the world or their lives.

Handle with Care

Misery may or may not like company. The psychic toll that results from complaining and blaming behavior is not worth any fleeting feelings of camaraderie that might surface in your relationship with your in-laws if you decide to join in.

Some people constantly fuel their conversational fires by complaining and blaming. For some, this has become such an ingrained part of their daily routine that they no longer recognize how much of their conversation and thoughts are consumed by negative thoughts. If you start playing their game, hoping to win them over, yours will be a shallow victory.

Social Psychology 101 tells us that if parties A and B have a common enemy C, parties A and B are united. However, that unity lasts only as long as C is present. Suppose that A is your in-laws, B is you, and C is every little thing they like to complain about, or someone in particular. Remove C, and A and B may find themselves at war with each other. Otherwise, they need D to come along, so they can renew their common dislike of a single target. This approach to forming a relationship does not create much of a union.

Realistically, you're not going to change your in-laws. It took them 60 years to become who they are, and they're perfect at it. They're not going to change in 60 minutes, 60 hours, or 60 days, even if you have a Ph.D. in psychology. You can politely decline to participate in their complaining and blaming routine by pointing out something to the contrary, as you'll see in the following examples:

➤ They say, "The government is always trying to squeeze every nickel out of us." You say, "It seems that way sometimes; but the government has sponsored some good programs such as the XYZ."

➤ They say, "TV is worse than a vast wasteland; it's a sludge pile of porn, violence, and inane sitcoms." You say, "Much of TV is; but, with all the channels we can receive today, there are some good programs on. Do you ever watch The Learning Channel, The Discovery Channel, or the Public Education Network?"

➤ They say, "I don't think that doctors have any clue about what I'm experiencing. With all the money they're making you'd think they'd have some answers." You say, "It's hard for anyone, no matter how educated, experienced, or equipped, to fully understand somebody else's health problem. There are things we can do for ourselves, such as ___ ___."

By now, you get the drift; no matter what their lament is, you can offer another way to look at the situation. The larger issue is, why bother offering them a counterpoint? Your argument may help, but then again, it may not. If you offer a counterpoint, it might start an argument. If you don't offer a counterpoint, then politely try to hang in there or change the subject. The choice is yours. At no time, however, should you become a party to their gripe-and-blame game.

Could You Say That Another Way?

Suppose one of your in-laws is notorious for his or her use of profanity. Every other word or sentence offends you. You're not sure if they use profanity for shock effect or if they simply talk this way to everyone. The point is, you don't like it.

It's hard to think of something to say to lessen this person's use of profane language. No matter what you say, you'll sound like a prude, a persnickety person, or a holier-than-thou type. One possible strategy, and this is certainly not for everyone, is to let the other party know you're also fully capable of using such language although you normally choose not to.

JUST THE FACTS MA'AM.

Just the Facts

In his book *Pulling Your Own Strings*, Dr. Wayne Dyer says that if you're offended by someone else's swearing, "Give it back in spades just for the shock value, and teach that you are capable of being assertive." After the next couple of times you let out a string of four-letter words following profanity from one of your in-laws, don't be surprised if you see him or her use it less frequently. Maybe they got the message.

If you're not comfortable with the idea of letting out a string of four-letter words following profanity from one of your in-laws (or anyone), and chances are you're not comfortable

165

with this approach, try excusing yourself from any conversation where you're subjected to language you prefer not to hear. You can always go to the bathroom, the front porch, the backyard, the car, or take a walk around the block.

Previously, you learned that rewarded behavior tends to be repeated. Likewise, you can help extinguish another person's behavior by saying something like, "That kind of language makes me uncomfortable." Or you can withdraw. If mother-in-law X swears profusely in your presence and so you disappear, mother-in-law X may realize that to continue talking to you, she needs to clean up her act. She may not get your message, though. Either way, you won't be subjected to such language.

Getting Anyone Else You're Close to to Listen and Respond

With anyone else with whom you are close, you want to avoid old, unproductive communication patterns, listen carefully to what's being said, and use assertive language when you want or need to speak or stand up for yourself.

Remember, the longer you are with anyone, the more easily you fall into communication routines. Therefore, it becomes more important to vary the structure of your sentences as well as the substance of your communication. Disarm your listeners on occasion by using bright, bold, colorful language that moves otherwise routine discussions to a new level.

For variety if nothing else, change your sentence patterns constantly. Instead of saying to someone, "I think I can help you here," try, "I see myself striding side-by-side with you as we take control of the situation and devise a system to make things stay in place."

Also, instead of saying, "I've heard what you said, and I'll get back to you," try something like, "What you've said is provocative and certainly merits considerable thought. I'm going to give your words serious attention and offer my plan as to where we can go from here. I appreciate how you've gotten the ball rolling and promise you won't be pushing it alone."

Too exuberant, you say? Disarming? Your communication partner will hardly believe it's you? Fine. That means that your words are likely to be all that more effective!

The Least You Need to Know

➤ The trouble you have with your spouse's parents may have nothing to do with you and everything to do with them. Conversely, check your own behavior and attitudes toward them—maybe you're the source of the problem.

➤ You don't have to silently endure behavior from your spouse's parents that you wouldn't tolerate from others.

➤ All of your relatives deserve respect and understanding. In turn, so do you.

➤ Sometimes the best way to get your message across is simply to withdraw from a situation and leave the room.

➤ It's a big and often lonely world, and your relatives can help make it a more hospitable place.

Neighbors and Other Acquaintances

When a problem involves someone who lives across the street, down the lane, across town, or in your county—or when you're arguing over a traffic ticket, speaking up at a town meeting, or negotiating with your landlord—being assertive makes a difference in the outcomes of your encounters. In this chapter, we'll look at both common and special situations you may encounter on any given day.

Dealing with Neighbors

They say that good fences make good neighbors. Mmmm…wonder if the reverse is true—do good neighbors make good fences?

If you're having or have ever had trouble with a neighbor, you're not alone. Across America, good relations with neighbors have become more difficult to establish and maintain.

In the book *The Day America Told the Truth,* by James Patterson and Peter Kim (Prentice Hall Press, 1990), a majority of survey respondents reported that they "have little or no sense of belonging to a community that is important to their lives." Here's the part that's going to keep you up at night—one in four admitted that "they don't really give a damn about any of their neighborhood's problems." The report indicated that people appear to be losing respect for private property.

> ### Just the Facts
>
> *The Day America Told the Truth* found that survey respondents felt fearful about the possibility of various situations occurring: 44 percent were afraid of being burglarized; 24 percent were afraid of being raped; 34 percent were afraid of their cars being stolen; and 14 percent were afraid of being murdered in the vicinity of their own homes.

While survey respondents generally may have resided in larger urban areas, these findings (even if the figures are off by as much as 50 percent, that is, only 22 percent of the respondents are afraid of their homes being burglarized) reveal that vast, deep, long-standing problems exist in many neighborhoods across the country.

Noise and Intrusion

Excessive loud noise is often at the root of neighborhood squabbles. The noise from your neighbors' power lawn mowers at 6 A.M., leaf blowers, chain saws, or car engines may keep you from having a tranquil morning. Adding television sets, radios, stereos, boom boxes, clarinets, and drum sets may make you wonder how you have any peace at all!

One word sums up another problem that has reached epidemic proportions: pets. In America alone, there are 62 million dogs. Nearly three out of five households in America have at least one dog, not to mention a possible second dog and other pets. The mind-boggling aspect of dealing with neighbors who have loud or intrusive dogs is that they often don't seem to regard their dog's behavior as a nuisance. Or perhaps they *do* realize their dog is annoying, but made the mistake of not training the dog well when it was young and are now paying the price.

Let's not leave out the problem our neighbors' children may present. There are loud, obnoxious, unruly, delinquent children in this world. Some of them play too close to your house, utter profanity within earshot at the drop of a hat, or leave their toys and possessions in your yard or near your front door.

So, how do you stand up for yourself and still live in a pleasant neighborhood? Fortunately, you have a variety of ways to do so.

Take Class Action

Suppose you have a neighbor who engages in behavior that offends not only you, but also many others in the neighborhood. Suppose that you're leery or even fearful of confronting this person even though you otherwise feel perfectly comfortable speaking up for yourself in your professional or personal life.

There is strength in numbers. Recruit other people from your neighborhood to sign a letter indicating the problem with a particular neighbor and then deliver it to him. The power of the group may be all that's necessary to "encourage" the neighbor to discontinue the offensive behavior. Since everyone feels the same way about his actions, he cannot reasonably focus his wrath on any one of you.

A group letter can be a gentle, less confrontational way to inform someone of behavior he may not realize disturbs others.

Handle with Care

No one likes to feel picked on or singled out by a group. Always maintain proper language and respect for the individual when you participate in a group against someone.

Remember the Golden Rule

Suppose you're awakened or kept awake by a loud party or a loud stereo playing in your neighbor's living room. You're angry and have no problem rushing over to his door, knocking on it, and telling him to turn the darn thing down or you'll yank it out of the wall. However, put yourself in your neighbor's shoes. To him, you are the intrusive one. After all, he's simply enjoying himself.

The most effective solution in this case is to politely request that your neighbor reduce the noise level. Then, on the following morning or afternoon, go back over to the offending party's home and apologize for making the request but explain that you simply found it impossible to sleep. If they are not home, leave a note to the same effect. The follow-up visit or note is important because that next day, the odds are great that your neighbor will have far more objectivity.

Handle with Care

If you're going to make noise, let the other people around you know in advance. Perhaps you can circulate a note saying that you'll be entertaining from 8 to 11 P.M. or something to that effect, depending on the situation. Merely indicating the times of your event may eliminate any feelings of anger or unhappiness that your neighbors may have toward you in response to the noise. After all, you thought enough about their welfare to write the note, giving them exact parameters.

Make Accurate Notes

Suppose you live in an apartment complex right next door to a noisy neighbor. The offenses come sporadically at first, then they start coming with regularity. If you make notes regarding the date, time, and duration of the noise disturbance, you arm yourself with sufficient ammunition if you end up presenting your case to your neighbor himself, a landlord, a housing commission, or even a court.

Handle with Care

Your neighbor may take offense that you keep any type of log on his activities. If the time comes to present such information, you could decrease any hostile feelings by using language such as: "I didn't want to show you this, but the frequency of these occurrences is increasing, and I want to be able to demonstrate exactly what I am talking about. You see here, just last week…"

Make It So

Whether you have a child, or own a pet, stereo, motor boat, or chain saw, you have an obligation to those around you to ensure that they, too, can enjoy a fair measure of domestic tranquility.

When keeping such notes, strive to be as accurate as possible. Don't round your numbers up or down. If a noise started at 9:06 and ended at 9:47, mark it as such. Your to-the-minute ledger will carry more weight because of its accuracy.

Don't Let Bad Feelings Fester

Do you sometimes stew because you find what your neighbor does offensive, but don't say anything to him? If the situation recurs, following a clear pattern, the longer you wait to say something, the longer you will fester.

When a new woman moved into my neighborhood, I began to notice strange deposits near my back door. One day, after I returned from a two-week speaking tour, I decided to assert myself. I dropped her a note:

"There is no easy way to say this: Your dog has defecated and urinated all over the grass, starting within four feet of my back door, and I would appreciate it if you would scoop this."

Fortunately, the note worked. Otherwise, I would have followed up with a different note:

"As I mentioned previously, your dog has defecated and urinated all over the grass, starting within four feet of my back door, and I would appreciate it if you would scoop this. If this occurs again, I'll be forced to inform Chapel Hill Animal Control. Meanwhile, I recommend that you read Section 2, Chapter 4, Clause 4 of the Chapel Hill Town Ordinance."

Perhaps you think I dislike dogs. That's not the case. If you own a dog, horse, pig, llama (Michael Jackson has one), or any other pet, that's your right, assuming that you manage the pet responsibly. When your pet, and by extension *you*, trample on the rights of others, you do not demonstrate assertiveness, but offensiveness.

Mediate

A growing number of towns offer no-cost mediation services that allow parties in a dispute to explain their sides of the story to an impartial judge. Sometimes, two or three meetings are necessary to achieve resolution.

You work out the resolution between you and the other party with the help of the impartial third-party judge. The majority of disputes that come to mediation are resolved. In some cases, however, particularly if there are requests for compensation in the face of damages, the parties simply may not see eye to eye. In that case, you need to take other steps to resolve the problem.

Word Power
When you and another party disagree, you can turn to a *mediator* who will listen to both sides and help resolve the situation.

The Law Says...

It makes sense to know what the actual law says regarding a particular offense. If your beef is related to noise, piled-up garbage, or a house painted day-glow pink, it's best to know your rights before you proceed.

Your city hall or municipal library contains all of the local ordinances ever written. Bring a roll of dimes so you can copy the appropriate pages.

You may come across some obscure clause on page 89C in the fourth column that is exactly what you're looking for. Then you can take that clause and work it in to your conversation, note, or whatever other form you desire to use for communication. Perhaps you will achieve resolution that way.

If you tell Ed Jones down the block, "I'm pretty sure that you can't use a leaf blower before 8 A.M. on Saturday morning," you may have said enough to sway Mr. Jones. A note to that effect may work just as well. State the letter of the law if the neighbor disputes your contention.

Legal Letterhead

If you need to escalate your campaign to make your neighbor stop doing something, a letter on a lawyer's letterhead is sometimes sufficient. You can keep the cost under $100, and in some areas under $50, if you first draft the letter yourself.

1. Cite whatever ordinance is applicable.
2. Keep the letter straightforward and factual.
3. Bring the letter to an attorney who undoubtedly will craft her own letter, but may model it after yours, saving time and money.

Word Power
The *litigious* among us have a high propensity to sue rather than resolve issues through other means. Their favorite expression is "I'll sue."

In our overly litigious society, the mere reception of a missive on legal letterhead is sometimes enough to induce the other party to permanently cease and desist their disruptive behavior forevermore.

If you don't want to pay an attorney a small fee to send a letter, send it yourself via certified mail. That way, your neighbor receives two messages:

➤ What you've actually written in your letter

➤ The fact that you may use this letter in case you have to build a case against your neighbor

Taking the Son of a Gun to Court

If you can't convince your neighbor to attend mediation, or the two of you cannot achieve an effective resolution through mediation and the offense is significant and recurring, then consider filing suit. If some type of damage has occurred, and you have a monetary claim of $5,000 or less, your local small-claims court will handle your case.

Handle with Care

The problem with taking your neighbor to small-claims court is that if you win, you're likely to have severed any possibility of a cordial relationship. Additionally, there's always the possibility that your neighbor may seek retribution at another time in another way.

The notes that you've made regarding the offense—a continuing log indicating date, time, and situation, accompanied by any pictures, third-party testimonials, or eyewitnesses—are the best evidence or documentation you have.

If the judgment is not in your favor, don't expect your neighbor to embrace you with open arms. He will probably be upset with you for bringing him to court in the first place. Therefore, you have to consider the decision to go to court thoroughly before beginning proceedings.

If you don't want to bring your neighbor to court but can't solve the problem, what should you do? Beats the heck outta me! At some point you might want to consider moving.

Arguing a Traffic Ticket

The phrase "arguing a traffic ticket" is highly misleading. When you deal with the actual traffic officer who's about to write you a traffic ticket, arguing will only hasten the rate at which he hands you the ticket. When you're in traffic court, you face a different situation, which I'll discuss shortly.

I've spoken to a couple of police officers and they pretty much agree—arguing with them over a potential traffic violation most likely will not cause them to change their minds. If anything, like umpires in baseball, they will cling even more steadfastly to their positions and you will get a ticket.

You see the red, white, and blue strobe lights pulsating in your rearview mirror. Your heart is beating a hundred miles a minute. By the time the officer reaches your car, you have done everything you could to remember where you keep your license and registration!

Now, put yourself into the police officer's position: The officer stops you because you have violated some traffic law. He or she pulls up behind you, checks your license plate, and then gets out of the police car and approaches yours.

Each time he or she approaches a motorist it is a potentially risky situation. Somewhere, nearly every day, an officer is shot at point-blank range and killed by a motorist who just happens to have a loaded gun.

Disarm Them

If the officer and you are both on edge, don't fan the flames by arguing. In fact, I suggest doing the opposite:

When the officer asks you for your license and registration in even, measured tones, respond politely with something like, "Sure, they're right here," and hand them over.

Instead of asking "What's the matter?", "What was I doing?", or "Why did I get stopped?", wait for the officer to speak. After hearing him out completely, respond in a calm and even manner with something like, "I try to be a good driver at all times. I'm not sure I did what you indicated, but it's possible. At any rate, I take full responsibility for my driving."

Handle with Care
Don't admit to the offense if you could end up in court and you want to contest it. Your admission could be used against you.

The officer has heard so many people flatly deny that they were going 85 in a 55 mile-an-hour zone, or did not roll past a stop sign or commit any one of a dozen other violations, that when he hears someone accept full responsibility for their driving, he is disarmed.

Here are some tips to remember (if you can remember anything at all when stopped):

➤ Throughout the encounter, remain polite and calm.

➤ Respond with, "Okay," to whatever the officer decides, even if he tickets, cites, or issues you a warning.

Then wait.

➤ If he says, "I'm going to issue you a warning," you've got it made in the shade—you don't have to pay a fine or appear in court, and you don't get any points added to your driving record.

Make It So
Regardless of circumstances, if you accept responsibility for your driving, you stand the best chance of receiving the least severe penalty.

➤ If he says, "I'm going to cite you," wait to see if that means a ticket, a court appearance, or only a warning.

173

➤ If he says, "I'm going to issue you a ticket," remain calm. You always have the option of contesting the ticket by appearing in court.

Your Day in Court

Suppose you feel you were wrongly ticketed, and decide to take your case to court. Surprisingly, you have a better chance than you might think of having the ticket reduced or dismissed. Here again, look at the situation from the judge's standpoint. A judge hears a variety of cases all day long. Nearly always, accused motorists plead that it wasn't their fault, they didn't do it, or there were prevailing circumstances.

If you stand up and say you believe the officer was in error but take full responsibility for your driving, you already register like few others that day. If you come in with carefully recorded notes, your case is even stronger. You might want to mark down several things, including:

➤ The exact location of the incident

➤ The exact time of the incident to the minute

➤ Weather conditions

➤ Traffic conditions

➤ Your speed

➤ Other people in your car

➤ How the officer approached you

➤ What you told the officer upon being stopped

Verdict: Yours

It's helpful for you to bring copies of any "good driving" commendations from your insurance provider with you. If you maintain other driving records, such as how many miles you drive per year or the last ticket you received for a moving violation, the judge will regard you as even more astute.

If the officer stopped you and cited you for something that needs to be handled, such as a broken headlight, expired license, or something else you can deal with before your court date, then handle it. When you come to court, bring a receipt for your new headlight or your new license.

At the appropriate time, tell the judge that you've fully taken care of the situation. Once again, your odds of receiving a dismissal are better than you might think.

Speaking Up at a Town Meeting

Someday you may want or need to speak up at a town meeting about zoning, schools in town, new sidewalks, taxes, etc.

JUST THE FACTS MA'AM.

Just the Facts

Civic participation appears to be declining. *The Day America Told the Truth* reveals that of the thousands of people the authors interviewed, "their level of community involvement was below three on a scale of one to ten." Two-thirds of respondents have never participated in community activities or solving community problems. More than half of respondents believe they have no influence on the decisions made by their local government.

Just showing up at a town meeting or speaking out sets you apart from the majority of people in your community! Many people find it difficult to speak up under these circumstances, or perhaps they just don't wish to make the effort to attend the meeting.

Take the Floor

In addition to what you learned in previous chapters on assertiveness and speaking up for yourself, here are some specific tips for speaking more effectively before town groups and groups in general:

➤ Come with prepared notes, ideally in bullet format.

➤ Start with a brief acknowledgment of the people chairing the meeting and those in attendance such as, "Mr. Chairperson, citizens of Gotham…"

➤ When presenting your points, proceed in a logical, sequential, and chronological manner.

➤ Address the group, not your piece of paper; that is, look up as often as possible.

➤ Speak in clear and even tones so that others can hear and understand you.

➤ Use emotion when appropriate, but don't make your entire presentation emotional. People tend to discount what you say if your whole presentation is overly emotional.

➤ If appropriate, distribute handouts, perhaps including a copy of the bullet points you're reviewing, supporting evidence, or contact information (names, addresses, phone numbers).

➤ Use overheads and an overhead screen projector if that helps you make your point.

➤ Wrap up your presentation succinctly.

You may find that you impact the town council far more effectively than you might have imagined!

Be the One They Remember

If you're one of many people speaking on a particular issue, try to be first or last on the docket. Studies show that the first and last presenters have the greatest impact. If you're buried in the middle, you will have a somewhat hard time standing out, regardless of how effectively you speak.

Whether or not you're stuck in the middle, make some personal gesture no one else has made that evening. For example, personally distribute your handouts to the committee members and smile or softly say to each person, "This is for you." Once again, you'll stand out, and thus, your points potentially will have greater impact on your listeners.

Here are some other ways to stand out:

➤ Use pastel-colored paper for your handouts.

➤ Wear a large button or name badge.

➤ If possible, leave your seat or the lectern and speak right in front of the group.

➤ Ask everyone to do something like look at their neighbor, stand up, raise a hand, or offer a verbal response.

Speaking Extemporaneously

Suppose you're in a meeting and didn't even intend to speak that night! You hear something you feel merits a comment, raise your hand or otherwise gain acknowledgment, and begin addressing the group. How do you proceed? You can of course rely on many of the steps presented above. In addition, here are some pointers to keep in mind:

➤ Depending on where you stand, turn to face other parts of the room so your audience can see and hear you better.

➤ Don't burden your audience by speaking for too long. Extemporaneous speech means quick and to the point.

➤ Speak with emotion (you probably feel this anyway), but don't let your speech wander.

➤ If appropriate, upon conclusion, say something like:

"I'd be happy to discuss this with the others afterwards," or

"If you want more information, contact me at _____," or

"If others feel the same way, meet me in the back of the room after the meeting."

➤ After you sit down, let others speak. You will have other opportunities to reiterate your points or rebut what else has been said.

The Need to Be Critical

Suppose you hear something in some public forum that simply is not correct, and find yourself compelled to refute what's being presented or criticize some action that's been taken. In this case, strive to offer constructive criticism, airing your views with as much tact as possible. Don't blame or accuse anyone, but state your observations and insights as objectively as possible.

Balance your criticism by offering positive remarks, particularly as a preface to whatever else you have to say. Stay away from remarks that focus on a person's appearance, voice quality, character, and so forth. Such remarks are likely to be regarded as personal attacks, and produce completely opposite effects from being assertive. They rile up the other party, often to the point where that person refuses to even hear you.

Make forward progress. Instead of pointing out what's wrong or not working, continue with recommendations for appropriate change. If possible, present these recommendations in chronological order.

Assertiveness All Around Town

Wherever you go you'll occasionally find yourself in situations where you'll want to assert yourself. Hailing a taxi, asking for directions, or simply maintaining your place in line are examples of such situations. Rely on the guiding principles in Chapter 1:

1. You have the right to maintain and convey appropriate self-interest.
2. You have the right to speak up for yourself.
3. While conveying appropriate self-interest and speaking up for yourself, it's important to uphold the rights of the other party as well.

After all is said and done in this world, a lot more is said than done. It's important to recognize that no particular strategy or set of guidelines will perfectly govern you in every situation. The noted German philosopher Friedrich Nietzsche remarked:

> "This is my way.
> What is your way?
> The way doesn't exist."

Make It So
Seek to uphold your rights as a person, taxpayer, consumer, group member, and audience member to voice your opinion, observation, or concern without impeding the rights of others who often are no less worthy than you.

The Least You Need to Know

➤ Neighbors engaging in offensive or noisy behavior often don't realize that they act that way.

➤ Try to work things out without going to court. You can win the battle but lose the war.

➤ When you know in advance you'll be speaking up at a meeting, bring a roster of the points you want to make.

➤ When you speak extemporaneously, mix logic with emotion and try to proceed chronologically.

➤ Never make a personal attack on someone when offering criticism.

Part 5
Assertiveness in Your Personal Life

The chapters in this section cover a variety of personal situations in which being assertive can keep you safe, make others notice you, and even save you money! It's not that recommendations for assertiveness prior to this section don't relate to your personal life. Rather, here I tackle highly specific subjects, such as those in Chapters 17 and 18.

In Chapter 19, I offer you a variety of ways to ensure that you get the product or service satisfaction that you pay for and that your tax dollars work in the ways they're supposed to; that is, you get bureaucrats to be responsive when you have an issue, question, or need.

Chapter 17

Special Assertiveness Situations for Women

> ### In This Chapter
>
> ➤ Asserting your rights as a woman
>
> ➤ Asserting yourself on dates
>
> ➤ Dealing with harassment
>
> ➤ Speaking so others respond the very first time

Let's be frank. I don't mean that you or I should change our names to Frank. Rather, I'll be entirely candid with you in this chapter about some rather sensitive issues. Depending on your gender or social status, special situations may arise in which you need to assert yourself.

In this chapter, I'll focus on some situations that only women are likely to encounter. If you're a man, keep reading—you might learn something useful, too.

I Am Woman, Hear Me Now

I know it's unfair, but simply because you're a woman you may have to work a little harder at:

➤ Standing up for yourself

➤ Saying no and having others understand that you mean "NO!"

➤ Receiving appropriate responses

Nevertheless, legions of women, of all ages and sizes and from all walks of life, do assert themselves. Now, for the first time in this quadrant of the universe, I will reveal the secrets of how women assert themselves in special situations!

Social Conditioning

Unquestionably, women face challenges in asserting themselves. This situation has significant ramifications in a woman's personal life as well as in her professional life. I'll deal with the professional side of the coin in Chapter 21, and in Chapters 23 and 24 I'll talk about dealing with your peers and staff. I'll deal with the personal side of the issue right here.

> **Just the Facts**
>
> Nearly every study and every psychologist of prominence finds that society conditions men to assert themselves starting at an early age. Women learn to exhibit responsive, submissive, and cooperative behavior, but traditionally have been discouraged from asserting themselves.

If you're a woman, from the moment you're born, you're covered with a pink blanket—figuratively, if not literally. Boys, on the other hand, are draped in blue. Without running through a litany of gender-based differences concerning how you're reared as a child, since you're probably aware of almost all of them, I will say the conditioning that women receive growing up is different from that of men. These gender-based differences range from the messages you hear, the toys you receive, and even to how your parents and others respond to you.

While we have made great strides as a society in overcoming much of the stereotypical thinking in defining and describing the sexes, you don't need to have a Ph.D. in psychology to know that false notions abound about the distinctions between females and males.

Squabbles Among Experts

In her book *Different Words, Different Worlds,* Professor Deborah Tannen, more widely known as the author of *You Just Don't Understand* and *Talking from Nine to Five,* observes that young girls receive encouragement that is vastly different from what boys receive. Girls learn to agree and compromise, engage in playing games where everyone has an equal role, and achieve some semblance of leadership by making alliances within the group.

In contrast, Tannen observes that boys engage in competitive games dominated by conflict. The boys scramble with one another to reach the top of the hill or the top of some hierarchy they have devised themselves. The stronger, more aggressive boys generally become the leaders who give orders. Even those below the leaders, however, continue to compete with the leaders for the top position.

John Gray, Ph.D. contends that men and women have inherent, fundamentally different emotional responses to stimuli, needs, and communication patterns. This all but ensures that they will not understand each other unless they take the time to learn about these differences in his universal best-seller, *Men are from Mars, Women are from Venus*, and all his follow-up books and tapes concerning the same general theme.

Dr. Julia Woods, of the School of Arts and Sciences at the University of North Carolina, feels that some popular gender-difference books distort and misrepresent both men and women. Woods says that when you tend to think of all women as being alike and all men as being alike, you lose sight of one's individuality: "It (our individuality) is submerged in the preconceived stereotypes of groups."

Woods also believes that when you maximize the differences and minimize the similarities between the sexes, you in fact, reverse the reality of the situation. Woods believes that the similarities between men and women far outweigh the differences.

People, One Person at a Time

In regard to this touchy issue, I tend to agree with Dr. Woods. I've met women who have exhibited what others would regard as masculine traits, although they clearly stayed within the bounds of exhibiting what one would consider feminine behavior. Some displayed the traits of aggressiveness and competitiveness, and some were calculating.

I'm not a "weak-willed" male by any stretch, but in some relationships I almost felt as if a role reversal had occurred. I became the less adventurous, less competitive, and less objective partner. These circumstances didn't make me any less male.

Make It So
Don't allow traditional expectations for female behavior to prevent you from acting in your own right. As Dr. Wayne Dyer says, you can give yourself permission to be whatever you elect for yourself, without giving thought to what sexual role stereotype you fit.

All women have the opportunity to assert themselves today more so than women of previous generations did in their personal and professional lives. Nevertheless, many women still feel reluctant to be assertive in a non-professional, small group or one-on-one setting. Some women grew up in nuclear families, where they observed a more assertive father and more passive mother.

When it comes to sex, Dr. Dyer emphasizes, "The woman who waits for a man to initiate a sexual encounter when she would really like to initiate one herself" chooses to abide by restrictions that may have applied in a previous era, which was dominated by chauvinism.

Conversely, Dyer observes that a man who occasionally prefers to be the more passive partner in an intimate relationship but invariably avoids such behavior similarly chooses to allow the mores of previous eras to confine him.

The Role of Physical Attractiveness

University researchers in the late 1980s examined the relationship between assertiveness and physical attractiveness, and found that more attractive females "exhibited more assertive verbal behaviors than less attractive ones did." Given that the researchers had some reasonable index for deeming who was attractive, there are reasons to believe that this study and others supporting the same conclusions are indeed valid. Of course, this is not necessarily the *desired* norm for human society; most individuals would verbally state that appearance is only skin-deep and physical beauty can sometimes be misleading.

Word Power
When you give preferential treatment to someone based primarily on their physical appearance, you're practicing *lookism,* an entirely human tendency that has persisted since the earliest recorded history.

Based on how our society is structured and human nature is in general, an attractive person, female or male, starting from an early age, is likely to receive more attention than others who are less attractive. The term in vogue for this phenomenon is "lookism." Studies have shown, for example, that more attractive defendants in criminal trials are more likely to receive favorable verdicts from juries.

Just the Facts

In 1995, the television news show *20/20* revealed that even weeks-old babies with virtually no social conditioning demonstrated by smiling a marked preference for pictures of attractive people, including movie stars, over those of more ordinary-looking people.

Word Power
A *genetic celebrity* is someone who noticeably attracts members of the opposite sex, even at an early age. Others often knowingly (or unknowingly) accord favors or preferential treatment to them because of their appearance.

People appear to possess a built-in characteristic that causes them to appreciate aesthetics amongst themselves. This produces the "genetic celebrities" among us, a term used by Dr. Warren Farrell in his book *Why Men Are the Way They Are* to describe people who, by virtue of their appearance, are more likely to engender favorable responses from others.

If people readily responded to you almost every time you said something, by age 5, and certainly by ages 10, 15, 20, and 25, you'd have a clear advantage in asserting yourself. After all, years of conditioning would probably have convinced you that people do in fact hear, understand, and heed you.

Solace for the Masses

If you're an average Jane Doe, or John Doe for that matter, take heart. While very attractive people may have advantages when it comes to being assertive, they certainly don't have a lock on the issue; there are opportunities for you to be just as effective.

For every six-foot-tall, curvaceous, Princeton-educated, Brooke Shields type, there are probably many more four-foot-ten, heavily accented, gravelly voiced Dr. Ruths who, at the least, can stand up for themselves and speak for themselves whenever they want to or need to.

Assertiveness When You're Dating

In the last generation or so, it seems to many people that the proverbial battle between the sexes has degenerated into the bitterness between the sexes. If you open your local newspaper to the "lifestyle," "style plus," "health and living," or similarly named section, you will find, at least weekly, some article or column dealing with:

➤ "How to get along with your spouse, boyfriend, or girlfriend"
➤ "How to make your relationship better"
➤ "How to cope with the loss of your relationship"

...and so on. And from the magazine racks, headlines scream out:

➤ "What to do when he won't listen"
➤ "Ten ways to know if he's playing around"
➤ "Five ways to make your relationship great"
➤ "How to have sex on your terms"
➤ "When relationships turn abusive"

The book *The Day America Told the Truth,* published in 1990, reports, "Women have changed during the past couple decades; that is clear..." Women report feeling more confident about themselves and more outspoken. Many men and a surprisingly increasing number of women agree that some of the rhetoric of the women's movement since the late 1960s has helped create the belief that men possess the characteristics of stereotyping and bigotry. Yet, both sexes face the problems of stereotyping.

Even if in reality men and women share more similarities than differences, because of communication gaps and misunderstandings, the sexes may continue to confuse one another.

I Date the Opposite Sex, Therefore I Assert

If it's true that men and women are having a harder time understanding each other, being assertive in dating is not just a good idea, but imperative! You can assert yourself as needed and still keep things rolling.

Here are some assertive phrases that can be said in a friendly tone:

➤ "I'd really like to keep things friendly for a while."
➤ "I'm enjoying myself, but I need to be home by 11:00."

➤ "If it's okay with you, let's go Dutch treat on this one."

➤ "I don't feel that way about you right now, perhaps I will over time."

➤ "I like it when you do xyz."

➤ "I'd prefer that you don't do that."

➤ "Yes."

➤ "DON'T, as in *do not*."

Men sometimes complain that they get mixed signals from women when dating. Personally, I don't understand how this happens. If somebody says "no" or "don't" even in a soft voice, I understand this as "no" or "don't." Some men, perhaps those who watch a lot of movies, may erroneously believe that a woman will offer a few "no's" just as a challenge, while secretly meaning "yes." This is an erroneous notion that's best tossed while it's still fresh.

The kind of guys who don't hear the word NO in a date rape situation are highly dangerous, and the woman's volume won't make a difference. However, volume can be a major factor in getting the attention of a friend, neighbor, relative, passerby—or best of all, a police officer—for help.

Saying NO, especially loudly, goes against the way many women were raised to behave, so this may be difficult for you. If so, practice yelling "no" in your home, backyard, shower, whatever—or perhaps enroll in a woman's self-defense class. One of the most empowering things about these classes is that you learn to yell "no" with force and without guilt.

Clearing Up an Age-Old Misconception

Many women think that a man's physical interest in them precludes any other interest in them. Not! Obviously, this has been the case billions of times, but read further. A man may be interested in you physically because he's interested in you mentally and emotionally as well.

Yes, men seem to be "ready" physically much sooner, and demonstrate more evidence of this than women do. Yet, it's unfortunate that so many in society dismiss the real issue when it comes to men's needs. If a woman wants to be hugged, kissed, or caressed, the prevailing thought is, oh how feminine, how tender. When a man needs affection, he too may seek simply a hug, a kiss, or a caress. Men can have the same physical needs to be hugged as women, and it doesn't always lead to sex.

Since AIDS and sexually transmitted diseases are likely to be with us in some form or another for the foreseeable future, and there are other hazards from lacking caution when you don't know someone very well, you should always go into potentially intimate relationships carefully.

Are You Setting Limits?

Getting to know somebody takes a while, and at one time or another, as the song says, "Everybody plays the fool." In general, women have more power and much more opportunity to assert themselves in a relationship than many give themselves credit for.

If men are more aggressive in society and their quest for power more apparent, they likely will assert themselves to what they perceive as the allowed limits. You largely set those limits.

Yet, you may lament, "Why should women have all the burden of setting limits?" Feel free to set limits, while recognizing that perhaps the type of man you're seeking should be able to control his own impulses and take responsibility for his own behavior.

If you're in a situation where your date wants to move faster than you do, say something. Try statements such as:

➤ "I'm attracted to you as well, but I always go slowly at first."

➤ "I don't want to get physical right now, but I would like to talk."

➤ "Besides getting physical, what else do you like to do?"

Asserting Yourself When You're Harassed

If you're being harassed in the workplace, you have a variety of options at your disposal. These include everything from simply walking away, to telling the other party off, reporting the occurrence, or filing a suit.

JUST THE FACTS MA'AM.

Just the Facts

Here is a streamlined version of the U.S. Equal Employment Opportunity Commission's definition of sexual harassment: "Unwelcome sexual advances, requests for sexual favors, and other verbal, non-verbal, or physical conduct of a sexual nature constitute sexual harassment when: (1) submission to such conduct is made either explicitly or implicitly a term or condition of an individual's employment; (2) submission to or rejection of such conduct by an individual is used as the basis for employment or decisions affecting such individual; and/or (3) such conduct has the purpose or effect of unreasonably interfering with an individual's work or performance or of creating an intimidating, hostile, or offensive working environment."

Many men have no idea what it feels like to be harassed. They may attend a course or read an article where they are asked to imagine that the tables are turned, but this simply doesn't work. They know that by the end of the exercise or the end of the day they can go back to how things are.

Although there are situations in which women in positions of power harass their male employees, they occur with less frequency. I won't cover them here, except to say that many of the same recommendations that apply to a woman being harassed also apply to a man.

Sure, a lot of guys would like to hear that they have broad shoulders, a great derriere, and who knows what else. Chances are, if they heard comments about their anatomy all day long, day in and day out, they'd start to feel differently. In time, they might even begin to understand how women feel when they hear inappropriate remarks.

Hands Off!

I had the unwelcome opportunity to know what being harassed feels like when I was 28 years old. It wasn't a traumatic experience for me and doesn't compare with the unfortunate situations many women have experienced, but it was bothersome nevertheless. For some inexplicable reason, a woman some 25 to 30 years my senior whom I had worked with for several months one day began making remarks that she evidently thought were endearing, such as: "Okay dear," "How ya doing, honey," "Hey doll," and so on.

> **Handle with Care**
>
> If you're a man, and you've had the guts to read this chapter, then listen up—sexual harassment is not macho, assertive, or attractive, and will hardly win you any friends or admirers. When you harass someone, you, in essence, attempt to *objectify* them; convert them to an object as opposed to dealing with them as a person.

I thought her remarks were inappropriate from the start, but I ignored them. After all, there was no great offense here. Besides, I was aware that many people routinely use such expressions, with no real meaning attached.

Her comments continued that afternoon and the next morning. She started saying things in a sing-song fashion that suggested she and I get to know each other in biblical terms, as in, "He knew her well." Quietly and professionally, after about the fourth or fifth remark, I told her I didn't appreciate what she said.

Around the middle of the next day, I realized that she was not getting my message, so I let her have it verbally, in the middle of the lobby with many people within earshot. I don't remember exactly what I said, but it was something along the lines of, *"Look, I've asked you politely to stop making such remarks, and now I'm telling you I don't want to hear this from you again."*

She looked a little shocked, but backed off. I didn't have any contact with her for the rest of the day or the next morning. By the next afternoon she appeared to be back to what I, at least, thought was normal. Nothing else remarkable characterized our encounters after that.

Perhaps I had stumbled onto something—a way to be assertive by publicly chiding another for unwelcome remarks, without in any way referring to the *nature* of those remarks. In any case, it worked and neither of us experienced any repercussions.

Grist for the Mill

Obviously, I didn't know that more than a decade later I'd write a book on assertiveness. Much of what you experience in life is, however, "grist for the mill." I did not enjoy the rather mild strain of harassment I endured for a day and a half. I can't begin to understand what women must feel like when they endure such behavior periodically for years on end.

An Attempted Power Trip?

In addition to demonstrating weakness or lack of self-confidence, men who harass women fail to achieve any goal.

The act of harassment is often used as a power play. A man harassing a woman, in essence says, "I can say what I want to you because I am powerful, and you are powerless." Often the age or marital status of either party doesn't determine the motives of the harassment. Fortunately, this is becoming less true today, as many progressive organizations have moved swiftly to uphold an environment where there are strict penalties for sexual harassment.

Understand It the First Time

There are certain types of assertive language you can use that can be very effective in the face of verbal harassment. The next time you have an encounter, try some of these:

➤ "I don't appreciate comments like that and I really don't want to hear them again."

➤ "I'm sorry, but I'm not here for your visual gratification, or any other type of gratification."

➤ "This type of language and these types of remarks are unacceptable to me."

➤ "I don't understand what prompts you to say such things, and I'm upset that you have. Don't speak to me in this manner again."

Each of these phrases is forceful, unequivocal, and to the point—they leave little room for interpretation as to their intended meaning. The same type of forceful language will be necessary, as well, if you encounter any type of physical harassment, no matter how slight. If you receive an unwelcome pat on the butt, for example, your retort should be immediate and direct, leaving no room for misinterpretation.

Repeat Offenders

Women who experience repeated harassment are wise to begin keeping a record of the incidents and/or try to enlist the help of any witnesses to the incidents. This is especially helpful if the woman begins to think about legal action or visiting the organization's "general counsel."

When you tell someone something like any of the above statements, once ought to be enough, but some perpetrators just won't get it! If you find yourself confronted by a repeat offender, you may need to escalate the level of your responses. Say something like:

➤ "Are you aware that what you just said to me is grounds for legal action?"

➤ "Perhaps you, me, and so-and-so in the office of the general counsel need to discuss how you've been speaking to me."

➤ "I've asked you to refrain from these types of remarks in the past, and now I'm *telling* you, if I hear a similar remark even once more, there will be serious repercussions."

➤ "I find your remarks demeaning. If I have to, I'll take whatever steps necessary to ensure that you stop making them."

As you may have guessed by now, if you hear even one more peep out of a repeat offender after saying something on the order of the four choices above, anything else you say to him probably won't work. Now the time has arrived to go to the legal counsel or whoever has responsibility for such incidences in your organization.

Especially Sticky Situations

What if the harasser is someone who has significant power and influence within the organization? What if the harasser is your boss? For potentially sticky situations, you might find it useful to inquire among other women concerning whether or not they have experienced the same treatment that you have.

Bob Packwood can attest to the fact that many voices speak with far more authority than just one. All of the women he harassed over all the years came forward to ensure that Mr. Packwood would no longer bear the title of United States Senator before his name.

Ideally, you shouldn't have to go hunting around your office to find someone else who's been subjected to the same demeaning behavior. But realistically, this is often your best route. The person who harassed you may have harassed others as well. There may be women who no longer work for your organization who were harassed when they did. The more senior the harasser, the more likely it is that he or she has harassed others before you.

So, what should you do if you find out that a bunch of women have been harassed by a senior executive? There is strength in numbers—knowing you have the backing of others may spur you on to confront the offender or report his behavior. I wish I could tell you that you'll prevail—that you'll keep your job with no repercussions. However, you run many risks if you report the behavior. In preparation for confronting the situation, you'll need to fully document the behavior. Be prepared to be ostracized by other employees if the boss is popular, or get horrible work assignments or passed over for a promotion.

You may succeed in curbing the behavior of the harasser, having him removed or relocated, or winning a court judgment, but the outcome may not foster a climate of tranquility and respect. Sometimes, though, you simply have to make a stand.

Harassment Away from Work

Harassment away from the professional setting may be more frequent but is often less insidious. Many women can relate to the experience of being subjected to inappropriate comments while walking down the street.

In most public situations where you encounter verbal harassment, your best move is to ignore it and keep walking. If in a bar or social gathering, move to the other side of the room, especially in the situation where you don't know anything about your harasser.

While moving away is common-sense advice, it may seem annoying that women have to be the ones to yield or adapt to men's bad behavior. This is unfair, but your safety is more important in such situations.

You don't want to verbally spar with individuals who harass you in a public place; some may take offense if you say anything back. Some may regard any response on your part as a sign of interest; some may be simply off the wall and looking for a world of trouble.

If Women Aren't Free, Men Aren't Free

It seems a shame that many women feel unsafe walking the streets at night, or uneasy walking down a busy street in the middle of the day, through a city park, or in other situations where men may make cat calls.

If women can't freely walk about in our society without being subjected to verbal harassment, then by extension, men aren't free either. When I see a woman walk down a street and I'd like to say hi to her, I banish the thought. I consider all the creeps that have probably approached her, and how she may be leery of the next guy, even if he's a nice guy. So, I say nothing and walk on by. In many ways, the bad guys ruin the reputation of all men.

All-Purpose Repellents

If you're being harassed, and due to the logistics of the situation (you're in a waiting room or predesignated location to meet a friend), some verbal response will apparently be necessary, toughen up and practice some of these responses. Most guys will get your message:

➤ "Buzz off."

➤ "Get lost."

➤ "Disappear."

➤ "I am not interested."

➤ "Beat it."

➤ "Leave me alone."

I look forward to the day when no one needs to write chapters like this one or whole books on the topic of harassment. People everywhere need to understand that as harmless as the action may seem to the harasser, harassment makes one feel objectified, demeaned, or insulted.

For now, I guess harassment will be a lingering, undesirable aspect of our society. It makes sense to have a few preplanned strategies and well-chosen words ready just in case.

The Least You Need to Know

➤ There are substantial differences between men and women, but there are probably more similarities than differences between the two.

➤ You don't have to be restricted by traditional gender roles.

➤ In a dating situation, you have the opportunity to set the ground rules or limits.

➤ Tell harassers in the workplace quickly and succinctly that you do not intend to tolerate such remarks.

➤ In your personal life, ignoring a verbal harasser is most often the best course of action.

Chapter 18

Assertiveness for Other Special Circumstances

In This Chapter

➤ Asserting yourself above and beyond...

➤ Assertiveness challenges for the elderly

➤ Assertiveness challenges for the young

➤ Assertiveness for the otherwise challenged

If your circumstances differ from those of the great masses of people around, often you may need to be a tad more assertive just to be even with the rest. Stereotypes do abound. Throughout the world, many people find themselves in a "second-class" citizens' status amidst all the others in "mainstream" society. Such groups, along with the elderly and the young, among others, may need to be more assertive.

Speaking with an Accent

Suppose you're foreign born and speak with an accent, or you have a first name or surname that's unfamiliar to others or is hard to pronounce. You will likely experience situations where you need to be assertive to be heard and heeded on par with others.

Just the Facts

If you emigrate to another country and learn that country's language, but speak with an accent, you may face some challenges to being assertive. The problem is acute for people who emigrate to America where English prevails. The problem is less severe in Europe where people are more inclined to speak multiple languages.

If you live in the U.S. and speak English as a second language, depending on how fluent you are in English, you may have noticed on occasion that:

➤ Third-, fourth-, and fifth-generation Americans may not listen to you as closely.

➤ People may ignore you or serve you more slowly.

➤ Others are always telling you what to do.

➤ You find yourself reluctant to speak up, particularly in group situations.

If you speak with an accent, you're less likely to be heard, understood, and heeded in the U.S. than, perhaps, in some other places. If this is the case with you, or for whatever reason you find that others do not readily understand or heed your words, the path of least resistance is relatively clear:

"When in Rome do as the Romans," or

"If you can't fight em, join em."

In other words, in addition to closely reading, absorbing, and putting into practice everything you're learning in this book, it would also benefit you to engage in one or more of the next several options.

Accentuate the Positive

Your cultural heritage—no matter where you came from—is a wonderful part of who you are and a contributing factor to how you speak. However, you don't want people to ignore or misunderstand you, especially in business dealings that can cost you money. If you're very concerned about this, you may wish to reduce or eliminate your accent (even if you're Southern, or from New York or Minnesota). There are several audiocassette, videocassette, and CD-ROM programs available to help you speak more clearly. That's not to say you should conceal your roots or be in any way shy about your heritage. You merely want to be understood in conversation.

Find programs through your local library, or, if you happen to be close by, a college library. One program I saw in my local library apparently gives users most of what they need to communicate with confidence and sharpen their communication skills. The program is designed so that you can work at your own pace. One version comes on audiocassette and another comes with an interactive CD-ROM program with voice recognition. Hence, you can compare your voice with that of native speakers. Both versions include a workbook.

Take a public-speaking course through any of a number of adult education courses, at the YMCA, local community colleges, a Dale Carnegie course, and the various "open university" types of courses offered in most communities with a population above 100,000.

Slow down. If you speak deliberately and enunciate to the best of your ability, others have a better chance of understanding what you say and are more likely to be responsive.

Make It So

A growing number of both municipal and college libraries today have extensive audiovisual resources. Go to the reference desk and inquire about any audiovisual aids related to English as a second language or to eliminating an accent.

Revel in Your Differences

For some people, no matter how hard they practice, some lingering trace will likely identify them as being from someplace else. That's okay; consider it part of your charm. Lots of famous, successful people have maintained foreign accents, including:

➤ Comedian and musician Victor Borge, with his heavy Danish accent

➤ Actor Antonio Banderas, with his Spanish accent

➤ Action star and bodybuilder Arnold Schwarzenegger, with his Austrian accent

➤ Action star Jean-Claude van Damme, with his Belgian accent

➤ Former Secretary of State Henry Kissinger, with his German accent

These people have all used their distinctive language pattern to their great advantage. As you learned in Chapter 13, differences, even impediments, can often be turned to one's advantage.

Heed Communication Norms

Respect the norms of the culture in which you're interacting. If you come from a culture in which people speak almost face to face, it's important to understand that there are other cultures where everyone's personal space is larger. In the U.S., for example, it starts at least 18 inches away from the body, and for some people, it's as much as three feet.

Handle with Care

No matter how persuasive or influential you are otherwise, if you invade someone's personal space, you won't be regarded as assertive, you'll be regarded as aggressive.

If you speak in high-pitched tones or tend to raise your pitch when you're excited or in a hurry, practice speaking in a lower pitch.

Hold your ground. Speak and interact with confidence. Maintain eye contact and employ all the earlier suggestions on self-confidence in Chapters 5 through 8. That alone will compensate for any potential assertiveness disadvantages due to a speech impediment or an accent.

Smile and maintain a sense of humor. In any culture, a smile is the universal indicator of friendliness and well-being. Researchers tell us that smiles originate in your brain, spread to your face, and then are transmitted to the other person.

I understand your reluctance to be assertive when you're at a disadvantage because of language skills. Nevertheless, if you remain poised and stay in control, you can minimize apparent disadvantages and ultimately make yourself heard, understood, and heeded.

Assertiveness Challenges for the Elderly

In some cultures, the elderly are revered. In youth-fixated cultures, on the other hand, the elderly are all too often looked upon as unnecessary reminders of what everyone will one day become. In any culture, the elderly are inclined to move a little slower than others, walk slower, and perhaps talk slower.

In his book, *Old Age is Not for Sissies*, Art Linkletter says that old age, like every stage in life, has both its benefits and its detriments. It can be a highly rewarding time while presenting challenges unprecedented in one's life.

Your Dignity Is Inextricable

It's rare today to find a senior citizen who at one time or another hasn't felt as if all eyes were staring at her, as she held up the line in the supermarket, the bank, or even the voting booth.

Through the first 17 chapters of this book I've emphasized the importance of self-confidence, vocal confidence, even posture. What do you do, however, when your voice is creaky, you walk with a cane, and you draw upon other inherent mental and physical attributes of younger days with difficulty? Maintain your dignity.

Although the example that follows is of a celebrity, consider the possible parallels with your own relatives or other elderly people that you know.

Kirk Douglas, at age 77, accepted an award for lifetime achievement at the Academy Awards presentations in 1996. What made the moment particularly memorable was that Mr. Douglas had suffered a massive stroke earlier that year. His motor skills were visibly diminished. Half of his face seemed frozen, inoperable. His mouth was contorted when he spoke, and some words were barely distinguishable.

Everyone who watched had sharp images of the swashbuckling Kirk Douglas from the film clips of him shown just moments before, juxtaposed with the sight of this contorted, if proud, figure before them. Yet, the image that will linger is Kirk Douglas's dignity, which reverberated throughout the hall and across the airwaves.

Sure, you say, who wouldn't buck up, summon their strength and energy, and show one-fifth of the world's population their best face?

If you saw Kirk Douglas that night, however, you know that the dignity, the presence with which he asserted himself, despite his incapacity, could not be feigned.

Not in My Theater

Katharine Hepburn, 90 years old as this book goes to press, has had a long history of asserting herself when and where she deemed proper. I had the opportunity to see her some time ago at Kennedy Center. While in the midst of delivering her lines on stage, someone took a flash picture of her.

Miss Hepburn broke out of character and said to the perpetrator, "How rude! How utterly rude." She then retreated to her position on stage, and became her character again. Katharine Hepburn was the master of her stage and of her dignity. Certainly no unauthorized photographer would "invade" her space like that again. She responded to the offending source and vigorously asserted her views. Then, she apparently moved past it, carrying no residue.

Some 20 years later, she is still known to handle reporters, interviewers, attendants, and service people with dignity so as to get what she wants, and to keep them on her side.

Here are some common denominators among the elderly I have observed who seem to maintain a well-developed sense of dignity. As a natural by-product of doing so, they also seem to maintain adequate levels of assertiveness. They:

➤ Enunciate their words as best they can.

➤ Speak slowly and distinctly if that's what serves them best.

➤ Maintain the best posture they can.

➤ Look directly into the eyes of the other party.

➤ Listen attentively.

➤ Appreciate any help offered to them.

➤ Don't move any faster than is comfortable for them.

With a Twinkle

Many elderly maintain what proverbially is regarded as a "twinkle in the eye." It is a certain something about them that lets you know they have more to share if you ask them. It's as if they've figured out some of the deep, dark secrets of life. And, having done so, they now proceed through life with an inner smile. I guess acquiring such wisdom is more than compensatory for having to move at a slower pace.

While they may encounter rudeness from younger people all around them, they seldom counter with reprimands. They take such incidences in stride, usually regarding them as trifling affairs in the overall span of things. When they need specific assistance they know how to ask for it:

➤ "Young man, would you be so kind as to help me with…"

➤ "Young lady, would you mind seeing if…"

➤ "Could I impose on you to…"

➤ "Would you do me the favor of…"

They pose such requests, in an upbeat manner that makes the other party feel good about handling the issue. Then, having received the assistance, they graciously thank their helper.

Assertiveness Challenges for the Young

The challenges that 17- to 25-year-olds face when it comes to being assertive often stem from elders who don't give them attention or respect. The young hotshot at work who may have brilliant ideas is ignored by others who see him as an upstart.

A too-youthful appearance in an otherwise adult world can be a detriment of sorts. Others may discount your experience, wisdom, or capabilities.

Hey, So What If I'm Younger

Here are some guidelines in the workplace, in social situations, and in general, if you find yourself facing special challenges because of your age:

➤ Dress at the same level as others in your position.

➤ Support others when they speak by being an attentive listener.

➤ Rely more on face-to-face encounters rather than notes, memos, and e-mail.

➤ Forgive a lot.

➤ Closely observe the superstars and emulate their characteristics.

➤ Find a mentor (or two or three) who can give you tips on how to come across more powerfully.

The Extra Mile

When I worked as a management consultant in the late 1970s and 1980s in the Washington, D.C. area, I used to speak to local civic and professional groups at lunch and after work. Thereafter, when I spoke up in and around my own company, people noticed that I did so with far greater ease and professionalism.

The practice that I put in as a public speaker paid off in terms of my assertiveness in my own company. Even though no one had seen or known that I was speaking to groups on the side, the effects were clearly visible to them. My bosses must have noticed, because at one point my salary increased $10,500 in a 14-month period. And, in the five-year period between 1978 and 1983, overall, my salary increased by $31,750. I don't relate this to boast, but rather offer it as a dramatic, attainable example of the dynamics at play when you go the extra mile, regardless of your age.

Make It So
A tried-and-true, if painfully slow, way to win over others in the workplace, is by doing it one person at a time. Go to lunch with someone different each day, so you can get to know others in a more professionally intimate way. Then you won't feel so out of it at the next group-wide meeting. Each person with whom you've had lunch will have his or her own more educated perceptions of you.

The Opportunity to Assert Yourself

If you want to grow as a person and minimize the "disadvantages" of youth, you have many options:

➤ Take a leadership position in a social organization, be it chair of the new member committee, programs and activities, or meeting registration or reception.

➤ Hang around with others who are more mature than you are (if they'll let you).

➤ Volunteer to participate in an election campaign; you're likely to be counted on based on your intelligence, energy, and creativity independent of your age.

➤ Join a debate club.

➤ Volunteer to take a role in a local play, particularly a role where you'll have some significant speaking parts.

➤ Take a course on acting. Ronald Reagan did.

➤ Take a Dale Carnegie course or other public speaking course where you have an opportunity to engage in exercises that verbally stretch your interpersonal communication patterns.

➤ Join a professional society, such as the Society for Technical Communications, or any other group cited in Chapter 12. This helps in the workplace, at least.

Assertiveness Everywhere Else

Beyond the workplace and specific social situations, look for other opportunities where you can flex your "assertiveness muscle." By that I mean take small steps forward by asserting yourself in situations where, perhaps, in the past you remained silent. For example, speak up if:

➤ Someone cuts in front of you in a line.

➤ A salesperson keeps you waiting unduly long.

➤ Some other adult makes a derogatory comment about youth in general when it has nothing to do with your particular behavior.

At 18 or so, I remember being somewhat slighted when it came to getting service at a department store. It seemed there was always some older man or woman, perhaps in their thirties or forties, whom salesclerks seemed to call on first, even if I had been at the counter first. On more than one occasion I found myself taking a half-step forward and saying, "Excuse me, but I was here first." Often, that was enough to acknowledge and get my request fulfilled.

Assertiveness Challenges for the Vertically Challenged

Handle with Care
Imagine how you would feel if there was a hit song that played on radio stations over and over again, mocking some physical or mental impediment that you had. You wouldn't enjoy it very much, and you certainly wouldn't like the singer or songwriter.

In the early 1980s, songwriter and singer Randy Newman produced a hit song called "Short People." Being six-foot-three and rather insensitive at the time to the obstacles that short people face in Western societies, I thought the song was funny. Apparently, many others did, too, because it became a hit.

We all need to be more sensitive to impediments that others may experience, even if such impediments seem rather harmless to us.

Not Imaginary Disadvantages

The challenge that shorter men and women face in society is real. Studies show that all other things being equal, they are:

➤ Likely to earn less money than their taller counterparts

➤ Less likely to be promoted into positions of leadership

➤ Less likely to win elections

Often, short people face the same form of subtle, social discrimination faced by people who are, say, hard of hearing, physically challenged, or follically challenged (bald).

As I stated in Chapter 5, the winners in life learn to turn obstacles into advantages. When five-foot-three Muggsy Bogues lasts more than ten years in the NBA, wow, what isn't possible?

Among the many things you can do to assert yourself in an often-insensitive society are the following:

➤ *Develop your vocabulary.* In his book, *The Ten Seeds of Greatness*, Denis Waitley says that a well-developed vocabulary is one of the predictors of success in business and in life.

➤ *Dress well.* A well-dressed man or woman, of any stature, is more readily noticed by others.

➤ *Maintain dignity at all times.* You don't have to apologize for not being tall. Certainly you can wear shoes that give you an extra couple of inches in height, but you don't need to appear taller, or wish to be taller.

➤ *Focus on your strengths.* If you have a great wit, or are particularly warm or charming, let these qualities shine through.

➤ *Keep your cool.* Don't respond to putdowns, however subtle or open they may be.

Work It Out?

Some of the most well-developed bodybuilders in the world are short. Perhaps they are building their muscles as a compensatory mechanism. Indeed, most of the Mr. Universes and Mr. Olympias of the past 20 years have been under five-feet-eleven, some well under.

An imposing physical presence in itself can be a form of assertiveness. However, I don't advocate that you go out and develop huge muscles. If you want to, go ahead, but it isn't necessary. Rather, I'd suggest that you focus on characteristics and capabilities that have enabled you to achieve what you have achieved.

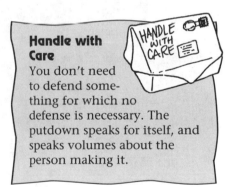

Handle with Care
You don't need to defend something for which no defense is necessary. The putdown speaks for itself, and speaks volumes about the person making it.

Assertiveness Challenges for the Horizontally Challenged

Fifty-eight million Americans are overweight. Obese people are at higher risk when it comes to heart disease and other circulatory and respiratory disorders. There is, however, conflicting data as to the long-term effect on health of being somewhat overweight, say in the 30- to 40-pound range.

Just the Facts

The number of overweight Americans has grown steadily over the past decade. One-third of people over age 20 tip the scales in the wrong direction, according to statistics in the *Journal of the American Medical Association*.

On average, adults weigh eight pounds more than they did a decade ago, reports Dr. Robert Kuczmarski and colleagues at the National Center for Health Statistics, Hyattsville, Maryland. "Comparisons...indicate dramatic increases in the prevalence of overweight people," Kuczmarski said.

Based on what's currently known, you'll live pretty close to what you would without the extra weight, as long as you don't smoke, get some exercise, and eat a variety of foods including fruits and vegetables. When it comes to asserting yourself, much of the advice that I gave to the vertically challenged is applicable.

Grant Me the Serenity...

You can do something about your weight, whereas a short person can't do much about his height. At the same time, you don't need to proceed in life with an air of apology for your weight. You are who you are.

Handle with Care

Imagine if we started calling people whatever we wanted based on observable physical characteristics such as pock marks, warts, skin discolorations, and what have you. We would degenerate to a "Lord of the Flies" society, in which physical intimidation and force would prevail over civility and reason.

Perhaps one of the reasons why you're less assertive today than you might otherwise be stems from your childhood. Suppose you were heavy as a child. Children can be cruel to one another. A friend of mine, whom I'll call John, told me that most of the names he heard in his youth have stayed with him in one form or another. In some way, they hold him back today. If that's the case with you, perhaps it's time to shake out the demons.

Please read the following list closely: Fatso, Butterball, Dough Boy, Porky Pig, Flabby, Fathead. Have you ever been called any of these names? Chances are you were. From the comic books' Little Lotta to Bill Cosby's Fat Albert, if you grew up heavy, you know that people had special names for you. As an adult, of course, you know that they were wrong to refer to you in such a manner. On some level you may still be restricted by such labels, however.

Put 'Em in Their Place

Contrary to the advice I dispensed for short people, if you are overweight, I think it's appropriate to address putdowns. Just because you can possibly reduce your weight doesn't open the door to others' comments.

Any one of the following responses should be sufficient:

➤ "Keep your thoughts to yourself."

➤ "Your statements are out of line."

➤ "Who gave you the authority…?"

➤ "I don't want to hear that from you again."

➤ "That's uncalled for."

➤ "Pardon me, that's none of your concern."

If responding in this manner is not for you, perhaps you can simply give a direct gaze at the offender so as to indicate, "You're rude."

The Ever-Worthy You

If you wear glasses, wear a hearing aid, or have some other physical, mental, or emotional challenge, this sometimes prompts in others an unwillingness to give you your due.

Self-worth is handed out at birth. You are worthy just for being you. You don't have to apologize, explain, or meet somebody else's expectations, unless you freely choose to.

The Least You Need to Know

➤ There are many tools available to help you improve your speaking if you feel that you're not being sufficiently understood or heeded.

➤ In any culture, a smile is the universal indicator of friendliness and well-being.

➤ When you're old and gray, at least you have your dignity.

➤ You don't need to proceed in life with an air of apology because you are different.

➤ You are who you are. You are worthy just for being you.

Chapter 19

Becoming an Assertive Consumer

In This Chapter

➤ Don't complain, assert!

➤ Using resource groups like the Better Business Bureau

➤ Composing effective complaint letters

If you buy an appliance and it turns out to be a lemon, don't get mad and don't get even—get assertive! In this chapter I'll show you what you can do to assert yourself as a consumer when the goods, services, or responses you deserve are not forthcoming. Let's start with something as simple as calling a company.

Dying on Hold

You call an organization and before you have a chance to say anything, the receptionist says, "XYZ Inc., will you hold?" If you think fast enough, say, "No, I'm sorry, I don't wish to hold."

Many receptionists will deal with your request there and then because, after all, they don't know who you are. You could be the president's brother, the major shareholder, or (yikes!) an IRS agent.

Often, the people who answer the phone for a living are in impossible situations. Some have to handle more calls per unit of time than any human being can comfortably handle. Therefore, you do your best to stay in control with the people who answer the phone. There are cases, though, in which you have a legitimate claim to assert yourself with the receptionist, such as when:

➤ You're calling long distance.

➤ You're returning someone's call, primarily as a favor to them.

➤ You truly do have limited time to devote to this call.

➤ You're calling from a pay phone and others are waiting to make calls.

➤ You're calling from an airport or other transportation hub.

If you're in one of these situations, good-naturedly let the other party know. Chances are the other party has been in the same boat and will do what they can for you.

Fingers Do the Walking

Everyone is doing more shopping by phone these days. Chances are you already know the routine, so you know how frustrating it can be. Have you ever encountered someone who says, "Hold on—I've got to get some paper (or a pen, or a desk, or a brain). When I get that response, I reply, "Gee, it might be advantageous to keep (said item) by the phone." So, just in case you'll be soon making your first purchase by phone, here are some fundamentals to remember:

Handle with Care
Never reveal your credit card number, checking account number, or other personal information to a telemarketer unless you are familiar with the organization, and the information is necessary in order to make your purchase.

➤ Maintain a record of the name, address, and phone number of the company, goods you ordered, date of your purchase, amount you paid (including shipping and handling) and method of payment.

➤ Mark down any delivery period that was promised.

➤ If the shipment will be delayed, write the date of that notice in your records and the new shipping date, if you've agreed to wait longer.

If you do these things, you'll maintain greater control of the issue, and you'll be able to easily assert yourself on subsequent calls because you'll have all the relevant information.

A Little Service, Please

Suppose you're in a store. You're waiting to buy a small item and none of the clerks seem to notice you. What should you do? You have a couple of strategies, the first being to wait until one of them does notice you. Usually, this happens after a minute or two. If you're still waiting, I suggest that you say something light, even witty, such as, "Who wants to take my money?", or make a ringing sound as if you had a bell you could depress to get somebody's attention. You could revert to the overused "Exxxxcuse me!" or "Hellllllloooooooo?" Too many people use these, however—they border on rudeness, and they don't help you increase your repertoire of assertive responses.

When clerks ignore you, strive to come up with something clever; work on it if you have to. Such spontaneity and creativity will serve you well in cases where you really need them.

So, You Bought an Appliance and It Turned Out to Be a Lemon

Suppose you bought a toaster and it went kaput three weeks after you bought it. You call the store where you bought it and they tell you that it was a close-out model and on sale for a special price. This is news to you; however, you've got breakfast to eat and no toast. You ask about the return procedure, only to learn that they won't allow you to return this particular item. Now you're livid.

As it turns out, you paid by cash for this item and can't find the receipt. Before asserting yourself with the vendor, you need to get organized. Allow me to recommend *The Complete Idiot's Guide to Managing Your Time,* written by yours truly, which contains every shred of detail you'd ever want or need on how to keep paper in its place and how to set up files that actually serve you. In a nutshell, hereafter you need to file all purchase-related paperwork. Include copies of sales receipts, repair orders, warranties, canceled checks, contracts, and any letters to or from the company.

Then, when you have a problem with something you paid for:

➤ Contact the business, even the same salesperson who sold you the item or performed the service. Calmly and accurately describe the problem and what action you would like taken. If it isn't resolved to your satisfaction over the phone, move on to the next point.

➤ Keep a record of your efforts to resolve the problem. Write to the company. Describe the problem, what you have done so far to try to resolve it, and what solution you want. For example, do you want your money back, the product repaired, or the product exchanged?

➤ Allow time for the person you contacted to resolve your problem. Keep notes of the name of the person you spoke with, the date, and what was done. Save copies of all letters to and from the company. If you are still not satisfied, escalate your efforts.

➤ Contact the company headquarters, if applicable, if you have not resolved your problem. Many companies have a toll-free 800 number. Look for it on package labeling, in a directory of 800 telephone numbers (available at your local library), or by calling 1-800-555-1212. Address your letter to the consumer office or the company's president. If your claim is valid, eventually you'll achieve resolution, since nearly every company today would like to avoid angry or embittered customers. The following sections give you some guidelines, courtesy of the United States Office of Consumer Affairs, on finding companies and on what to include in a complaint letter.

Finding a Company's Headquarters

First you've got to figure out where to send your letter:

➤ Check the product label or warranty for the name and address of the manufacturer.

➤ For additional help locating company information, check the reference section of your local library for the following books:

Standard & Poor's Register of Corporations

Directors and Executives

Standard Directory of Advertisers

Trade Names Dictionary

Dun & Bradstreet Directory

Handle with Care
Only do business with companies you will be able to find later if you need to. It can be difficult to find companies in other states which only list post office boxes as addresses. Also, even if you have an address, it might be only a mail drop, so be sure you know where the company you are doing business with is actually located.

➤ If you have the brand, but can't find the name of the manufacturer, the *Thomas Register of American Manufacturers* lists the manufacturers of thousands of products.

➤ Each state has an agency (possibly the corporation commission or secretary of state's office) that provides addresses for companies incorporated in that state.

Public libraries also have other directories that might be helpful.

Guidelines for Writing a Complaint Letter

Here are some tips for writing a complaint letter to a company:

➤ Include the obvious, such as your name, address, home and/or work telephone numbers, and account number, if any.

➤ Keep your letter brief and to the point. Include the date and place you made the purchase, who performed the service, information about the product such as the serial or model number or warranty terms, what went wrong, with whom you have tried to resolve the problem, and what you want done to correct the problem. (See the following sample complaint letter.)

➤ Include copies (never originals) of all documents.

➤ Be reasonable, not angry or threatening, in your letter.

➤ Type your letter, if possible, or make sure your handwriting is neat and easy to read.

➤ Start a file of correspondence to and from the company.

➤ For important issues or high-ticket items, send your letter with a return receipt requested. This will cost a bit, but offers you proof that your letter was received and tells you who signed for it.

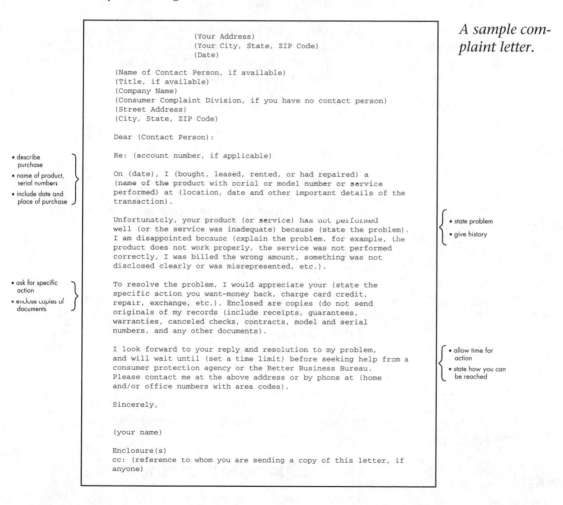

A sample complaint letter.

Negotiating a Lease

There are some life events where your single best opportunity to get a fair deal comes at the initiation. For example, if you're going to rent equipment or premises, you have

Handle with Care

Once you sign a lease, you remove most if not all of the leeway you have in negotiating major items with the lessor.

the best chance to get what you want at the time of the lease signing, rather than afterwards. Suppose you're about to move into a $750-a-month, two-bedroom, two-bathroom apartment, not including utilities. You know that the rental market has been slow and the landlord would be lucky to have someone like you as a tenant. Now is the best time to ask to have utilities included.

Call, then Write; or Write, then Call?

Suppose you move in, and the apartment needs repairs or some type of alteration. To assert yourself, write a letter and make a phone call. Often, the sequence doesn't matter much. The call is important because it allows your landlord to gauge the urgency of the problem through the tone, volume, and pitch of your voice.

The letter is important because it provides documentation of your request and clearly spells it out.

I'll Just Hold on to the Rent Check

If you're in a situation where repeated requests don't receive action, I suppose you have the option of withholding rent. Nothing speaks louder than not showing your landlord the money. However, I don't recommend that you do this often, and if you can help it, avoid doing it at all.

Handle with Care

Holding up rent money waves a big red flag to your landlord. In most cases, you're far better off paying your rent on time and continuing to assert yourself about the issue.

Make It So

When it comes to landlord-tenant relations, you always want to create a clear and unimpeachable paper trail, regardless of which role you play.

You might be thinking, well, what if I just deduct the cost of repair out of the rent and send it in? I advise you not to do this for several reasons. First, if you haven't received the permission to do this, you may make your landlord mad. Perhaps more importantly, when you pay your rent in full, and are reimbursed for repairs afterwards, you receive written documentation concerning the proper amounts due to the respective parties.

Tenants rights associations exist everywhere, although they are more active in major metropolitan areas. They can provide you with all kinds of advice about your rights, plus mediation services.

The Multiple-Date Method

One technique I use seems to work rather well, whether I'm dealing with landlords (a problem of yesteryear) or encountering anyone else with whom I've made a repeated request. I send the same letter, a second, third, and if necessary, a fourth time, always including the latest date directly under the date of the earlier letter. For example:

A Multiple-Date Request Letter

Memo to: Hardhead Properties Management

From: Jeff Davidson

September 16
September 24
October 1

Dear Manager,

The caulking around my bathtub tile is coming apart and requires immediate repair to reduce any possibility of water getting into the drywall. Please call me at 555-8625 as soon as possible so we can arrange for this repair.

Yours truly,

Jeff Davidson

If you need a variety of repairs, structure your letter in bullet format.

The common denominators of these letters are:

➤ Clear descriptive language of what needs to be done

➤ Items that are individually highlighted using bullets

➤ A sense of urgency

➤ A request for scheduling, a call back, or whatever other consideration you need completed

Your Home, Your Castle?

It's not your imagination—it is getting harder to get some peace and quiet even in your own home. Let's examine a variety of situations where you may wish to draw upon your power of assertion when you *don't* want to be a consumer.

Door-to-Door Sales

Suppose somebody comes to your door to try to sell you something. Obviously you always have the option of saying, "Sorry, not interested."

Perhaps you are mildly interested. If so, here are some tips to stay in control of the situation:

➤ Ask to see the salesperson's personal identification (and license or registration if that is required where you live). Jot down his or her name, the name and address of the company, and whether the salesperson carries proper identification.

➤ Ask for the salesperson's sales literature. Then give yourself time to call retail stores that might sell the same items to compare prices. Some door-to-door products can be greatly overpriced.

➤ Feel free to say no—you never want to let yourself be pressured into buying anything. Pressure tactics include an offer of a "free gift" if you buy a product, an offer good for today only, or a story about a neighbor making a purchase.

➤ Ask the salesperson to leave if you feel threatened, intimidated, or even mildly uncomfortable.

If You Decide to Buy

If you do choose to make a purchase or sign up for whatever's being offered, you need to know about the "Door-to-Door Sales Rule," sometimes referred to as the "Cooling Off Rule"). This law is in effect in all U.S. states and gives you the right to cancel certain purchases costing $25 or more. You have to notify the vendor in writing by midnight of the third business day following the sale. Saturdays are considered business days. Sundays and holidays are not.

If you decide to accept what the seller is offering, the seller is supposed to give you two dated copies of a cancellation form showing the seller's name and address and explaining your right to cancel. Many vendors don't do this! Depending on where you live, your state might also have additional laws that protect you as a buyer. Your state or local office of consumer protection can send you a summary of your rights as a consumer. If you choose to cancel a contract you've initiated, sign and date one copy of the cancellation form and mail it within the three-day limit! It must be postmarked before midnight of the third business day. Send it by certified mail if you want to show proof that it was mailed. (There's more on mailing in the next chapter.)

Getting Assertive with Telemarketers

Telemarketing as an industry probably continues to exist because most people are too polite to give the intruder short shrift. To terminate calls politely and quickly, you may need to cut in and say "Excuse me, I'm just not interested" and that should do it.

Over the years, I've heard stories and anecdotes about clever and creative ways people have stopped telemarketers in their tracks. Here's one of the better ones, which happened to appear in *Reader's Digest*: A woman told a telephone solicitor who was trying to sell cemetery plots that she couldn't call her husband to the phone because he was using his plot.

If you really want to put a chill into the telemarketer's campaign, tell the next caller: "To comply with the Telephone Consumer Protection Act, Telephone and Consumer Fraud and Abuse Prevention Act (ref: Telemarketing Sales Rule, Part 310) you are directed to remove my name, phone, and fax number from your rolls and to make no more calls/

faxes to me. Under the 'do not call' provision, calling or faxing a consumer who has requested not to be called is rule violation, for which you risk a $10,000 civil penalty, per violation. To protect yourself and your company, please have your supervisor send a copy of your 'do not call' policy."

Everything in the above paragraph is accurate and true. If you want a complete copy of the telemarketing sales rule, write to:

Direct Marketing Association
1120 Avenue of the Americas
New York, NY 10036-6700

Better Business Bureaus

Regardless of what type of consumer issue you're facing, you can always give a call to your local Better Business Bureau (BBB). BBBs are non-profit organizations supported primarily by local business members. The focus of BBB activities is to promote an ethical marketplace by encouraging honest advertising and selling practices, and by providing dispute resolution.

BBBs provide consumer education materials; answer consumer questions; provide information about a company, particularly whether or not there are unanswered or unsettled complaints or other marketplace problems; help resolve buyer/seller complaints against a company, including mediation and arbitration services; and provide information about charities and other organizations that are seeking public donations. BBBs usually request that you submit your complaint in writing. Then they will take up the complaint with the company involved. If the complaint cannot be satisfactorily resolved through communication with the business, a BBB may offer an alternative dispute settlement process, such as mediation or arbitration.

JUST THE FACTS MA'AM.

Just the Facts

BBBs do not judge or rate individual products or brands, handle complaints concerning the price of goods or services, handle employer/employee wage disputes, or give legal advice.

More Consumer Help

Did you know that you can get a free copy of the Consumer Information Catalog, which lists approximately 200 free or low-cost Federal booklets with helpful information for consumers? Well, you can! Topics in the catalog include careers and education, cars, child care, the environment, Federal benefits, financial planning, food and nutrition, health, housing, small business, and much more.

The catalog is published quarterly by the Consumer Information Center of the U.S. General Services Administration. To obtain a single copy, write to:

Catalog
Consumer Information Center
Pueblo, CO 81009

National Consumer Organizations

There are many organizations whose sole purpose is to offer consumer assistance, protection, and/or advocacy. Many of the groups discussed on the next few pages distribute consumer education and information materials. The American Association of Retired Persons (AARP) Consumer Affairs Section advocates on behalf of mid-life and older consumers, and develops and distributes consumer information. AARP addresses such issues as housing, insurance, funeral practices, eligibility for public benefits, financial security, transportation, and consumer protection, all with special focus on the needs and problems of older consumers. You can reach them at:

American Association of Retired Persons
Consumer Affairs Section
601 E Street NW
Washington, DC 20049

An organization that can help you with marketplace problems is Call for Action. An international non-profit hotline, Call for Action is affiliated with radio and television stations and helps consumers and small businesses through mediation of marketplace disputes. A list of the affiliated radio and television stations is available by contacting the hotline. For more information, contact:

Call for Action
5272 River Road
Suite 300
Bethesda, MD 20816

The Consumers Union of U.S. is a non-profit, independent organization which researches and tests consumer goods and services. They then write up the results in their monthly magazine, *Consumer Reports*, as well as in other publications. For more information, contact:

The Consumers Union of U.S.
101 Truman Avenue
Yonkers, NY 10703-1057

Avoiding Car Repair Blues

You brought your car in for servicing, and after a few minutes, the mechanic reports to you that your car will need this and that and that. The bill will come to $480. You are aghast. In this case, even if you don't know a lot about cars, and don't have much experience with this particular repair shop, you may ask some questions to stand up for yourself and keep your bill as low as possible.

The following are examples of such questions:

➤ "On that third item, what factors led you to this conclusion?"

➤ "If I don't take care of that one today, how long can I go before I do have to take care of it?"

➤ "Are you sure about that one? I just had that examined about two weeks ago and everything seemed fine."

If the mechanic or service person is emphatic about your need to get the repairs as indicated, perhaps you need to get the work done. If the mechanic hedges a bit, you probably don't need to have that particular repair done at this time.

If you decide to go ahead and have the repairs done, you can always ask about the warranty or guarantee of the parts, labor, and so forth. You can also ask for the worn-out parts. Thus, you will have the opportunity to have someone else examine the old parts and what was done to determine whether or not the repair was needed.

You may ask, "What good will that do me, since I've already spent the money?" If it appears that the old parts didn't require replacement, you have recourse against the original repair shop. All states now have a hotline number for car repair fraud.

> **Make It So**
> When having repairs done, in particular auto repairs, always err on the side of caution. You're better off if you go ahead and pay a car service center for a repair that could be delayed for several weeks or months from now. The value of having a car that continues to run smoothly has no price.

The few times in my driving career when I've broken down on the highway were highly disruptive. You probably feel the same way. Therefore, while I certainly will assert myself in an auto repair shop to the extent that I need to, I am also willing to pay a few extra dollars when necessary. In those cases where I do drive off with the least amount handled, I will then quickly visit a repair shop I am familiar with and ask them to assess the situation. About half the time, they concur with the first repair shop, and the other half of the time, they do not. I guess that's how the car repair biz works!

The best advice I can give you is to find a repair shop that you trust and use them whenever possible.

Problems When Buying a Car

If you have a problem with a car you purchased from a local dealer, first try to work it out with the dealer. If the problem is not resolved, contact the manufacturer's regional or national office. For U.S. cars, most of the headquarters are in Detroit. If you still cannot resolve your problem, contact the local Better Business Bureau, which may have a special department for handling auto purchase-related problems. Also, contact your local or state consumer agency to see if your state offers state-run dispute resolution programs. If you suspect you have a vehicle problem that might fall under your state lemon law (in which you've apparently been sold a car of dubious performance), call your local or state consumer agency to find out about your rights. Often, you'll find that the deck is stacked in your favor!

Also, draw on your assertiveness skills to get the best price on a car. The purchase of a new car is an area where many people feel at a disadvantage. Assertiveness can change that experience by conveying to the salesperson that you intend to get a good price and will stand your ground until you get it, or you are prepared to walk away. (For a good guide to negotiation in general, pick up *The Complete Idiot's Guide to Negotiation*.)

Dispute Resolution Programs

Companies that manufacture similar products, such as car manufacturers, or that offer similar services, such as attorneys, often belong to industry or professional associations. These associations help resolve problems between their member companies and consumers. Depending on the industry, you might have to contact an association, service council, or consumer action program. If you have a problem with a company and cannot get it resolved with that firm, ask if the company is a member of an association. Then check the following list to see if the association is listed. If the name of the association is not included here, check with a local library.

Here are some additional groups that may be able to lend consumer assistance:

American Arbitration Association
140 West 51st Street
New York, NY 10020-1203

This is a non-profit public service organization with three dozen regional offices across the country. The AAA offers consumer information on request.

American Council of Life Insurance
1001 Pennsylvania Avenue NW
Suite 500
South Washington, DC 20004-2599

The ACLI consists of life insurance companies authorized to do business in the United States.

216

National Association of Professional Insurance Agents
400 North Washington Street
Alexandria, VA 22314

The NAPIA offers consumers practical advice on personal insurance buying through its national outreach program.

American Society of Travel Agents, Inc.
1101 King Street
Suite 200
Alexandria, VA 22314

The ASTA is the prevailing national association for travel agents.

Direct Marketing Association (DMA)
1111 19th Street NW
Suite 1100
Washington, DC 20036

The DMA consists of members who market goods and services directly to consumers using direct mail, catalogs, telemarketing, magazine and newspaper ads, and broadcast advertising. The DMA operates the Mail Order Action Line, Mail Preference Service and Telephone Preference Service.

For problems with a mail order company, write: Mail Order Action Line, 1111 19th Street NW, Suite 1100, Washington, DC, 20036.

To remove your name and home address from national mailing lists, write: Mail Preference Service, P.O. Box 9014, Farmingdale, NY, 11735-9014.

To remove your name from telephone solicitation lists, write: Telephone Preference Service, P.O. Box 9014, Farmingdale, NY, 11735-9014.

In all, there are more than 40,000 trade and professional associations in the United States, representing all manner of industry and professions. Some of these associations and their members have established programs to help consumers with complaints not resolved at the point of purchase. Trade associations have various consumer functions, which are described in *National Trade & Professional Associations* of the United States. This directory is available in any city or college library.

State, County, and City Government Consumer Offices

State and local consumer protection offices can help you resolve consumer complaints and provide you with consumer education information. These agencies might mediate complaints, conduct investigations, prosecute offenders of consumer laws, license and regulate professions, promote strong consumer protection legislation, provide educational materials, and act as advocates in the consumer interest.

When you have a hot case of suspected fraud, misrepresentation, or simply a worthy complaint, governmental agencies want to know, since consumer complaints form the basis of most consumer protection law-enforcement actions. If you want to file a complaint, call your local consumer protection office to learn what you need to do. You can usually find a list of state, county, and city government consumer protection offices in the "blue" or government pages of your phone book.

Many states also have special commissions and agencies to handle consumer questions and complaints about aging, banks, insurance, utilities, vocational and rehabilitation services, weights and measures, and securities.

City, county, and state consumer protection offices can also provide you with vital services. Since you're paying for them via your tax dollars, you might as well use them if the situation merits. Consumer protection offices may mediate complaints, conduct investigations, or even prosecute offenders of consumer laws.

The Least You Need to Know

➤ If you call an organization and are told, "XYZ, will you hold?" feel free to say "No, I'd prefer not to hold."

➤ Never reveal your credit card number, checking account number, or other personal information to anyone by phone unless you are familiar with the company.

➤ File all purchase-related paperwork, such as sales receipts, repair orders, warranties, and contracts. Then when you need to assert yourself, you'll have "documentation power."

➤ If you choose to cancel a contract for over $25, you have three days to do so.

➤ No matter what the issue, there is a private or public group that can help you find resolution.

Chapter 20

Becoming an Assertive Citizen

In This Chapter

➤ Calling on government

➤ How to get a little attention

➤ How to communicate by phone with a bureaucrat

➤ Be forceful when you have to

➤ Don't get mad, get assertive!

If you've got a beef with government, say the IRS has held up your refund check for more than two months, or some techno-twit at the Department of Commerce keeps ignoring your calls and letters, you've come to the right place.

In this chapter, I'll cover talking to bureaucrats on the phone in a way that will make it difficult for them to ignore you, writing a complaint letter, and making sure that you get action.

Calling on Washington, D.C....Is Anybody Home?

Perhaps you've had an experience such as the following: You place a call to the federal government to check on something personally important to you, such as to inquire about a regulation that may affect you, to find a certain form, or to answer a question that you can't get answered locally.

Yet, on any given day, it doesn't seem as if anyone is home. Why is it that when you call the federal government, or state or local government for that matter, you so often get the old voice mail run-around?

Just the Facts

Earlier forms of the bureaucratic shuffle included phones that continually rang and no one ever answered, messages saying that the number you'd reached had been disconnected, or receptionists who couldn't seem to get you to the right party no matter how many buttons he or she pushed.

If you've been subject to the run-around even once, let alone a dozen times, you're probably reticent to give a call to the federal government again, even for a pressing issue. Take heart, you have in your hands the formula for getting bureaucrats to respond—sometimes even the first time!

First, Get Organized

Perhaps you're trying to correct an inaccurate wage statement, apply for a benefits program, or you simply need information. Before you assert yourself as a citizen, whether you're dealing with the federal, state, or local government, there are some prerequisites:

1. Get a file folder for whatever documents you currently have on hand related to the issue and for whatever documents you'll be accumulating.

2. Get stamps, envelopes, and Post-it pads. Get some notepaper and, obviously, a pen.

3. Hopefully, you have a copier and a fax machine nearby. If not, these services are available at copy shops across the country.

4. Before actually making the call, check the time. Give yourself 15 minutes for the call. Three to four minutes will probably be spent simply getting the right party on the line. Another three or four minutes will be your discussion of the issue you're facing, for two or three you'll be put on hold, and the rest will be the bureaucrat responding in some fashion. Don't short-change yourself; you're going to kill 15 minutes for this call any way you cut it. In fact, 15 minutes might turn out to be a bargain.

5. Now, prep yourself. Remember, you may not get the right party on the first try. You may get shuffled around. You may be fuming because it's a long-distance call. But don't. Keep focused on what it will feel like when this particular issue is resolved. Keep your eyes on the prize!

Be the First on Your Block

Okay, suppose you get a letter in the mail from a government agency, or some government benefit that you're supposed to be receiving is not forthcoming. Before picking up that phone, there's a little something I'd like you to do. Go to your local library and ask the reference librarian for the latest copy of the *Federal Yellow Book* or the *Federal Executive Directory*.

The *Federal Yellow Book* is a large volume directory of direct-dial phone numbers breaking down each federal government agency into its subagencies, department, divisions, groupings, special offices, and so forth. It also provides contact names, address, mail stops, and zip codes. It is updated annually and can be found in the reference section of any municipal or college library. The *Federal Executive Directory* (FED) is a viable alternative providing much of the same information.

Your task is to find the agency in question in the *Federal Yellow Book* or the FED. Once you find the appropriate section, copy all of the pages relating to the agency with whom you have an issue. Then bring the pages with you to your home or office and take the three or four minutes required to find the closest department, division, or office that corresponds to your current issue.

For example, if you find out that your employer of three years ago failed to list the proper amount of withholding tax for you, you would get in touch with the Social Security Administration, find the department or division in question, find a couple of key names and phone numbers, and highlight them.

If you've received a letter from the Social Security Administration informing you of the problem, obviously you have the address and possibly the name of the person to contact. When you have an address to respond to, and an actual direct-dial phone number, consider yourself ahead of the game.

If you're lacking a specific person's name, a direct-dial phone number, or any other critical information for getting back in touch with this agency (to right this grievous wrong), you'll find that the pages you've copied from the *Federal Yellow Book* will serve you well.

> **Make It So**
> The most important thing to remember when dealing with any bureaucracy is to always follow up. If you mean to assert yourself in a way that will end in effective resolution for you, you have to let the party on the other end know that you intend to stick to him on this issue like a fly to flypaper.

The Fun Begins

When you're ready to get back in touch with the Social Security Administration (or any other federal agency, for that matter), you can use the call-mail-call approach discussed in Chapter 19, or the mail-call-mail approach. You can take your pick.

Taking the path of least resistance for openers, simply proceed as you would in any other case—send out your letter, make your call, do what you normally do to achieve resolution.

Make It So

If you decide it's necessary to go over someone's head, try to reach someone who is as close as possible in geography to the person with whom you're speaking. This increases the probability that mentioning the third-party name will have impact. If you can find the boss of the person to whom you're speaking, all the better. Sometimes, the person to whom you are speaking is already listed in the *Federal Yellow Book,* and hence you have the name and number of his or her boss.

If you find that the other party is not responsive or is apparently dragging things out, use the information about the agency that you copied to great advantage.

The next time you have the bureaucrat on the phone, and you're obviously being jerked around, mention that so-and-so in the office of xyz would approve of the way you're executing your responsibilities as a civil servant. The mere fact that you can refer to someone higher up in the organization who, presumably, this underling knows or has heard of, may be all that's necessary for you to get some responsiveness.

Remember, however, that while you may feel like you're being jerked around, it may not be the fault of the person you're talking to, but instead the amount of red tape that exists. Perhaps this person can't do anything but tell you to put it in writing or fill out form x, y, or z, or call someone else. It could be the system that's a mess, not the bureaucrat. This person may just be trying to do his job. You always have the option of asking, "May I please speak to your supervisor?"

In addition to dropping names over the phone, you can also "cc" letters—circulate copies of letters—all over creation. While this practice may get you some response, it probably won't win you any friends and could make future dealings a bit tricky, so it's appropriate only in the "major offense/never going to see this person again" category.

Double Your Pleasure

One technique I've used to get a response is to find the name of a second party within an agency, and then put both names on the address of my letter. If I'm dealing with Mr. Jones but not getting anywhere, and I happen to know that Mr. Jones reports to Ms. Withers, I address my next correspondence to Mr. Jones and Ms. Withers.

When I feel particularly affluent, I send a letter to each with *both party's names on both letters*. This tells Mr. Jones that I'm perfectly capable of making end runs or going over his head. This tells Ms. Withers that I'm not the typical citizen and will not tolerate the typical runaround.

Refining Your Approach

During that same trip to the library to copy the pages of the agency with which you have an issue, consider copying the first page of *all* the major agencies with which you have issues. Then you can write to each agency and ask for the agency's directory. Many agency directories are free.

Write first to the agency's Office of Public Information and simply ask for a directory of agency personnel. It helps if you include a self-addressed mailing label. You may have to write more than once (sorry, that's just the way government works).

The directory may cost some small sum, but in my opinion, it's more than worth it. Once you have the agency directory, you have pretty much stacked the deck in your favor. Some listings may have fax numbers. Some may even have e-mail addresses!

Dealing with Bureaucrats 101

It may seem to you that many civil servants have been at their posts for life plus 75 years. Maybe you think they don't have quite the same orientation to time that you have. Just remember, many civil servants are overwhelmed, and are battle-weary from having dealt with so many overly aggressive citizens who have spared no energy in conveying their wrath.

Stand in My Shoes, Man

One of the verbal strategies I've used and will continue to use until my dying day is to relate the issue at hand to the life of the person on the other end of the phone.

Suppose there is an error in my Social Security tabulations. Once on the phone with the appropriate party, I would say, "Gee, have you ever been in a situation where you knew that some financial information about you was incorrect and no matter what you did, it didn't seem to get resolved?"

At one time or another everyone has "been there." By bringing up such issues with your conversation partner, you're likely to get a more human, action-oriented response.

And I'll Stand in Yours

It helps tremendously if you acknowledge what you surmise to be the other person's situation:

➤ "I know you're very busy and probably don't have the resources you need..."

➤ "I can appreciate what it's like working for the federal government these days, with all the cutbacks..."

Make It So
The more ways you can get in touch with bureaucrats—calling, mailing, faxing, e-mailing—and the more proficient you are at letting bureaucrats know you can get in touch with them in a plethora of ways, the more you'll see that they actually respond. What a country!

Handle with Care
Your strategy when dealing with bureaucrats is to always stay as even-tempered and objective as possible.

223

➤ "You're probably under a lot of pressure all the time, and so I'm especially grateful for your assistance in helping me to…"

➤ "Talking with someone like you really helps restore my faith in government…"

➤ "I really need your assistance; I don't have any place else to turn…"

It helps if you let the other party know that you're going to do everything on your end to assist him in any way that you can. For example, if you can send duplicates of the documents at hand so he doesn't have to do any copying once he receives them, that might make the other person's day.

Here are some other ideas to help grease the skids:

➤ Faxing the documents at hand

➤ Sending along several of your own mailing labels

➤ Making a call at the other person's request

Would You Be Willing to Receive Praise?

There's an option for gaining the person's cooperation that works like a dream: Ask the other party if there is a boss or superior to whom you can write a quick note in praise of this person's efforts. You might be thinking "What drudgery. Why should I have to write a note just to get service from government that ought to be forthcoming?" The answer, my dear reader, is that you live in the real world.

In the real world, people crave appreciation. In the real world, you often have to go an extra measure in order to achieve what you want. And there's an even more compelling reason: The brief note that you write in praise of the bureaucrat or civil servant who helps you will actually be *less* work than if you try to slug it out the old-fashioned way.

Think about the times you had to make follow-up calls, send follow-up letters, make follow-up copies, and so on. If you get someone on your side in a hurry and send a nice note, you may have an ally at a government agency forever. Remember, many of these people are there for a lifetime (plus 75 years).

If you're at a loss for words, here are a few choice paragraphs that you may wish to use in your letters in praise of civil servants:

> I'm writing in high praise of Mr. So-and-so, who admirably helped me with my problem concerning xyz. It's a pleasure to know that your agency employs such a dedicated, professional staff.

Or

> On March 14th, Ms. Conner helped me with a nagging issue I feared might take weeks or months to resolve. Thank you for having such a responsive, highly trained staff in place.

If the recipient of such a letter doesn't keel over (they probably get one like this about every 50 years) he or she is likely to make copies and send it all the way up the chain. Heck, even the cabinet level secretaries will probably get a copy. After all, they're looking for any shred of evidence that their agency is doing something right, some of the time, for someone!

Even if it's been a year or two since you've been in contact, you can always say, "Hi, Jim Smith, I'm the one who sent that letter praising you for helping me to accomplish xyz." If you're concerned that the bureaucrat will let you down in the future, having received your letter of praise, and now thinking that, "Gee, I don't have to do any more for this guy, I'm never likely to get another letter and it's already on record that I helped him," fear not.

If you have to, you could always mention that you "would hate to have to write a letter that diminishes the impact of the first one."

Getting Some Extra Mileage

There are additional uses for the nice notes that you send in praise of bureaucrats. Assuming you have a PC and that you save such letters on your hard disk, when you correspond with the agency in the future, include a copy of that letter (independent of the new issue at hand). You'll send a clear signal: "I'm not just a typical citizen complaining about something or trying to get service. I'm someone who appreciates the assistance I receive."

All the while, no matter how tough a son-of-a-gun you come up against when trying to resolve some personal issue, remember that the person you're dealing with is a human being. He or she probably has a family, certainly has bills to pay, and is facing all the same stresses and strains of living in modern society that you are. A little humor in your conversation, a little empathy, and even some good cheer can work wonders.

Handle with Care

If you fear that the person you're writing about won't get a copy of your letter of praise, you can always send him or her a copy. Hereafter, every time you deal with that person, you're likely to have an edge—he or she will remember that you sent that letter.

Make It So

You could enclose a copy of the letter you sent to one agency when dealing with other agencies on different issues. Why? Any civil servant opening your package will see that you're a cut above the rest. (You could include a note saying "Here's the type of praise I'm capable of giving.") It may even prompt them to render good service to you so that they get a letter from you as well! However, they have to earn it.

Just the Facts

In his book *The Human Animal,* anthropologist Desmond Morris says, "No matter how far humans feel they have evolved, human instincts and behavior are and forever will be rooted in their animal past." Despite oceans of "superficial cultural differences that divide us," human behavior is "universal."

"As long as we can smile at one another, laugh, embrace, hug, point, and nod, there's hope for a friendly future. The more I travel the globe making observations of the language of the human body, the more optimistic I become." This says to me that whatever your issues with people—in this case bureaucrats—you have more in common than you may acknowledge.

Could I Get a Little Attention Here?

To further facilitate your assertiveness efforts, consider the packaging that you use to mail to the civil servant in question. Do you use an overnight express service for $8 to $10? If so, you're wasting money. In my experience, most people do not respond to the overnight packages on the day they receive them (unless there is MONEY involved). They respond to the package a day or two later.

You're better off using good old first-class mail.

What Does Your Envelope Look Like?

Aside from the ways you can get a message to a bureaucrat, what does your actual package look like? Consider the impact if it says "We love the federal government" on the outside of your envelope. What impact would a handwritten note, label, or sticker to that effect have on the person who receives it?

Just the Facts

Dave Yoho, an author and speaker from Fairfax, Virginia, put a message on his envelopes that literally said, "We love the U.S. Postal Service, that's why we entrusted this package in their care." Did that increase the probability that the recipient would notice his letter? Yes! In fact, the U.S. Postal Service authorities noticed and wrote a column on Dave and his envelopes in their monthly newsletter to their thousands of employees.

Here are a variety of low-cost ideas you can implement today to help make your envelope stand out and to increase the probability of a more rapid response from the recipient:

➤ Affix gold stars throughout.

➤ Attach one of your kid's stickers, for example, *Barney, the Little Mermaid,* or the *Power Rangers.*

➤ Use lots of small-denomination stamps that add up to the proper amount. For example, a 4-cent stamp, a 5-cent stamp, a 12-cent stamp, an 8-cent stamp, and a 3-cent stamp add up to 32 cents, currently the amount for a first-class, one-ounce envelope. Because you used five stamps instead of one, chances are your package will stand out from anything else the recipient got that day or that week.

➤ Use your computer and printer to create a label that says, "The U.S. federal government—the world's best government."

On occasion I've written on the outside of my envelopes such messages as, "Do not open until Thursday." Naturally, whoever receives this is going to open it immediately because they're curious.

The point is to make your envelope stand out from the masses.

A Package of Distinction

How about sending distinctive packaging as an alternative to normal packages? For example, you can send a letter in a tube. It's likely to get opened right away. Or go to your local stationery store and buy some distinctive stationery. Then fold your correspondence so it fits appropriately and mail it off.

Make It So
Stay focused on your goal: to get some attention, get your issue resolved, and move on with as much grace and ease as possible.

Because it's not a standard white business envelope it will likely stand out. The recipient may be lulled into thinking they have received a greeting card from someone.

How to Communicate by Phone with a Bureaucrat

When you're on the phone with a government representative, there are a few things you need to do to make sure that you are most effective, that you don't run up a huge phone bill, and that you don't wind up having to make repeat calls.

Basic Phone Tips

First, always keep a pad and pencil ready. Whenever you get a party on the line, ask the person you are speaking with to slowly repeat his or her full name, position, and direct-dial phone number, particularly if you were switched over from another party. Don't do this in an accusatory manner. Simply do it as a matter of fact.

It's also important to let the other party know that this is a particularly nagging issue that you would like to resolve *today*, or at least get in motion today, so that it can be resolved shortly.

If you get bumped around an agency, you're likely to get upset. My goal is to help you avoid getting too upset. If it turns out that you're not speaking to the right person, spend an extra couple of seconds with this person ensuring that the next transfer will in fact put you in touch with the correct party.

Now, About Solving My Problem

Once you get to the right party, ask him or her how long it will take for the matter to be resolved. If it's anything other than today, try asking, "What would it take for this to be resolved today?" If he says that's not possible, try giving the person another timeframe (one that still works to your advantage).

Even if you continue to get resistance, this gives the other party a clear message that you intend to resolve this as quickly as possible. Whatever timeframe he does give you, write it down and say as you're writing, "Let me just jot this down. Okay then, you're saying that by next Tuesday we should be able to accomplish xyz." Again, keep your tone friendly and non-accusatory.

Proceed with whatever details and conversation you feel are necessary. At the end of the call, include a summarizing sentence such as, "So then, it's my understanding that we can accomplish xyz by so-and-so. You need to receive xyz, and I need to abc. Have I assessed the situation correctly?"

If the other party says yes, conclude by saying "Okay, I'll call you on xyz" or "You'll receive the documents by abc." In other words, *keep the conversation pointed toward resolution, timeframes, and action!*

Handle with Care

When fishing for contact information by phone, always ask courteously, "Could I get your name?", and, "What's your direct-dial phone number?" If it's helpful, start at the top of a blank piece of paper. Then, if you get bumped around in an agency, you can proceed downward on the page using arrows so that you know who led you to whom.

Handle with Care

Too many people on the other end of the phone line are happy to pass you along to someone else, no matter why you called. Hence, you get to the next person, and then he passes you along to someone else. By the fourth party, you're upset. If you'll be a little patient and spend some extra time with the first party, chances are you can cut down the chain dramatically.

Make It So

Your goal is to get the people on the other end of the line to help you, not to be one of hundreds of callers who "demand service."

Depending on the size of your request and how ambitious you are, you might even summarize what the other party just said or agreed to. Then send that to him in a letter or fax. This cements in his mind that you intend to follow up on the issue in ways that few others do.

More Tips for Dealing with a Bureaucrat

If it turns out that the other party needs to send you something, ask if they can do it by fax. You know how slow the mail is in general? Well, it seems like it's even slower when you're waiting for something from a government office.

Almost everyone has access to a fax machine. You'd be far better off having whatever it is you're waiting for faxed to you if you really want to close the issue, rather than wait for the mail.

If you don't have your own fax machine, have the sender send it to a local Kinko's or Copytron. You can also try looking in the phone book under "Printer." Find the nearest quick press near you, ask if they have fax reception capabilities, and if it costs anything to receive one. In many cases, it costs nothing or a nominal fee. Then, when you make your call to the bureaucrat, you have a fax number ready should he or she actually relent and offer to send you documentation by fax.

It's also fitting and appropriate to ask for the other person's business card. If they don't have a card, ask them for an agency card, on which they can write their name, direct-dial phone number, and fax number if applicable.

If follow-up is needed or required, exchange with the other party the best days and times when each of you can be reached.

That Pesky Voice Mail

When trying to reach your party, what should you do if you encounter voice mail on your first try? I suggest that you call back until you get the person live and on the phone.

Even if you have to hang up a couple of times, it's worth your while. Why? It's far too easy for someone in government to delay your request for a long, long

Make It So

There's nothing like having somebody's business card in your possession to give you that feeling of being in control when you know you're going to have to get back in touch with them a time or two more. Having a card with all the relevant info on it is convenient.

Handle with Care

If you leave a message on voice mail and don't get action for a while, you may end up calling back several times anyway. So, you might as well wait for that first connection, get the other party on the phone, and get your issue at the top of the pile.

229

time if you leave a message on voice mail. In fact, you might be one of dozens of callers leaving a message that day or that week. You have no idea where you are in the queue.

Closing the Conversation

As you're about to finish the conversation, remember, the other party is facing all kinds of pressures. No matter how irritated you may be, you want to leave that person feeling at least appreciated, and at most praised. No matter how many calls it took to get to this person, how many times you had to explain the issue, or whatever other rigmarole you encountered, try to say something that leaves the other party feeling good.

Even when I've been totally irritated, I on occasion have been able to utter:

➤ "I appreciate you hearing me out."

➤ "Thank you for being patient and staying on the line with me."

➤ "Sorry I got a little upset—thank you for your understanding."

If the other party has truly extended herself, close the conversation with a higher order such as:

➤ "I think you're doing a valuable service."

➤ "I'm glad I was able to connect with you. It sounds like you have a handle on the situation."

➤ "I appreciate the time and attention you're devoting to my concern."

➤ "I wish I could always encounter someone as effective in listening as you."

Same Thing, Less Bureaucracy

Pretty much all of what I've talked about can apply to state and local government. The exceptions are:

1. You may end up getting less of a run-around because there's less bureaucracy involved.

2. The phone calls may not be long-distance.

There are many directories listing the phone numbers of state and local officials, among them:

Directory of City Policy Officials
National League of Cities
1301 Pennsylvania Avenue, NW
Washington, DC 20004

In addition, Omnigraphics, a Michigan-based publisher, offers an amazing array of directories covering many subjects. The *National Directory of Addresses,* for example, contains many government phone numbers. Write to:

> *National Directory of Addresses*
> Omnigraphics, Incorporated
> Penobscot Center
> Detroit, MI 48226

Having a key directory in your possession is power. Again, you only need to go to your local library and copy the appropriate pages.

In terms of local government, often the phone numbers you need are listed in the blue section of your phone book. If your phone book doesn't have a blue government section, call your city hall. Often, they have a directory that's free.

If there is a charge for it, if it's nominal, go ahead and get it. Or explore the alternative ways of getting such information. For example, your local Chamber of Commerce, the League of Women Voters, and other groups around town often maintain and distribute free directories of local government officials.

Let Me Say It a Different Way

Sometimes, no matter what you do and how hard you try, you cannot get action. Weeks or even months roll by, and the issue is still unresolved. You've leaned over backwards, did somersaults through flaming hoops, walked over hot coals, or traversed the high wire, and still, no satisfaction.

Tell the other party that you're prepared to go over his or her head. Here is the order in which you should proceed:

1. The boss of the party to whom you are speaking.

2. The boss's boss, who might be the division or department head.

3. The ombudsman, a special agency official whose task it is to resolve grievances that haven't been resolved through normal channels.

4. The general counsel or corporation counsel, depending on what term is used. These are the agency's lawyers.

    Often, when you call the general counsel, and somebody from the general counsel calls the department or person with whom you're having problems, you tend to get

Make It So

City government directories are so valuable to have on hand that even if you have no particular burning issue right now, open your phone book and make a couple calls to round these up now, while the idea is fresh in your mind. Hey, if you never use them, my hat's off to you! But if you have to use them, you'll be in far better shape than otherwise.

resolution much faster. This is because you've given a direct message to the party who is not cooperating that you know how to make big trouble if you have to.

5. **The head of the agency.** If you have an issue that is not resolved, write to the head of the agency. It may take a while before things get moving, but often they can move swiftly. Obviously, the Secretary of Labor or other cabinet-level official is not going to deal directly with your issue. In fact, it will never even get to him or her.

   It will filter back down to the party with whom you had conflict. This person will *now* be motivated to take care of it! Be prepared to wait it out, because it will take time for all of this to take effect. Nevertheless, if you go this route, you've told everybody in between that *you're through messing around*.

6. **The General Accounting Office.** Do you realize that there is a government agency in place that does nothing but audit the practices and performance of federal agencies? Yes sir, it's the General Accounting Office. Now don't get me wrong, by writing to the General Accounting Office, you're not going to get any action on your low-level issue.

   Merely introducing the notion of you going to the General Accounting Office, however, can put fear and trepidation into the hearts and minds of officials and underlings of the agency with which you're having problems. They know that if the GAO heads their way, and finds deficiencies and incompetence, a stinging report will make its way to the President and to Congress. Budgets may be cut. Heads may roll.

7. **Any federal agency hotline that may be in place.** If you have a problem with the Small Business Administration, for example, try dialing 800-555-1212 and asking for the SBA hotline. In this case, you get the SBA answer desk at 800-827-5722. From there you play the voice-mail game, but it's another entry point, another prong in your multi-pronged attack.

8. **Congressional representatives.** Going to one of your senators or congressional representatives is another possible route toward resolution. Like going to the head of the agency, however, again, be prepared to wait. Your little piddling issue, which it will look like to people at this level, must compete with the hundreds if not thousands of issues that people present to their senators and congressional representatives.

   Still, if you're not getting resolution any other way, going to the top will provide psychological satisfaction, if not ultimately some form of resolution.

You Don't Have to Actually Use Any of This Stuff...

I've presented all this information first so that you'd know what avenues are available to you. Knowledge is power! Fortunately, you may not have to use them. In conversation with the uncivil servant who's blocking your path, you may wish to mention your potential use of one of these vehicles. When the other party knows that you know how to make waves, he or she may more readily capitulate.

Or, you might run into that tough son-of-a-gun who couldn't give a flying funnel cake and seemingly remains unintimidated while on the phone. Don't fall for the con. He or she knows that in terms of your issue, it would probably be best to get off the pot and actually do something about it.

The Least You Need to Know

➤ Before you assert yourself as a citizen, you need to get organized and to treat your problem as a campaign.

➤ In dealing with any bureaucracy, assume nothing and follow up, follow up, follow up.

➤ Having key government directories is power.

➤ Bureaucrats secretly crave appreciation, and whatever you can offer will be to your advantage.

➤ If you're not making any progress, let the other party know about your arsenal of hardball alternatives for getting action.

Part 6
Assertiveness in Your Professional Life

Now we come to that arena in which being assertive can make the difference between a career that continues to progress at a healthy pace and one that is stifled. Being assertive in the workplace, that modern-day jungle, is a prerequisite to higher pay, respect, and the corner office. If you doubt it, think about the people with whom you work who are not assertive. Chances are they're the wimps. They do a good job, perhaps earn a decent wage, but they get passed over time and time again.

Each of the chapters in this section focuses on helping you to be more effective in the workplace and beyond. You'll learn how to naturally and easily be more assertive at appropriate and opportune moments. If you're in the corporate ranks, the chapters in this part will be of special importance to you. And if you're an entrepreneur, this section may be the most important of all, since you'll be dealing with customers and clients, peers, staff, suppliers, creditors, and service providers.

Being Assertive at Work

In terms of practicing assertiveness skills, the workplace is a special arena. Never mind all that stuff you've seen on inane television shows and movies where executives spar with each other in grandiose ways. There's enough real-life drama that you don't have to draw upon the false images the media conveys.

In this chapter, I'll explore the assertiveness issues that could make a difference in your job.

The Difference Between Progress or Failure

How, you ask, can assertiveness be a substitute for accomplishment, competence, and effort? Study after study shows that if you and a co-worker have similar education, training, and experience, and all other things about you are equal, the one who is effectively assertive will predictably rise faster in his or her career.

Make It So
Given that you are a competent employee who dutifully executes the requirements of the job, the nature of your interpersonal communications at work—how assertive you are—largely defines your progress.

Suppose two managers are alike in every respect—they have the same background, education, training, aptitude, skills, and so on. You know what this is leading to. One has no problem being professionally assertive in the following areas:

➤ Airing his views

➤ Speaking up for himself

➤ Defending his turf

➤ Persuading others

➤ Speaking up at company meetings

➤ Making his ideas known

The other manager is marginally effective in these areas. Who is more likely to rise faster and go further in his career? Okay, you say, this is a no-brainer. Anyone will say the first manager.

Door Number One or Door Number Two?

Now let's complicate the issue a bit. Suppose that two managers are alike in most respects, but the first is not quite as sharp, and doesn't quite have some of the technical knowledge possessed by the second manager, but is very good at expressing himself.

The second manager is very conscientious. He is a planner. Generally, he executes his tasks with precision. When it comes to expressing himself, however, there are some gaps in his ability. Sometimes he rambles on. Sometimes he's not forthcoming with his views when the situation calls for it. Sometimes, to know what he's thinking you practically have to *pry it out of him*. Nevertheless, he does a consistently good job and unquestionably is an asset to the organization.

Now, who's likely to rise faster and further in his career? The answer isn't so easy this time, is it? The odds remain that the first manager will rise faster even if he is lacking in some categories as compared to the second manager. Why? He has the ability to assert himself.

Much More than Schmooze

Before you start thinking, okay, well, the first manager has the gift of gab, he's a schmoozer—he talks his way up the chain—think again. The professional who is able to assert himself as necessary enjoys significant advantages over his otherwise more talented counterparts who are unassertive. For example, the assertive professional can do the following:

➤ Adroitly express himself to others.

➤ Identify obstacles, hazards, and pitfalls of proceeding with a given plan.

➤ Better guard against requests of his time when he already is stretched to the max.

➤ Be more persuasive when influencing others to attain a desirable performance level.

➤ Establish alliances that can aid him in accomplishing his goals and the goals of others.

What might befall the more technically competent manager who is not as good at asserting himself? The following are all possibilities, although it's not likely that any one manager would be confronted by all of them:

➤ He ends up taking on more work than he can comfortably handle because he lacks the ability to indicate to others when he's overloaded.

➤ He may have trouble expressing frustrations over daily occurrences, how a project is going, and so on.

➤ He may not be as effective in supervising others. He may allow performance levels to slide because he is uneasy when it comes to verbally appraising others' efforts.

JUST THE FACTS MA'AM.

Just the Facts

Until we can read each other's minds, the otherwise talented but unassertive manager is more likely to be stuck in terms of his overall career progress. He's more likely to stay at the same level longer than his more assertive counterparts. And, sadly, he's more likely to be overlooked for raises and promotions.

Test-Drive It

If you doubt that any of this is true and you work in a large office with lots of other career professionals, make a few observations. On a scale of one to ten (with "one" being highly unassertive, and "ten" being highly assertive) quickly and mentally rate who's in the larger or corner offices within your organization.

If there's only one corner office, who has it? If there are two, three, or four, who's occupying them? Chances are, you'll find assertive types occupying this prime real estate.

Why Wimps Get Passed Over

To be sure, there are absolutely brilliant, talented, highly accomplished, non-assertive career professionals. Someone like that may be seated in your chair right now. However,

Handle with Care
Recalling what you learned in earlier chapters about how all career professionals today are overloaded with too much information competing for their time and attention, you have to acknowledge the reality that even your own boss, on far too many occasions, may give little more than passing notice to your accomplishments.

if you're not able to convey a sense of importance and even enthusiasm about your accomplishments—not able to "toot your own horn," even though what you've done may be a matter of record—hardly anyone will know what you've done.

Not even your own boss is likely to grasp the magnitude of your achievement. How could this be? You were asked to do xyz and you did xyz. Doesn't the performance speak for itself? Many times it does. Just as often, probably, the performance does not speak for itself. Perhaps:

➤ Others take it for granted.

➤ Others discount in their minds what you've done.

➤ Others don't recognize the true significance of your deed.

Cool-Hand Luke

Let's face it, sometimes you may not even understand the value of what you've accomplished, and, if that's combined with an inability to assert yourself, you might as well be working in the basement of the building.

I had a young man help me create a macro on my computer that enabled me to instantly convert any file that I had on disk to any ASCII or generic text format. He called me over to show me how it worked. He seemed pleased to have finished the task, but otherwise showed no enthusiasm or excitement over accomplishing what certainly was a challenge. I was very excited about this newfound capability, and my enthusiasm washed over the room. Eventually he caught hold of it and began to show some signs of life himself.

I'm not equating enthusiasm and assertiveness. However, the young man's inability to express himself in the situation I described merely portended his inability to express himself when he needed to speak up for himself, air his views, or ask for help.

Nose to the Grindstone Makes for a Very Sore Nose

The dedicated, hardworking professional in the typical office who consistently does the job day in and day out but otherwise is unassertive, unfortunately gets passed over when it comes to the goodies and the kudos of work and of life. Here's an exercise to show you how this happens.

Draw up a list of the people in your office. Now go back to the list and put a star next to everyone who got a raise, got a promotion, got recognized, or was rewarded in some way recently such that others in the office including yourself have knowledge of it. For example:

*Bill Williamson

*Ahmad Maresh

Courtney Adams

Chris Colie

Roxanne Havers

Art Conners

Angela Freeman

Zack Debagan

*Katharine Ayers

After you've finished placing stars by the appropriate individuals' names, review the list again. This time put an "A" at the end of the names of all individuals who on a purely personal and subjective scale you deem as being assertive:

*Bill Williamson A

*Ahmad Maresh A

Courtney Adams

Chris Colie A

Roxanne Havers

Angela Freeman

Art Conners

Zack Debagan

*Katharine Ayers

When you're through, look back at your list. What do you notice? Do most of the people with a star at the beginning of their name have an "A" at the end of their name? Is there one with simply a star or simply an A and not both? If there are, I'll bet the number is small.

The conclusion? Raises and assertiveness appear to have some significant correlation.

Assert and Grow Rich

Given that you're doing a good job, being assertive is probably the most important attribute you can have for getting pay raises.

When I was a full-time management consultant supervising a staff of eight, I had two young women on my team who had, in fact, nearly similar capabilities. However, one was assertive and one wasn't. The assertive one came to me after a couple of months on the job and said flat out, "I'd like to talk to you about my salary." I knew what was coming next and I also knew she would present a convincing argument.

She took the floor and waxed eloquently about how she had been doing consistently good work, sometimes putting in extra hours, helping others on the project, doing things she knew needed to be done that she wasn't asked to do, and even anticipating challenges down the road. She talked about how others her age in competing firms were earning more and how she was actually more valuable to the firm since she first came to us months ago.

> **Just the Facts**
>
> What most people asking for a raise don't understand is that the cost of replacing them can be inordinate. Depending on what you do and how well you do it, your organization may well prefer paying you 5, 10, or 15 percent more than you're currently making to having to place an ad, interview more people, bring somebody on board, get them up to speed, and see if they can actually do the job. The smaller the company, the more costly it becomes to replace good staff.

Her arguments were sound and I could see that she was determined. Still, I used an old manager's trick of saying, "Okay, let me think about it and we'll discuss it again in a little while." She said fine and left.

In two weeks, when I hadn't brought it up again, you can be sure that she did. This time she added to her pitch. She discussed how she was helping out other members of the project team and how she was requiring less and less supervision (both true), and how eventually she'd be able to assume more of the burden while maintaining her productivity.

I told her I'd have to discuss it with the big boss. She seemed to know that I was going to stall some more, so this time she pinned me down as to when we would get back together. She had a specific increase in mind. I said I'd do what I could.

We had the meeting and she ended up getting the raise she sought.

Asking for a Raise

By now, you're probably drooling with anticipation. What exactly do you have to do to get a raise? What are the words, what are the gestures, how does the whole thing work? Actually, it's not complicated at all.

The tactics and words used by my staff person as just described will work rather well. In somewhat chronological order, here's how to assert yourself when it comes to asking for a raise:

1. Determine in advance how much you want. This has to be in line with other factors, such as the pay range for your position and the budget allocated to your department. If you can't find these things out, try to determine what a reasonable percentage increase would be. For example, have others in your firm received 8 percent raises? Or is 4 percent a more predictable figure?

2. Ask your boss for an appointment, or if that's too formal for your setting, at least reserve some time. Perhaps you can take him or her to lunch. In any case, you want it to be known in advance that you have something important to discuss. Don't go into detail about *why* you want to meet—telling your boss you want to meet to discuss a raise would give him time to prepare his response.

3. Once you're face to face and ready to talk, make sure that both of you are seated. If you're standing, it's too easy for the conversation to be curtailed. The boss might be called away, or you may feel uncomfortable standing your ground for so long. Besides, you'll get more time with the boss if you're seated.

4. Cut right to the chase. By now, your boss knows there's something important on your mind. Let it out.

5. Use the classic irrefutable arguments: You've been doing very good work, you're requiring less supervision, you're anticipating challenges to be better prepared for them, you're helping others on the team, you're going the extra mile, you're becoming more valuable to the organization, and so on. If it helps, bring up the parity issues. Other people with your experience, your education, or your age in similar positions in other organizations are earning x amount, and so forth.

   Your boss may pooh-pooh your arguments in person; nevertheless, your points will register. If you can, come equipped with specific facts—preferably on paper—to back up these assertions. Instead of just saying you require less supervision, show evidence of a project that you handled solo.

6. If you can get approval at this one meeting, wow, you're a winner! It's more likely that your boss will ask for a follow-up meeting. Agree to it.

7. In the interim, continue to work hard, but *don't bring up this issue.*

8. When it's time to meet again on this issue, have some new points ready to add on top of the old ones. For example, just last week you were able to accomplish xyz. Also, you took it upon yourself to straighten up the abc project, and you made a few extra calls to make sure that ghi. Emphasize all the little things you do that nobody tends to notice in addition to those things you do that are more apparent and visible. (For more on emphasizing your contributions, see the next chapter.)

9. If you encounter additional resistance, move to, "Okay then, by when?" Get your boss to commit. If she says "next quarter," "by next June," or by next anything, you've done well. Remember, in some cases, your boss truly is restricted as to what she can offer. Her budget may be fixed for the coming period.

   However, *there is always some financial slack in an organization when it comes to rewarding and retaining superior performance*. You have only to find out what the CEO of your organization is making, including bonuses, and it will be abundantly clear that your organization can find the extra couple dollars per hour or thousands per year you're seeking.

10. Everything you've learned throughout this book about being assertive comes into play when seeking a raise. You need to be a good listener. You need to give the other person a chance to respond. You need to look her directly in the eye. You want to be professionally assertive but not overbearing or cantankerous. You want to end the conversation on a cheerful note and march proudly back out the door.

You Talk Too Much

I'm frequently asked if it's possible to over-assert yourself. The answer is yes. Recall the oft-quoted line in Hamlet, "Methinks the lady doth protest too much." By asking for something too vigorously or too aggressively, you can actually diminish your chances of accomplishing it.

> **Handle with Care**
> Overstating your case is an indication to others that you're grappling with some other issue internally.

If someone is constantly complaining, say about the weather, the reality is he probably isn't so concerned with the weather as something else.

When you assert yourself, make sure that the time, place, and person are appropriate. It doesn't matter how assertive you are if you ask someone to do something that he:

1. Can't understand in 100 years of explanation
2. Has no capacity or authority for undertaking
3. Might be able to accomplish but doesn't know where to begin

And Another Point...

Offer your points in sequence based on chronology, order of importance, or other useful criterion. Some communication experts tell you to present your best point first, and your other points in descending order of importance.

Other communication experts suggest that you present your points in ascending order; that is, start with the least important ones and work up to the most important one. In this manner, the last point that you make is your best and most important and the one most likely to be remembered by your audience.

In my opinion it doesn't matter in what order you proceed —ascending, descending, or even offering your best point in the middle. More important is that you did a good job to begin with, you prepped your boss so that he or she knew that you were coming in to talk about something important, you reviewed the tips on assertiveness throughout this book, and you were your best self when you finally sat down and got around to talking about your value to the organization.

Buddy, Can You Spare a Job (at Executive's Wages)?

Many of the same principles apply when you're interviewing for a job. Joe Sabah, author of the popular book, *How to Get the Job You Really Want and Get Employers to Call You,* advises his readers to push for action during the first interview using his three-step formula:

1. Stop the Ping-Pong game by asking, "Is there anything else you'd like to know about me during our first interview?" Then stop and listen.

2. Summarize what's gone on before. "I feel with my background, education, and experience I could do a great job for your organization and help us both accomplish our goals this year."

   Having said such a statement, sit back and let the other party take the floor. They'll have to either agree or disagree. Most of the time they'll have to offer some form of agreement.

3. Close the interview by asking, "By the way, Mr. Jones, I'm available right now. How soon would you like me to start?"

> **Make It So**
> Whether your best point is first, in the middle, or last, what's most important is the *impact* of the message that you impart to your boss. What impression did he or she receive? Did he get the notion that you're serious about getting this raise? If you present your case as, "Gee, wouldn't it be nice if I could get wxyz," you're not likely to get it. If you present your case as, "I intend to be at the next level of compensation next quarter," you've increased your chances dramatically.

Some people think this is aggressive, but it's not—it's merely being assertive, notes Sabah. Unfortunately, "Most applicants are too passive," Sabah says. "They say something wishy-washy like I hope to hear from you soon, or it was really nice meeting you. This conveys a message to the interviewer: You're a nice person. What it does not convey is that you're ready, willing, and able to start on this job."

Sabah asserts that this closing technique *works*. He's been a guest on 625 radio talk shows and counting. To procure all these guest spots, he always closes every interview with the show host or producer with these three tips!

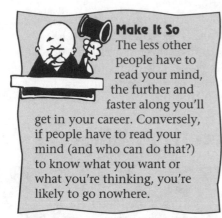

Make It So
The less other people have to read your mind, the further and faster along you'll get in your career. Conversely, if people have to read your mind (and who can do that?) to know what you want or what you're thinking, you're likely to go nowhere.

Directness Has Its Place

Sabah's advice is valuable for many reasons. He's saying to get directly to the issue. Whether you're interviewing for a job or asking for a raise, or asking to be transferred to another department, go ahead and say exactly what you mean.

Suppose you want to be transferred from the orders and processing division to the routing division. Instead of saying, "I hear that the routing division is doing some great things and it's a pretty good place to be working these days," try saying, "I'd like to be transferred to the routing division."

Assertive Women in the Workplace

In Chapter 17, I discussed the special problems women have being assertive, especially in male-dominated circles. Can a woman be *professionally* assertive in the workplace on par with her male counterparts and get the same general results? Happily, increasingly the answer is yes.

Since women represent a large share of the workplace today and will continue to do so in the coming years, a growing structure and network of resources will continue to form, giving women the support they need at various points along their career paths.

Same-Sex Support

Researchers Pamela A. Geller and Stevan Hobfoll recently reported in *Sex Roles: A Journal of Research,* that "gender bias is clearly evident" in work-related settings. "When women act appropriately assertive at work," they say, "they may actually alienate support."

Handle with Care
Researchers found that if a woman's assertiveness on the job is misread as aggressiveness, support may not be forthcoming from men or women.

A woman should assert herself in the workplace when the situation calls for it, even if the men working with her ostracize her at first. Eventually they may change their behavior toward her when they realize she makes a valuable contribution and has valuable opinions. If she remains passive, she limits her opportunities to advance.

If you're a woman, you may be upset that what you have to say may be interpreted by men as aggressiveness. Yet, women aren't going to get anywhere by continuing to "play nice." The dilemma is the long-standing cultural patterns that may be at play. The same action taken by a man and a woman often is perceived as aggressiveness in the woman and assertiveness in the man.

Evaluate your own reactions. For example, when your female supervisor calls you on the carpet for being late, do you react differently than when a male supervisor asks you why your report is late? If so, ask yourself why you have this different reaction.

The Least You Need to Know

➤ All other things being equal, a manager who is assertive will predictably rise faster in his or her career than his non-assertive peer.

➤ Most people asking for a raise don't understand that the cost of replacing them can be inordinate. So ask for a raise.

➤ It is possible to over-assert yourself and actually diminish your chances of getting what you want.

➤ Whether you're interviewing for a job, asking for a raise, or seeking to be transferred, go ahead and say exactly what you mean.

➤ Unfortunately, it's still true that assertiveness in women is perceived by some as bossiness or pushiness. Nevertheless, don't let others diminish your right to be heard.

Chapter 22

Who's the Boss Around Here?

In This Chapter

➤ Being assertive with your boss

➤ Smile when you say that

➤ Give-and-take often extends beyond the lines of authority

➤ Showing the boss how much more you can absorb

➤ Working together for higher productivity

➤ Influencing your boss for his or her own good

"Of all the gin joints in all the world she has to walk into mine. You played it for her, you can play it for me. If she can take it, I can take it. Go ahead Sam, play it!"

—Humphrey Bogart, as Mr. Rick, in *Casablanca*

"Of all the people in the world that you may be least inclined to be assertive with, your boss is at the top or near the top of the list. If you can be assertive with others, you can be assertive with your boss. If your boss can be assertive with you, you certainly can be assertive back. Go ahead Sam, or Samantha, be assertive!"

—Jeff Davidson, as author, in *The Complete Idiot's Guide to Assertiveness*

In recent years there have been all kinds of books with titles such as *Never Work for a Jerk, How to Manage Your Boss,* and *Influencing Others When You Are Not in Charge.* The underlying theme, I suppose, because I didn't read any of them, is that in any boss-employee situation there is give-and-take that often extends beyond what the employee might surmise. In other words, you have more leverage when it comes to working with your boss than you might presume.

The chief way to wield this leverage is by being assertive. Obviously, there are some things you wouldn't dare try with your boss that you can get away with when dealing with others. In this chapter, I'll explore how being assertive can help you to enjoy all the potential bennies!

Okay, Rehearse Your Lines

You hear about it all the time. Someone has to go in and talk to the boss, and they fret for days before the big event. They practice in the mirror, talk to their spouse, even talk in their sleep. Clearly, for many of us, talking to the boss can be an anxiety-laden event.

Understandably, a range of anxieties and concerns can bubble to the surface when it comes to having to be assertive with your boss. After all, he or she has authority and leverage over you that other people simply don't have. For example, your boss may:

➤ Have the power to fire you, and fire you on a moment's notice without even consulting anyone else.

➤ Conduct performance appraisals of you that dramatically impact your ability to advance in the company, or conversely, keep you stagnant.

➤ Define your job responsibilities. Indeed, he may have personally written your job description, or perhaps he used to do your job.

➤ Schedule your work activities. In this respect, your boss may have control over each and every hour that you spend at work, what you work on, how quickly you have to work, and what resources you're provided.

➤ Have leverage over what benefits you receive.

As if this weren't enough, in addition to the authorized power that your boss is likely to have over you, he may also have other forms of power, including the following:

➤ She may be older, wiser, and likely to be earning more. Depending on your interpersonal dynamics, that could mean you're intimidated by your boss.

➤ Your boss could be physically imposing.

➤ Your boss might have connections throughout your organization or profession or industry that you don't have and are not likely to acquire.

➤ Your boss may have a working style that is radically different from yours.

➤ Your boss may have a style of interpersonal communication that results in anxiety and frustration for you.

➤ Your boss may have vastly different expectations from your own as to why you were hired, what you're supposed to do, and how you're supposed to perform.

These factors and many others add up to the likelihood that on occasion, if not often, you'll have some difficulty in asserting yourself with your boss! Despite all of the advantages your boss seems to enjoy, you have some leverage too. As such, you may want to do some exercises in preparation for the times when you'll wish to assert yourself.

First, Know Thyself

Please get a blank piece of paper and a pen. On the top page, write "Outstanding Attributes." Now, list everything you can think of about yourself that is outstanding, particularly your innate skills and attributes. For example, your list might include wit, charm, stamina, endurance, tolerance, and affability.

You might add phrases such as "keen powers of concentration," "the ability to set priorities," or "the ability to meet deadlines." The list you generate should contain at least 15 or 20 items. Many people can reach 30, 40, or more. If you can't think of that many, refer to Chapters 5–8 on self-confidence for ideas.

Professional Skills

When you've finished with this list, write another heading, "Specific Skills." Now list every blessed thing that you've learned professionally over the past several years. For example, do you know how to use Microsoft Word 9.0? List that. If you know how to use Internet search engines, include that as well. Run through all the software that you know how to use, office equipment that you can operate, and office procedures that you are knowledgeable about.

> **Make It So**
> If you have trouble generating a list of your skills and attributes, recall what others have said about you either verbally or on paper. Or perhaps you have letters others have written to or about you that contain phrases that describe you.

Then list any other professional skills that you have, such as mastery of a foreign language, the ability to use other equipment, and so on. This list may exceed 30 items and if it's double or more, all the better!

Who Can I Turn To?

Finally, under the heading "People," make a list of the empowering people in your life—those people who have an effect on your professional and personal life. This should include everyone you can get on the phone and share information with at the touch of the keypad. It also includes any mentors that you have, coaches, advisors, team members, or helpers of any nature.

Make It So

Go through your Rolodex, address book, or database software file. Who are the key people that you count on as resources?

This list, too, may reach 30 people or more. If you've been in the working world for a while and have been fairly active in your industry or profession, your list could exceed 100 people. You have my permission, however, to stop at about 50 or 60 names.

If you find it hard to list 30 people, set a lower goal, such as 10 or 15.

Go Away, Come Back Another Day

When you've completed all three lists, put the page away, and take it out another day to review it. This list serves as a reminder of who you are, what you can do, and who you know. Think of it as a resource tool, a confidence booster if you find yourself being less assertive than you'd like when confronting your boss.

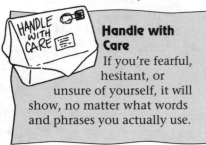

Handle with Care

If you're fearful, hesitant, or unsure of yourself, it will show, no matter what words and phrases you actually use.

Recalling the words of Dr. Janet G. Elsea in Chapter 13, you cannot *not* communicate. In other words, every time you speak to your boss, regardless of the actual words and phrases that you use, you're communicating. If you've recently reviewed your resource list as well as Chapters 5–8 on self-confidence, your sense of self-confidence and assurance will come through to your boss the next time you're in conversation.

Bricks and Mortar

In addition to preparing a resource list, you should begin laying the groundwork now in conversations with your boss. This will come in handy later, for those times when you seek to assert yourself. Here are a variety of tips for doing so:

➤ Praise your boss when he merits praise. Many employees forget that the boss is a person, too, who needs psychological strokes just like everyone else.

➤ Assemble your evidence. If you have a point to make, come in armed with supporting evidence.

➤ Do some pencil pushing. If it's not clear whether the department is going to pick Plan A or Plan B, map out the costs and benefits as you see them and present them accordingly.

➤ Don't dump on your boss. Your boss is not a shoulder to cry on for what went wrong at home or at work. Yes, depending on your relationship, you certainly can seek empathy from him on occasion. He may be the type with whom you can commiserate. Generally, though, keep your lamentations brief and move on to what's next. Keep thinking solutions.

➤ Use "we" and "us" phrasing instead of "I" and "my." Think, speak, and convey "team."

➤ Pace your communications. Don't overwhelm your boss with more than she can comfortably take on at one time.

➤ Take personal responsibility for any department-wide activities or projects in which you're participating. Take responsibility when things go wrong as well. Nothing lays the groundwork faster and more effectively for you to be assertive than when you have a reputation for taking full responsibility for your actions.

➤ Don't drone on. Present your situation or problem as succinctly as you can.

By engaging in these behaviors, you'll find that often you have more latitude later, when you may need to assert yourself.

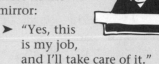

Make It So
Practice saying these in the mirror:
➤ "Yes, this is my job, and I'll take care of it."
➤ "I accept complete responsibility for that."
➤ "That's definitely in my department; I'll handle it."
➤ "That's something I will handle personally."
➤ "That sounds like something in my department."
➤ "I'll get the situation under control."

Emulate Your Boss's Communication Pattern

Martha Peak, group editor at American Management Association Magazines division, said in an editorial in *Management Review* (February 1995): "Correctly sizing up your boss's communications preferences may mean the difference between getting your project off the ground or watching it fall moribund before it gets a fair chance of survival."

"The most effective style is not one that follows some preferred textbook approach," says Peak, "but rather, one that the listener is most attuned to." Thus, if your boss prefers that you sit down and chat for a few minutes, get good at doing that. If he prefers that you stand by the door and give a quick report, so be it.

The Good, the Bad, and the Beheaded

Convey the good and the bad as it transpires. If you have to deliver bad news, however, it's best to have a strategy already mapped out.

Too many employees are afraid of falling prey to the Persian Messenger Syndrome. As the story goes, in ancient times, whoever brought bad news to the king was beheaded. Soon enough, no one brought bad news to the king.

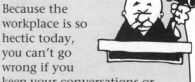

Make It So
Because the workplace is so hectic today, you can't go wrong if you keep your conversations or communications brief and to the point.

253

The great paradox of this situation is that to be an effective king, or a boss for that matter, one has to have accurate information about what's happening in the kingdom, or in the department. If your boss is only being fed good news or a sugar-coated version of what's happening, he's likely to fail as a leader.

If you're the one staff person who can deliver bad news without blinking and also have some ideas or solutions to impart, you'll have far less trouble when you need to assert yourself in major ways, like asking for a raise.

So, what strategies can you employ for delivering bad news? Try following this plan:

1. Start with some good news.
2. Give the bad news, and follow it with some possible solutions.
3. End with some other good news.

Going for the Big One, Asking for a Raise

Earlier I asked you to develop a resource list that contained a roster of your attributes, acquired skills, and human resources. Concocting that three-part list undoubtedly took a few minutes, but if you did it (did you do it?) and review it often, it's likely you will experience the benefits.

Now, I'm asking you to create another list, and this one is going to take a while. I call it your "Internal Achievements List." It is a clear, detailed, and accurate list of what you've done for your team, department, or division in the past six months, year, or two years.

Here are some examples to get you started:

> January—Received credit as one of eight associates contributing to the annual report.
>
> January—Appointed by team as chair for the first-quarter meetings.
>
> February—Completed second appearance before industry council representing the organization's philosophical viewpoint.
>
> March—Participated in the reorganization of the department library.

Armed with such a list, you will be your most effective self when asking for greater rewards due to your contributions and value to the organization. Memorize these before sitting down with your boss. You can also type them up concisely so that you can position a single piece of paper on your lap and look down to see an instant reminder of all you've accomplished.

Here are some examples of assertive language that you can use, having discussed your various contributions to the organization:

➤ "In light of what I've presented, I think that my request is fair and certainly merits consideration. Can we get back together on this at this time next week?" (Use this approach with a boss who is highly organized and detail-oriented.)

➤ "I've stated my case clearly. I'm trusting that you'll do what's best for you, me, and the organization. I believe I've earned this; now it's a matter of making it a reality." (Use this approach with a boss who is very loyal to the organization, perhaps having been employed there for 10 years or more.)

➤ "I appreciate your listening to me. I know you've got lots of important issues to deal with, but understandably, this is an extremely important issue to me. Can we wrap this up in the next couple of days?" (Use this approach with a boss who maintains a clear desk—someone who doesn't let issues accumulate.)

➤ "Hey, I know I'm asking for something significant, but I also believe that I'm more than worth it. Besides, once I get this, I won't come in here with this issue for at least another three months [said jokingly]." (Use this approach with a boss who appreciates a sense of humor.)

➤ "There it is, all laid out on the table. I'm trusting that my points were clear. I think my case is pretty much irrefutable. I know you've got a lot of other things on your mind right now. By taking care of this one quickly, [said in a light, good-natured way] you'll be able to turn your attention back to everything else." (Use this approach with a boss who is analytical in nature and who will probably assess your request point by point.)

Obviously, some of these statements work better with some boss's personalities than others. Without meeting you or your boss, I can't tell you what approach will be most effective with your boss.

Mastering the Performance Appraisal

Depending on the size and nature of your organization, you may receive an annual, semiannual, or quarterly performance appraisal. The appraisal might be tied in to a raise or be independent of it.

Some people look forward to performance appraisals—especially if they're linked to raises. Also, for many people it's the only time they get positive feedback from frantic, over-extended bosses. Hence, a performance appraisal can be a positive experience. But for many people, this may not be true. You probably don't enjoy performance appraisals. Your boss probably doesn't like them either. This is why you should make the performance process far less upsetting, and, in fact, even somewhat enjoyable, by asserting yourself!

The Man with the Plan

As you would do when asking for a raise, bring along your Internal Achievements List. In addition, spend 10 or 15 minutes a few days beforehand mapping out a little strategy:

➤ What issues is your boss likely to bring up? How would you respond?

➤ What didn't you do so well that might be a topic of discussion? How would you skillfully address shortcomings and offer solutions that minimize or eradicate them in the coming period?

➤ What if your boss says something you think is inaccurate? How would you respond? How will you maintain your level of composure?

Mentally rehearse what you'll say in each instance, so that you'll feel confident and do your best when it counts—during the actual appraisal.

Equal Footing

It's vital to remember during a performance appraisal that you're not some waif who by the grace of God was given this job, and every now and then given a cookie and a pat on the back for your efforts. Your performance is being appraised so that you can obtain feedback, formulate strategies for improvement, and understand your role and position in the organization.

Concurrently, your boss gets your views on how you're doing, which can be valuable information for him. He also gets the opportunity to learn more about his effectiveness as a boss, and the opportunity, potentially, to reward you.

All of this points to the notion that you want to engage in this discussion as someone on an even plane, almost an equal partner to the performance appraiser.

If performance appraisals are a time of high anxiety for you, Marsha Reynolds, a personal and business coach based in Minneapolis, Minnesota, has an idea that's an interesting variation on an earlier theme. She suggests that you make a brief roster of your strengths, such as intelligence, compassion, and creativity. Put these on a pocket-size card. Then, before you enter some potentially intimidating situation, whether it be a performance appraisal or a phone conversation, find a quiet place and actually read the card out loud, saying "I am" before each item.

By the time you get to the end of your list, Reynolds says that your sense of self will be stronger. You'll approach the encounter feeling powerful and centered.

Taking the Reins

Here's how to get the best from your performance appraisal, stand up for yourself if necessary, and leave the meeting feeling good about what transpired:

➤ Listen as closely as you ever have listened to anyone speaking to you. Take notes. Write like a son-of-a-gun. Take down as much as you can.

There aren't many other times in life when you get such pointed, potent information about your capabilities and performance. (If you could tape the performance appraisal all the better, although I doubt that many performance appraisers would be comfortable having such a device present.)

➤ Take responsibility for whatever did not go right on the job, when in fact it was your responsibility.

➤ Remain on an even keel. Don't get flustered or upset if you hear things that you think are inaccurate or overly critical. You'll have your turn to speak.

➤ Ask probing questions that require more than a yes or no answer. For example, rather than asking, "So, you'd like the quota to be above 10 percent?" to which your boss could respond yes or no, try asking, "What do you see as the optimal quota target and how do you arrive at that?"

➤ Recap what you learned during the performance appraisal. If there are any action items that you and your boss agreed on, reiterate your willingness to initiate them.

> **Make It So**
> Your self-performance appraisal actually helps to reduce some of your boss's burden. Each time you objectively assess your own performance, you're giving her information she can stick in her file on you and use once it's time for the formal performance appraisal.

Preempting the Appraisal Process

Why wait for an annual, semiannual, or quarterly appraisal? Get in the habit of producing your own. Yes! On a weekly, monthly, or other interim basis, provide your boss with a one-page, unsolicited appraisal of your performance. Make it as accurate and as objective as you possibly can.

At first, your boss may be a little dumbfounded that you even went to the trouble. Assuming you aren't explicitly told to stop, by the third or fourth time you've done it, your boss may begin to expect it. Thereafter, he may even look forward to it.

> **Handle with Care**
> If you produce your own performance appraisals, say on a monthly basis, and submit them to your boss, remember: This is your own career-related strategy and you don't need to share it with others.

When the formal-appraisal time rolls around, guess what? More than half the stuff that you've submitted makes its way back to you as part of your boss's feedback. In other words, you get to assert yourself in a grand way. *You end up influencing, if not dominating, a process you might have once feared.*

When You're Asked to Do Too Much

When you're asked to take on too much at work, stay too many hours, or handle more than you're comfortable handling, the ability to assert yourself is valuable indeed. Suppose you work for a boss who's a full-fledged workaholic. How do you keep your job, turn in a good performance, maintain sufficient relations, and still have a life? You say "no" without having it sound like "no":

➤ "That is something I'd really like to tackle but I don't think it would be in our best interest since I'm already on xyz."

➤ "I can certainly get started on it, although because of the abc deadline and the xyz event I'm certain I won't be able to get into it full fling until the middle of next month."

➤ "If we can park that one for a while, I'm sure I can do a good job on it. As you know, I'm already handling the hij and wouldn't want to proceed unless I could do a bang-up job. If you need to have somebody get started on this right away, I wouldn't hesitate to suggest Tom."

➤ "I'm not sure what level priority this should be in light of the lineup I'm already facing."

Don't Wimp Out on Yourself

Handle with Care
Don't say "I'm sorry," advises Patricia Wiklund, a Ph.D. from Fair Oaks, California, who offers training programs on dealing with or managing difficult people. She finds that many people (and not just those in the workplace) have trouble declining to take on extra tasks. "I'm sorry" weakens your credibility and the strength of your refusal, Wiklund says. "The other person will jump right in to play on your guilt."

You don't want to fall into the trap of declining every time you're asked to take on more work, because it can have ramifications on your career health and peace of mind. Too many professionals today, fearful that they may lose their job as well as health insurance and other benefits, suffer various forms of work-related abuse because they lack the ability to assert themselves.

Here is some additional language, mildly more forceful, that you may need to draw on, depending on circumstances:

➤ "I'm stretched out right now to the full extent of my resources and I'm fearful that if I take this on, not only will I not be able to give it my best effort, but the other things I'm handling will suffer as well."

➤ "I'm going to request that I not be put on assignment jkl, if that's okay with you. I've been going long and hard for several months now and if I don't regain some sense of personal balance I feel I'm putting my health at risk."

➤ "Is there anyone else right now who could take that on? I need to get a better handle on what I've already been assigned. In a couple weeks, or perhaps a month or two, when things calm down, I may be able to work something else into the lineup."

➤ "I wish I could—I've been burning the candle at both ends, and if I start to burn it in the middle there will be nothing left."

➤ "I'm honored when you ask me to take on some tough assignments, because that means you have strong confidence in me. By the same token, I think you'll agree that I have a good idea of when it wouldn't be prudent for me to handle another responsibility. This is one of those times."

Asserting Yourself in Dire Situations

Suppose your boss is one tough son-of-a-gun and despite your protestations to the contrary keeps piling on the work and responsibilities. No matter how effective you are at asserting yourself and how often you do it, you seem to be besieged with more assignments, more projects.

If this is the case for you, the first thing is to stop and assess the situation. Here are the basic options:

➤ You can leave your present position, department, or organization. This is radical, but sometimes it's the best alternative.

➤ You can push for a compromise situation in which you take on some of the new work. Or, you take all of it on, but you receive additional resources such as more staff people, a bigger budget, or more equipment.

➤ You can knuckle under and simply take on the added assignments with no additional resources.

Since the middle option is most desirable in those situations in which your boss simply won't stop dishing out the assignments, assert yourself for the purposes of at least making your situation easier. Here's some language you can use if you're willing to only take on some of what's been assigned:

➤ "I believe I can handle the stu assignment, but the rest simply has to go to the other department. I'm snowed under now and it won't be of any value to anybody if I can't deliver."

➤ "Of all these projects, which is the one that is most important? That's the one I probably ought to tackle, and we need to assign the rest of these elsewhere."

➤ "I can appreciate what you must be up against. I'm already working over the max, but I would like to help you by taking on the xyz assignment."

Using this kind of language doesn't necessarily mean that you would be happy to handle the assignments, but that you're doing what you can to accommodate your boss given your already demanding workload.

Get the Resources You Need

Having adequate resources to tackle what's assigned to you can be important. You already know how to structure your requests. The only thing I have to recommend at this juncture is to prepare a memo that will help your boss understand and accept your resource requests. By putting down on paper precisely what you need and why, you give your boss the ammunition he may need to "make it so."

Make It So
Succinctly convey that what's being asked of you is not something you can simply add to the fray, but rather will require blood, sweat, and tears, (whoops, I mean money, time, and effort).

For example, you could compute how many hours would be necessary to tackle the new assignment, how much that would cost in terms of bringing another staff person on board, and what the overall return would be. Proceed in a similar fashion if you need a bigger budget in general, new equipment, or other resources to be successful in handling the added assignments.

When Nothing Works

If the situation looks untenable—no level of assertiveness on your part is sufficient—you may be forced to either consider leaving the organization, getting transferred elsewhere, or taking on the extra work against your better judgment.

If you take on the extra work, do so for a finite period of time, until you can make a major job change. When you see a light at the end of the tunnel it makes whatever you have to endure in the present a little more tolerable. Your long-term health and well-being are far more important than any job situation in which they are put into jeopardy.

If you have to take on the work, but you don't want to make a major job change, keep in mind that even crunch periods come to an end. Hang in there!

A Parting Word

John Caposy, author of *Why Climb the Corporate Ladder When You Can Take the Elevator?*, has some sage advice, particularly when dealing with your boss, with which I will close this chapter:

➤ "Most consultants first ask corporate executives what advice they are seeking and then later give them that advice." (Do you see any corollaries here with giving advice to your boss?)

➤ "A career should be a quest not for perfection, but for a high batting average." (I'll bet this one applies to you all day long.)

➤ "If you think something is wrong, it probably is."

➤ "Better to ask twice than to lose your way once."

The Least You Need to Know

➤ Draw up a list of who you are, what you can do, and who you know, and use it as a resource tool and confidence-booster when being assertive with your boss.

➤ Before asking for a raise or listening to a performance appraisal, plan what you're going to say and how you will respond.

➤ Preempt and dominate the performance appraisal process by conducting your own appraisal and delivering the summaries to your boss.

➤ If you're asked to take on a large burden, ask for more resources.

➤ Your long-term health and well-being are far more important than any job situation in which they are put into jeopardy.

GANG, LET'S GO BACK TO WORK.

Assertiveness with Your Peers

In This Chapter

➤ On being one of the guys/gals

➤ Being more influential right where you are

➤ Effective verbal sparring

➤ For the good of the group

In the book and subsequent movie, *The Lord of the Flies*, by William Golding, a group of boys are marooned on an island. After several weeks, they resort to tribal behavior with each other. The stronger, more influential, and more assertive children take the lead. The weak, passive children become the whipping boys. The culture that ensues is not a pleasant one—it's built on a hierarchy based on strength and influence. The lower castes are stigmatized and brutalized. By the end of the story, if it were not for adult intervention, the weak, passive types would have been killed.

Now, about you and your peers at work. Being assertive is going to make a big difference in how you're treated, what advantages come your way, and what kind of relationships you form. This chapter tells all.

You and Your Peers

To be one of the guys or gals, you have to be able to stand your ground as well as any of the other guys or gals, maybe even better. Although you may have less trouble being assertive with your peers than you do with your boss, chances are there's a thing or two more you could be doing to be more assertive with your peers.

Poor Substitutes

Many studies reveal that if one co-worker feels slighted or upset because of the actions of another co-worker, the first party is likely to engage in any one of a number of activities, many of which are not helpful or productive to either party. For example, when upset with a co-worker, professionals report that at various times they have resorted to:

> Avoiding the person throughout the day

> Giving the other person the silent treatment

> Talking behind the other person's back

> Ratting on the other person to his or her boss

> Making derisive comments to the person

> Unobtrusively deciding not to support or cooperate with the other person

> Using various means to try to get even

> Asking to be transferred out of the department

Make It So

Being assertive in your home life, with friends, and relatives, in your community, and everywhere you roam can certainly help you get more of what you want more of the time. Being assertive in the workplace, particularly among your peers, is not just helpful, it's mandatory.

> Engaging in a shouting match

> Pulling rank on the other person (if applicable)

> Coercing the other person into an apology

> Attempting to have the other person leave his or her job or the organization altogether

> Taking a pill for stress or anxiety and trying to forget about it

> Taking a drink and attempting to forget about it

> Making friends with others in the organization who may not like the person as well

> Resigning from one's position or at least looking for a new job

> Talking about the incident with other co-workers, ostensibly trying to gain empathy

> Talking about the issue with spouse, friends, or others away from the workplace

These are not happy outcomes. The strategy that makes the most sense most of the time is to talk about the situation directly with the person involved. If that comes hard for you, then this chapter is for you.

Chapter 23 ➤ *Assertiveness with Your Peers*

Conflict Is Not Inherently Bad

Although you may have been slighted, offended, or otherwise upset, not all conflict at work is necessarily bad. People sometimes believe that conflict means that there's a breakdown in communications or that one party simply doesn't get it. Even fully functioning, rational people, however, can view a situation differently. Thus, conflict may help bring differing views and opinions to the surface so that ultimately a team can achieve great synergy and the desired results.

How Do Others See You?

To get a handle on how you might be perceived by others at work, think about four or five terms others might use to describe you. Would they call you aggressive, sensitive, loud, caring, egotistical, intelligent, careless, thoughtful, or uninspired?

Taking the notion a bit further, what would your co-workers see as your four or five strengths? Might it be your tenacity, accuracy, inventiveness, listening ability, assurance, leadership, or simply positive attitude? Then, what would they see as your four or five most notable weaknesses? Be honest here. Might it be that you rush your work, are always looking for shortcuts, are not a team player, miss deadlines too frequently, or don't plan your time well in general?

Handle with Care

There may be some co-workers with whom you will never see eye to eye. This doesn't mean you can't be effective working with and around them. You both can be assertive if you understand that your individual differences need to be subdued for the overall good of the project, team, or organization.

Not Everyone Is Going to Like You, No Matter What!

I once had a job where one co-worker in particular flat out didn't like me. It didn't matter what I did or said, or whether I tried to avoid or befriend this person. Maybe I looked too much like someone from the past. Who knows?

After a couple weeks of subtle hostility, I decided to assert myself. Rather than confront this person directly, I determined that the best strategy would be to write a note. It simply said:

> I acknowledge your personal dislike for me. We are both professionals and I believe we can put aside our differences for the good of the firm.
>
> Yours truly,
>
> Jeff Davidson

It must have worked. Although we never discussed it, I was thereafter able to have semi-pleasant exchanges with this person in the hallways.

Some Nuts Are Tough to Crack

Of course, it doesn't always work this easily. I could have written that note, and ended up fanning the flames even hotter. I felt I had to do something, however. By acknowledging that I knew I wasn't liked, and then drawing upon the fact that we were both dedicated, hard-working, talented management consultants, I "bonded us" in a novel way under less than ideal circumstances.

On Being One of the Guys/Gals

Your decision to be one of the gang is uniquely up to you. Many people go along with the crowd because they feel that it gives them social advantages. When they want or need to stand up for themselves it's certainly a heck of a lot easier if they're doing it within their own circle. For most people it seems "safer" as well.

There could be problems with trying to be one of the gang when you're the boss. Employees always treat the boss a bit differently and may not welcome your efforts to befriend them, so play it by ear.

Yet, "being one of the guys or gals" is not a prerequisite to effectively asserting yourself with individuals within the group or with the whole group itself. I'm sure you've known mavericks, lone wolves, or outsiders who, when they needed to assert themselves, could do perfectly well.

Getting to Know You

If you want to form a stronger relationship with your co-workers or simply to get to know them more quickly, you have lots of strategies. You can engage in any one of the following:

➤ Just start talking

➤ Involve them in what you're doing

➤ Attend the same convention, outing, or task force, and meet and converse early on the first day of that event

➤ Communicate honestly from the outset

➤ Convey more interest in them than in yourself

➤ Touch them emotionally

➤ Find a common cause

➤ Share a mutual deadline

Each of these strategies can bring you closer to another person.

To Befriend or Not to Befriend

Much has been written on networking as a strategy for career advancement. Networking works best when there is truly some element of friendship involved. There are few people I can think of offhand with whom I network on a regular basis who I'm not otherwise friends with or at least friendly with. It's probably the same for you.

Focus on activities and behaviors that tend to give you a stronger bond with your co-workers, with the understanding that for most people it's easier to be assertive with a friend than a nonfriend.

Among a boat-load of strategies for upping your friendship quotient with your co-workers, here are several, many of which may be right for you:

➤ Begin exchanging letters, e-mail, etc.

➤ Support their cause

➤ Serve as a sounding board

➤ Tell the truth

➤ Convey gladness to hear from them

➤ Share a common need

➤ Mutually admire something about each other

➤ Work through a crisis together

➤ Remember their birthdays and surprise them!

Word Power
Networking is strategically connecting with others for purposes of friendship, career advancement, or information exchange.

Just the Facts

Dr. Bernard Guerin, a member of the Department of Psychology at the University of Waikato in New Zealand, recently conducted a study in which he found that participants were able to be more assertive with a friend than with a stranger. Hence, a sound strategy for being more assertive among your co-workers if this has been a lingering problem for you is to get to know them better, and even become more friendly with them.

Listen Up, Partner

The greatest single courtesy you can give to a co-worker and at the same time lay the groundwork for you to be assertive when you need to be is to be a better listener.

I've alluded to listening throughout the book, and in the context of working with others, listening takes on an added measure of importance. After all, to meet tough challenges, critical deadlines, and stay profitable, you need to work as effectively and efficiently as possible much of the time. Being a good listener is effective and efficient.

Being More Influential Right Where You Are

With all the talk about teamwork today, many people don't realize there are times when individual assertiveness is called for.

In the quest to avoid conflict, do you find yourself not speaking up with co-workers when your insides are telling you to do so? Here's a quick quiz to see if you're being too reluctant to speak up with your co-workers:

---

1. Now and then I feel that some co-workers take advantage of my good disposition.   Yes ___   No ___

2. I feel uncomfortable when co-workers ask me to help solve an argument.   Yes ___   No ___

3. When a co-worker asks me to participate in a project, I feel anxious saying no even when it's not practical for me to participate.   Yes ___   No ___

4. I find it difficult to delegate some project I'd rather not personally tackle even though I have the authority to do so.   Yes ___   No ___

5. I hesitate to bring up anything that might diminish group harmony, even if I have an important point to offer.   Yes ___   No ___

Make It So
Recognize that conflicts at work are not only normal, but can actually be healthy in terms of finding solutions more quickly, airing grievances that would have otherwise festered, and staying focused on the best way to meet challenges.

If you answered yes to three or more questions, assertiveness with your co-workers is a problem for you. If you answered yes to four or five questions, you need to reread all the chapters in this book several times (just kidding).

Because being assertive is part and parcel to open and straightforward interpersonal communications, I suggest that you reexamine this quiz. Then, the next time any of the situations described in the quiz occur, level with your co-workers. Tell them how you feel and what outcome you think can be accomplished.

Say Your Peace

Here are some phrases you can use in situations where you need to speak up with a co-worker or the group and you're concerned that you might upset the harmony or balance that seems to prevail:

➤ "I'm not trying to upset the apple cart or anything, but I need to point out that..."

➤ "This is just a suggestion, but one that I think everyone ought to strongly consider..."

➤ "Before we go any further, there's something I feel compelled to say about..."

➤ "We've been through a lot together, so I'm asking you to hear me out about..."

➤ "There's something that's concerning me that would probably be best to get to now..."

➤ "I'm somewhat troubled that..."

What is it about the language of the preceding phrases that makes them effective? You're being vulnerable and respectful, yet assertive.

For a particularly sticky situation where you feel you need to assert yourself, use language that draws the other person in. For example:

➤ "I need your help on something that I haven't been able to get out of my mind..."

➤ "Could I ask a favor of you? Right now I'm feeling as if xyz and I'm not sure if you understand your part in that..."

➤ "One of the things I like about you is that I can shoot straight from the hip with you..."

➤ "This is not easy for me to say, but..."

➤ "I have a burning issue and I need to call upon your keen powers of attention..."

The unifying theme of these statements is that you *ask* for help.

Start with One and Move On to Others

Generally speaking, it's easier to be assertive with a single co-worker than with a group of co-workers, likewise with a friend than with a stranger. Thus, if you're reluctant to assert yourself among a group of co-workers, for now, don't do it. Start with just another co-worker, one on one.

Handling Criticism from Co-Workers

When someone lets you have it, either fairly or unfairly, constructively or nonconstructively, first consider who is making the charges. In his book, *A Strategy for Winning*,

Carl Mays suggests that you assess each of your co-workers by asking yourself the following questions:

➤ Is this person helping to build me up or tear me down?

➤ Is this person helping me reach goals and objectives I've set for myself?

➤ Does this person have his own goals?

➤ Have we been able to support each other?

➤ Do we have similar value systems?

If the co-worker who is criticizing you scores well after you've made this assessment, then give him or her the benefit of the doubt, and listen as closely as you can.

If this co-worker does not score well when assessing him based on these questions, continue to listen as best you can. Remember, there are always grains of truth in even the most malevolent of criticism. While you're listening to the co-worker, try to engage in some of the following behaviors:

➤ *Don't go on the offensive.* It's not going to help if you launch a counterattack, however emotionally satisfying that might seem.

➤ *Don't feign agreement when you really don't agree.* It may help things in the short term, but soon enough, when there's no activity or behavioral change on your part, the other person will see through your ruse.

➤ *Stay focused on the issue at hand.* If someone says you weren't supportive on the xyz report, he's talking about the xyz report, not the last five years of your career.

Verbal Sparring

What can you say to assert yourself, stand your ground, let the other party know how you feel, and not exacerbate the situation? Plenty!

First, acknowledge the other person's input. You can say something reasonably nice along the lines of, "I acknowledge you for what you've said, but I don't see it that way." Or acknowledge any part of what they said that you can agree with while expressing your lack of agreement for the rest. Acknowledging the other person's input is important and effective because on some level, everyone loves acknowledgment.

Next, take five to cool down or collect your thoughts. Tell the other party, "You've laid a lot on me and I'm going to need time to ponder what you've said. I'll get back in touch with you after the weekend."

If the criticizer wants more immediate responsiveness, try saying something like, "Okay, that's a lot to drop on somebody. I just can't respond this moment, let me take it up again with you in a few minutes." In those few minutes you can regain your composure, perhaps, or approach the issue with greater objectivity.

You also have the option of asking the other party to refine her observation. For example, say, "Could you say that a different way?" or "Could you elaborate on that?" In both instances, you may get the other party to shed more light on the situation.

Another response (one that you should practice with greater frequency) is saying, "You know, you're right. I flubbed that one. It's my responsibility to get things back on track."

Sam Horn, an author from Hawaii who has written the helpful and amusing *Tung Fu: The Art of Verbal Self-Defense,* says that when you make a blunder, sometimes the best and easiest thing to do is just to say, "Oops! I really blew that one."

Repellent Strategies

There may be times when someone who is criticizing you is being totally unfair, and it's someone who is not supportive of you anyway.

I don't advocate escalating any situation so that you have a permanent long-standing enemy within your organization. That's highly counterproductive. Try using one of the following phrases:

➤ "I think your criticism is unfounded."

➤ "I think you've overreacted."

➤ "Let's look at this objectively."

> **Make It So**
> Agreeing with your criticizer when he has valid points, even if he comes on a little too strong, will disarm most rational people. They won't have much to say after you've admitted responsibility for the faux pas.

Dealing with Coy Behavior

Every now and then, a co-worker might ask you a question to which they already know the answer: "Did you turn in the report on time?" (when he or she knows that you didn't). Or they might really be trying to get at something else. If you dutifully respond, you play right into their hands. Short-change the process by using one of the following responses:

➤ "What are you really asking me?"

➤ "What's behind your concern?"

➤ "Okay, what do you want to know?"

➤ "I'm sensing that this isn't what you really want to know."

Said without emotion, all of these represent fair and effective assertive replies. Stand up for yourself without trampling on the rights of others. You also have the option to offer a short answer, such as a yes or no, and say nothing more.

You don't have to tolerate coy behavior, but don't be rude, either. If you do offer a short answer, do so with sincerity and a smile, and then turn to something else.

271

Being Assertive for the Good of the Group

What should you do if, to the best of your knowledge, your entire group is headed in the wrong direction? Here's where you earn your stripes. There's a variety of strategies for asserting yourself for the good of the group. Let's tackle them one by one.

Make a Flat-Out Appeal

If the group is assembled, take the floor, and, using everything you know, make your case. If the group is scattered, send an e-mail, write a memo, or connect by conference call.

Trying to redirect a group is the fastest way to evoke change, but also the riskiest. You risk the distinct possibility of one person disagreeing and others joining in. You also risk being subject to group-think, wherein the group simply can't make a change because they're so heavily invested in the plans already in place.

Proceed with caution, however. If you're not the most senior person, it could be dangerous to send such an e-mail to superiors. You may commit career suicide by trying to tell your superiors that they're going the wrong way. You might try calling first, tempering your message one-on-one over the phone, and then send a follow-up e-mail if appropriate.

The Behind-the-Scenes Approach

With this strategy, you visit or communicate with each member of the group, one on one, one at a time. Obviously, this takes longer and requires more effort on your part, but the risk is lower. If you can convince one person, you can use that victory to go to the next person, and so on.

Eventually, when you have half the group or more on your side, or even one of the most influential people in the group on your side, it's a safe bet that you'll be able to sway the rest.

Again, proceed with caution. You run the risk of people (especially those who may have championed the strategy you're disagreeing with) feeling that you're sneaking around. Once you get some people on your side, tell the rest that these people agreed with you. There is strength in numbers!

Bring Up Your Issue as a "What If" and Ask for Input

In this scenario, you approach the group, perhaps when you're already meeting. You voice your concerns as if you're not absolutely certain, but you have strong reason to believe that xyz will happen. Although a response like this may seem to go against the notion of assertiveness, sometimes the best tactic is to act less certain than you are, especially if you sense you've come on too strong in the past.

You then ask the group to consider this possibility and various alternatives they might take if it were true. If you have the opportunity, you might ask them to engage in brain-storming.

Your quest is to get the group to grapple with the issue that you raise, so that by the time they're through talking, it's a group concern and not necessarily your concern.

The Least You Need to Know

➤ Conflict may help differing views and opinions surface so that a team can achieve synergy and the desired results.

➤ It's easier to assert yourself within your own circle.

➤ The greatest single courtesy you can give to a co-worker is to be a better listener.

➤ Remember, there are often grains of truth in the criticism directed toward you.

I'D LIKE TO SEE A LITTLE MORE EFFORT...

Chapter 24

Assertiveness with Your Staff

In This Chapter

➤ An assertive staff is more productive

➤ Helping your staff become more assertive

➤ Having to say things only once

➤ When to let your staff members have space

Let's take what you've learned thus far and apply it so that you can both be assertive with your staff and help them to be more assertive. Why bother to help your staff be assertive? An assertive staff will be more productive in the long run, and you'll see less turnover and less burnout because they'll feel less frustrated.

Think of all the bosses you've had. Have you ever felt totally bottled up because the climate was suffocating? Have you been in a situation where you couldn't air your views without being fearful of your position? I once left a job for that reason. Perhaps you know people who have done the same.

In this chapter, you'll learn how to avoid being a boss like the ones I describe.

Helping Your Staff to Be More Assertive and at Their Best

Because you're the boss, you have more latitude with your staff in helping them to be assertive than you do with your co-workers. For example, in preparation for the next group meeting, you could assign one of your staff people to lead a significant part of the session.

If that's going too far for you, appoint one of your staff people in advance to have some responsibility for airing his or her views during the meeting.

Just the Facts

The best leaders throughout history in politics, commerce, and even religion routinely surrounded themselves with the best staff people—advisors—that they could find. Sure, a few autocrats here and there kept their own counsel, and some of them actually did manage to retain power for longer than anyone might have predicted. The odds, however, are with the leader who surrounds himself with the best people he can find. Not "yes men" or "yes women," but people you know you can count on for the straight dope about critical issues.

Open in Word Only

So often in business and industry you hear of managers who proclaim with great pride, "I have an open door policy. Any of my people can come in and talk to me at any time." If you were to poll such managers' staffs as to how open the open door policy is, and exactly what can be said during such meetings, you'd find that the staff has completely different views.

Just the Facts

A study conducted in the early 1990s by Psychological Associates Inc., a St. Louis consulting firm, found that executives often rated communication among themselves as their main area of difficulty. This was more problematic than handling conflict, holding better meetings, or making decisions. Moreover, if corporate executives find it difficult to have conversations among themselves, how much better are they when communicating with staff members throughout the company?

True communication, the kind that will help maintain committed employees, and probably show on the profit sheet as well, is communication in which workers feel they have a stake in the company's success, and a chance to be heard as well.

What About You?

If you are a supervisor or manager of even one other person, have I got a quiz for you! On a scale of one to five (with one being the lowest and five being the highest), rate yourself on the following ten items:

1 2 3 4 5   Is it easy for your staff to get hold of you? In other words, is your door open most of the day, or can you be summoned via intercom, e-mail, beeper, and so on?

1 2 3 4 5   Do you have a scheduled time each week, month, or (my goodness!) quarter in which each of your staff members gets to sit down with you for an allotted time?

1 2 3 4 5   Do you encourage your staff members to be open and straightforward with you by using language that unmistakably requests that they be candid?

1 2 3 4 5   Do you encourage suggestions by installing a suggestion box, encouraging staff members during group meetings, or by other means?

1 2 3 4 5   Can a staff person take issue with you without you becoming upset?

1 2 3 4 5   Are you a skillful listener to your staff?

1 2 3 4 5   Do you give your staff the latitude to make errors occasionally, knowing that they still have your confidence and support?

1 2 3 4 5   Do you openly seek feedback from your staff regarding your performance as a manager?

1 2 3 4 5   Do you offer constructive criticism to your staff members when each needs it so as not to thwart their confidence?

1 2 3 4 5   Would you say that your staff members regard you as easy to communicate with?

If your answer to each question is a four or five, congratulations, you're probably someone that others would like to work for. If your answer to each question is a three, certainly you have room for improvement. Use this quiz as a way to check yourself in one month and in two months to see if your own rating improves as a result of the new measures you put into practice.

Handle with Care
A boss may think he is accessible (and rate himself highly on these points) when actually he is not. If you're a boss, you might ask your employees to answer these questions about you.

If your answer to each question is a two or less, guess what? The atmosphere in your department is probably stifling. There are many things your staff would like to tell you, for the good of the department, but they don't feel safe to do so. This is a difficult situation for them, and an unfortunate one for you, because you're not getting the best from them.

Knowing When to Drop Back and Punt

Kevin Martinson went into work early one morning to finish up a project. By 11:30 a.m., he had accomplished a great deal. The project was completed, and Kevin was pleased with it. He was also ready for a break. Near lunch time, Kevin took the elevator down to the main floor and was walking to a sandwich shop when he passed his boss, Ed Seals.

Ed was preoccupied in thought and hadn't really noticed Kevin. When Kevin passed by with a big "Hello," Ed managed to say "Hi, Kevin" and then proceeded on. Suddenly he stopped, turned around and said in a louder voice, "Say, Kevin. I've got some figures I'd like you to check, and also the Taddle Company report from last month should be revised, and…"

By this time, what Ed was saying really didn't matter much to Kevin. You see, Kevin had put in a good morning's work and was now on his way to lunch. While he would normally be ready to tackle any assignment given him, at this particular moment he was simply not interested.

Handle with Care
Discussing assignments and responsibilities during chance meetings in the lobby of the building or in the sandwich shop is not being assertive; it's being overbearing and not of benefit to anyone.

When Ed finally finished talking, Kevin muttered, "Okay, just gotta grab a bite to eat." He then made his way to the sandwich shop with about one-tenth of the enthusiasm of several minutes ago.

This situation, unfortunately, occurs thousands of times every working day. Ed and Kevin have a fairly sound working relationship, and it's not Ed's intention to suffocate Kevin.

Why does an otherwise well-meaning supervisor often forget that there's a proper time and place to discuss work assignments and job responsibilities? The discussion of either of these at the wrong time or place can have the opposite effect of assertiveness—it can demotivate or dampen the spirits of the most loyal and hardworking employees.

One reason well-meaning supervisors may inadvertently and inappropriately "collar" staff outside of the office or on otherwise "neutral" ground is that they happen to think of the task at the moment they're passing the employees and don't wish to lose that particular train of thought.

Okay, so occasionally we all have thoughts we want to unload in the moment. If you want to be assertive, however, discussing or issuing an assignment on the spur of the moment can only be a reflection of poor planning.

278

Some supervisors mistakenly believe that discussing an assignment in the stairwell is a time saver. Not! Most staff will not be mentally prepared to hear and act upon your message, no matter how effective you are at expressing yourself otherwise. So, if you provide instructions at the wrong time, the chances are you'll have to repeat them!

Make It So
Assuming the employee is doing his or her job, and the manager has effectively coordinated planning responsibilities, no employee should have to be collared in the lobby or in the washroom unless there is a company emergency.

Beyond Where: When?

If you seek to be assertive, "when" can be as important as "where." When should you bring up a difficult assignment or sticky subject?

DON'T bring up a sticky subject::

➤ The very moment someone gets to work

➤ Just before lunch

➤ After an argument has just concluded

➤ When the other person is otherwise heavily distracted

➤ Right after someone else has brought up a sticky subject

➤ When you're unprepared to be assertive

➤ Just before quitting time

DO bring up a sticky subject:

➤ When you're both seated

➤ When the other party is calm and relaxed

➤ When you have the other person's undivided attention

➤ When the other person tells you it's a good time to do so

➤ When delaying any longer will result in serious consequences

➤ When, in your best judgment, the time is appropriate

You'll have to play it by ear sometimes, but usually these guidelines will serve you well.

Having to Say It Only One Time

In the military, when a superior officer gives an order, you can bet the troops jump. There are immediate and sometimes severe penalties for not responding the first time you're told to do something. In the working world, there are penalties as well, but usually not as acute.

Handle with Care

In supervising people who don't seem to "get" assignments correctly, you need to pull out the stops to ensure that they hear, understand, and follow your directions explicitly. You need to create reinforcing backup systems, such as taping the instruction (discussed below). Yes, it takes some time, but hey, it takes a lot more time to try to correct something that's been turned in and unfortunately widely misses the mark.

How do you get to a point where you only have to say something once? How do you get each and every one of your staff people to be responsive, independent of their skills, aptitudes, and backgrounds, and orientation toward work?

Assuming that you communicate effectively and that the instructions are finalized, it's useful to assess your staff based on their demonstrated ability to understand your instructions.

There are staff people who get assignments right the first time. These are the people you love to work with, and to whom you will give the most amount of latitude when making assignments.

Then there are those people who seem to get the assignment right the first time, but then ultimately get something wrong. With these people, you need to show some patience, and engage in some reinforcing communication techniques.

Finally, there are those staff people who consistently don't get the assignment right. These are people you'd like to ax, but for one reason or another, you're stuck with them at least for awhile.

May I Have Your Attention?

Once you've assessed your staff people based on their ability to understand and act upon instruction, here are some strategies for conveying what you want to have done and only having to say it once.

You can use these techniques with all levels of staff, acknowledging that those in the last category will still require the greatest effort on your part. The payoff, however, is worth it when you find that even your least effective staff member has to only hear you once to get the assignment correct.

Tape-Record Your Conversation

Tape-record your conversation with individual staff members as you dole out an assignment, and give the tape to the staff person. I've used this for years to great effect. It's especially handy when the assignment I'm giving is new for the staff person, if it's quite involved, or if it simply takes a lot to convey.

The tape does not take the place of having the boss available to clarify the assignment or answer questions, but rather, it's a tool to help someone remember all the details of the assignment.

Dictate the Assignment

Dictate the assignment and have it typed up, or type it yourself, then print two copies so that you and the staff person can each have a copy while you're reviewing it face to face. Another option is to e-mail the assignment to the staff person so that he can download it and have it on his computer.

You might also request that a staff person provide a written running commentary on each aspect of the assignment. That way, you'll have a written record of what was assigned and a report from the staff person as to his or her progress on the various aspects of the assignment.

Make It So
Audio-taping your instructions to your staff is advisable if it's a multi-part assignment or if there is specific wording that you want a staff person to use as part of successful completion of the task.

Just the Facts

Touch means much. Studies show that if one adult lightly touches the arm or shoulder of another while imparting information, the person being touched has a much higher probability of receiving the message. If you or the climate in which you're employed are too worked up about harassment issues, or if there is a corporate policy specifically forbidding it, feel free to skip the light touch. Remember, however, that emotions play an important part in the messages you convey to others. Managers who appeal only to the logic and rationale of their followers are rarely as assertive and, hence, effective as leaders who combine both the rational and emotional pleas.

Say It Back to Me

Another effective technique is to make your assignment and then request that the staff person repeat it back to you, in her own words, so that you're sure she understood it completely. You might even request that she make notes as you're issuing the assignment. Obviously, if you use this in conjunction with the tape recorder, your PC, and printer, or e-mail, you'll have double and triple reinforcement.

Okay, So It's More Work

If this sounds like a lot, consider that miscommunication and misunderstanding of assignments is probably the single most costly element in business today. Even if you deliver your assignments with the oratory skills of the Reverend Billy Graham, the charisma of Tom Cruise, the prose of Abraham Lincoln, and the presence of Sylvester Stallone, it's not likely that your staff people are going to hear an assignment once and execute it to perfection, except in one itty-bitty circumstance: if the assignment is singular in nature, short-term, and to be acted upon immediately. So, a football coach can bark orders at a player, who runs back into the game, and follows what was just drilled into his head at a high decibel level. Otherwise, people—being rather imperfect creatures—will get some things wrong.

At work, you also can get away with saying it once if the assignment is singular, short-term, and to be executed immediately. In such an instance, your staff person only needs to hear it once. Otherwise, you're managing erroneously if you think your words are perceived like golden tones coming from on high.

When to Let Your Staff Have the Floor

How do you help your staff when they want or need to be assertive? In a word, you give them space. You give them the opportunity to air their views, reversing all those things you learned about being assertive yourself.

> **Make It So**
> Be your magnanimous self and on occasion clear the floor so that someone else can make their views known.

Be a good listener, don't butt in, maintain eye contact, and hear them out. Offer feedback based on what you heard.

If you're in agreement, say so. If you have to take issue with something that's said, do so in a responsibly assertive manner so that staff person still feels good for having asserted himself.

You can give space by saying things like, "Say, Ted, I imagine you might have some pretty strong feelings on this..." Here are some other phrases you might want to consider in support of helping others in your group to be assertive:

➤ "Roberta, I'd be interested, and I think the others would be too, in hearing your views on this."

➤ "John, did you want to add to that? I know you have a strong background in this area..."

➤ "I'm not sure what to make of this, but you know, Carla, I'd be eager to know your feelings on this..."

➤ "You know, Albert's been working in this area for quite a while and I think his thoughts would be valuable..."

➤ "...but I've said enough, let's give the floor to Terry."

Silently but surely, as you give others the opportunity to express their opinions, you win a vote of thanks from everyone.

Encourage Your Staff

Here's a long list of actions, not just words, to encourage your staff to open up, be more assertive, and, as the U.S. army ad says, "Be all that they can be":

➤ Welcome their suggestions even when you don't agree with them.

➤ Occasionally have lunch together as equals.

➤ Help them to be their best, but don't expect them to be perfect.

➤ Take what they say at face value—believe them.

➤ Trust in them, and demonstrate your trust.

➤ Acknowledge them when they accept a tough challenge.

➤ Strive to be as fair and consistent with them as you possibly can.

➤ Show enthusiasm when you see them.

➤ Follow through on any promises you make, however big, however small.

➤ Answer their questions as completely as you can.

➤ Let them take the lead in areas where they have the most competence.

➤ Offer praise, recognition, and reward immediately following a good performance.

➤ Now and then, ask them about themselves.

Some Staffers Will Present a Challenge

On occasion you may need to handle significant difficulties such as high absenteeism, insubordination, and dishonesty. A good way to win confidence is by describing a problem with a staff person as "one that you both have to work at solving."

If possible, be seated next to the person instead of across the table or desk. This also helps symbolize that you are on his or her side and decreases the possibility of confrontation.

By approaching the situation at hand in a professional, controlled manner, you can be assertive and actually increase morale rather than decrease it. Your staff members are often well aware of their unacceptable behavior and know that they will eventually be confronted by you or some other authority.

Here are some guidelines for ensuring that you tackle problems in a way that resolves them:

Handle with Care

Inexperienced or first-time supervisors sometimes have trouble dealing with serious personnel problems. The worst thing that can be done, however, is to pretend the problem doesn't exist or to look the other way so as to avoid a confrontation and the responsibility of administering corrective action.

1. Be certain that any organizational policies and procedural guidelines that do exist are understood by your staff.

2. Highlight and make clear from the beginning any specific activities that you deem inappropriate.

3. Keep a log or chart of inappropriate behavior or activity that can serve as the necessary documentation if the situation grows worse and you have to take more drastic action.

In general, if you lay the groundwork in advance to head off problems, you'll reduce the chances of being caught unprepared to deal with the issue.

Helping Your Staff to Work Better with You

When you work with people daily, it's easy to fall into unproductive communication patterns. You need to stay aware of what's being said, and use assertive language when you want or need to gain attention. The longer you are around someone, the more easily you fall into communication routines. Therefore, it becomes more important to vary the structure of your sentences as well as the substance of your communication.

Disarm your listeners on occasion by using bright, bold, colorful language that moves otherwise routine discussions to a new level. Instead of saying to someone, "I think I can help you here," try, "I see myself striding side by side with you as we take control of the situation." Instead of saying, "I've heard what you said, and I'll get back to you," try something like, "What you've said is provocative and certainly merits considerable thought. I'm going to give your words serious attention."

Too exuberant, you say? Disarming? The staff person will hardly believe it's you? Fine. That means that your words are likely to be remembered.

Telling the Truth

In addition to using colorful, descriptive language, there's something about speaking the truth that your staff will find refreshing. Be forthright about what you can or can't do, what you have or haven't done. Also acknowledge the reality of the situation. Try saying something like:

➤ "I know I'm asking a lot, but it's important that you…"

➤ "This may seem as though it's coming out of left field, but I'd like you to…"

➤ "I haven't mentioned this before, but I want you to…"

➤ "It's going to require more effort than usual, but I want to have…"

➤ "You might see this as kind of a challenge; my request is to have you…"

When you're asking someone to do more or to do something special, letting them know that you recognize the magnitude of the request can make all the difference in the world.

The Least You Need to Know

> ➤ An assertive staff will be more productive in the long run, and you'll see less turn-over and less burnout.

> ➤ The leader who surrounds himself with the best people he can find has the best chance of long-term success.

> ➤ To maintain employee commitment, your staff needs to feel that it's safe to speak up when they feel it's necessary.

> ➤ If you seek to be assertive with your staff, "when" is as important as "where."

> ➤ When you ask someone to do something special, let them know that you recognize the magnitude of the request.

Handling Clients or Customers

Of all the people you encounter in life, your clients or customers are arguably some of the most important. After all, they're the ones who pay you. To keep your relationships vibrant and long-term, there are plenty of instances in which you need to be assertive. If the quality of your relationship has changed, and especially if it's changed for the worse, being assertive is the order of the day. In this chapter, we'll look at how to examine your relationships with your clients or customers to determine where and when assertiveness is desirable.

Customers Are King

Customers may not always be right, but they certainly do pay the bills. The renowned management consultant Dr. Peter Drunker observes "that of all the elements that make up a business, customers is the only one that is essential." Whether you work with customers in a retail setting, or with clients providing some type of professional service, the fundamentals of effectively handling your patrons and being assertive are nearly the same.

Handle with Care

Checklists like the ones throughout this book can help you develop good listening skills. You can't boil down the process of conveying real interest in what a customer is saying to a checklist, however. Your interest has to come from within. You can convey strong interest by offering your rapt attention, asking relevant questions at the appropriate junctures, and not jumping ahead of the customer.

Make It So

As hard as it is to remember, a person's name is important to him. Using a person's name is generally helpful in all encounters, but be sure that you don't overuse it (dropping it in every other sentence).

Handle with Care

Hypnotic pacing helps establish trust and rapport. It does not work as a gesture, however. Anything other than an honest attempt to understand the other person and his or her frame of reference in a particular situation will be seen as mimicking, which will lessen trust.

Do You Care?

Perhaps the crucial element of interpersonal communication is conveying a sincere interest and appreciation for what the other person is telling you—in other words, to be concerned and interested with what the other party is saying. This is no easy feat.

The Sound of My Own Name

Many advocates of good customer relations suggest using the customer's name, either their first name, if you know them well enough to do so, or Mr. or Ms. in all other cases. This seems like a simple gesture, but it works. It offers the customer a form of personal recognition that helps put him or her more at ease.

Tell Me to My Face

In recent years, research has revealed that emulating a person's communication pattern and body language in face-to-face encounters, or emulating their rate and pattern of speech over the phone, will enable you to quickly communicate with them efficiently and effectively. Dr. Donald J. Moine, a California-based psychologist who heads his own sales and management training firm, compared the sales techniques of high-achieving salespeople with those of mediocre salespeople. Moine found that top sales personnel use what he calls "hypnotic pacing" and instinctively match the customer's voice tone, rhythm, volume, and speech rate. Career marketers take note!

"The good salesman or saleswoman matches the customer's posture, body language, and mood," explains Moine. "If the customer is slightly depressed, the salesperson shares that feeling and acknowledges that he or she has been feeling a little down lately. In essence, the top sales producer becomes a sophisticated biofeedback mechanism, sharing and reflecting the customer's reality—even to the point of breathing with the customer."

Once you're able to get on the same communication wavelength, at least in terms of energy and rate of speech, you'll be able to better tap in to the customer's emotional state as well. Moine and others have then postulated that as you begin to build rapport you can change your rate of speech and mental state, such as going from placid to enthusiastic, and the customer may actually follow!

Keeping Your Relationships Vibrant and Long-Term

Everyone wants to feel important. Everyone is tuned to the station WIIFM—What's In It For Me. Hereafter, with customers or anyone else, you can accept as a given that when you convey through your words and action that you regard the other person as important, you've won a lot of points already when it comes to being heard, understood, and heeded.

> **Make It So**
>
> For optimal assertiveness when speaking with a customer, telephoning a client, or even writing a letter, consider that person's likely mood and reaction. What effect is your message likely to have? And how can you phrase that message for maximum benefit?

> JUST THE FACTS MA'AM.
>
> **Just the Facts**
>
> One of Dale Carnegie's 21 rules in his legendary book *How to Win Friends and Influence People* is to "make the other person feel important." The advice must be good—the book has sold more than 15 million copies during its 50-year run.

Don't Treat "A" Customers Like "D" Customers

One of the keys to customer service and, therefore, assertiveness, described in my book *Marketing Your Consulting & Professional Services* (Wiley, 1997), which I co-wrote with Richard Connor, is that you can't be all things to all customers. A more viable strategy is to identify which customers are more important to your business or practice. An easy way to do this is to classify them. Classify your existing customers or clients by estimating their potential for providing you with business opportunities or problems that you can solve. Use an "A," "B," "C," and "D" approach, as shown in the following table:

Characteristics of Customers or Clients

Client Type	Characteristics
"A"	Has a realistic notion of a situation Spends a lot Willingly accepts large fees Is a prestige client Provides contacts/referrals

continues

289

Client Type	Characteristics
	Has a need that you can serve and satisfy
	Has compatibility, or "chemistry" with you
	Offers challenging work
	Is enthusiastic about your company
"B"	Pays willingly
	Has repeat needs
	Is a growing business
	Is generally easy to work with
"C"	Presents fee or collection problems
	Presents temporary problems
	Can be educated to become a "B" but probably not an "A"
	Able to openly and fairly discuss fees
"D"	Is difficult or impossible to work with
	Holds up payment
	Offers ultimatums
	Asks for unethical, unreasonable services

An "A" client is a key client. This type of client provides you with substantial revenue. This client may make referrals in your behalf, provide you with potential for additional services, and so forth.

Your "B" clients are your fair-to-good clients, who might be called your "bread-and-butter" clients. They pay their bills, make a few demands, and seldom provide you with additional service opportunities.

Your "C" clients are your marginal clients who fit one of two categories: (1) They constitute fee problems because they represent excessive discount situations or are slow payers; or (2) They make you vulnerable or upset with their actions because they give you or your staff a hard time.

Your "D" clients must be dropped immediately. "D" clients routinely ask you to compromise your standards or ethics. These are clients you wish you'd never met.

Since "A" clients are more valuable to your firm, and you can talk with them more easily, you may wish to go out of your way to meet their needs. With "B" clients you may feel a little less so, and so on. With "D" clients, collect whatever they owe you and then bow out. (Chapter 26 is all about collections!)

What Is Your Quality of Relationship?

In general, if you think there is a problem with a client or customer, there most assuredly is. Suppose you created a grid of your clients and ranked them according to how strong your relationship is with them? Five is a great relationship, and one is the pits. If you plotted your quality of relationships, or QORs, with seven "A" or "B" customers and subjectively determined that these were the scores, how might you choose to strengthen each relationship? (Remember, it's easier to be assertive with people you know and like.)

Generally you would have good relationships with your "A" and "B" clients and poorer relationships with your "C" and "D" clients. But even among "A" and "B" clients there may be strong potential for better relations.

Potential answers are located in the Strategy column.

Clients	Quality of Relationship	Strategy (Varies by Client)
ABC Co.	5	Take to lunch, maintain a great relationship
Bill Jones Group	3	Call to ask about how you can better serve them
ACME Supply	2	Visit in person to see what's not working
Dworkin Brothers	5	Send thanks for their last order
Sloopies	1	Invite over for a tour and lunch
Z-Barts	4	Send tickets to the Bears game
Olson and Sons	3	Help find them a client

As you review your list and plot your strategy with each key customer or client, consider these questions:

1. How many relationships such as attorneys and bankers do I have in each category?
2. Among those with a QOR of 5, what makes these particular relationships strong?
3. How frequently do I contact these people to thank them for their efforts and seek additional leads?
4. How frequently do I reciprocate by making appropriate referrals to them?

The Customer Service Blues

It will happen. Some customer decides to let you have it, and offers a stinging barrage of verbal attacks or criticism. Should you let him have it right back? Maybe, but not usually, especially if it's an "A" or "B" customer.

Let's take a look at some assertiveness strategies under various troubling scenarios, regardless of what type of client is involved.

When a Customer Criticizes You

There's an old saying that goes, "It is easy to avoid criticism, say nothing, do nothing, be nothing." Since you don't have those options, you need to have some strategies and specific language you can use when confronted by criticism, particularly unfair criticism.

Television correspondent Barbara Walters, who obviously has the gift of gab, once handled criticism in a way that was so effective I never forgot it. She was co-hosting with Harry Reasoner on the *ABC Evening News* in the early 1980s. This was the first time a woman had ever been an anchor or co-anchor for a major network's nightly news. If you were around back then it's not likely you recall ever seeing her on the news, because the job ended abruptly.

Walters and Reasoner were replaced by a single anchor, Patrick Reynolds. One evening while being interviewed as to why the ratings were so low, and whether the higher-ups at ABC were unhappy with her performance, Walters looked directly at her interviewer and said in a soft, low, but nevertheless commanding voice, "I guess I'm a pretty easy target these days."

Her response much disarmed the interviewer and if he had any other tough questions to bring up, apparently he let them slide. When you're besieged with criticism, sometimes the best response is to just say "Okay, hit me some more, everybody else is doing it" or something to that effect. If you want to disarm a customer in seconds, try this:

"You're the 8th (or whatever number is applicable) person who has strongly voiced the same concern this very day. Apparently, we messed up big time, and we're going to listen to all criticisms carefully so that we can devise the best resolution."

Thereafter, what reasonably fair-minded person could continue the same level of attack?

A Strategy for Diffusing Hostility

The next time you're criticized by a customer, remember these other ways to stand your ground and avoid blowing your stack:

1. Listen carefully for any shreds of wisdom that are helpful to you. Even in the most vitriolic attacks there may be some grain of truth. However personal the attack may be, try not to take it personally. Try to remember that it's based on something your company has done or behavior you've exhibited, and generally not on you as a person. (Of course, if someone is attacking you as a person and trying to diminish the very root of your being, that's another story!)

2. Understand that nearly all criticism is subjective. Someone who says you did a crummy job is voicing his opinion. You might actually have done some aspects of the job quite well. However, the customer's perception, to him, is EVERYTHING! Also, recognize that there probably are times when you have done a crummy job.

3. If you can, let the customer finish. The temptation is to try to cut them off, but this only fans the flames.

4. When the customer is finished, try to respond graciously. If you can't say something that's reasonably pleasant, at least say something that's not derogatory or belligerent; for example, "Thank you for expressing your concerns."

Righting Wrongs

Suppose the customer is making an honest attempt to rectify what he sees as a grievous wrong. How might you receive such input?

1. Receive it like a champ. Look for the good in whatever the other person is saying. Avoid attempting to read between the lines. Don't add meaning or implications where none were intended. Offer signs that you are listening: Nod your head on occasion, maintain at least occasional eye contact, and give the other party some respect.

2. Respond as appropriate. If you have to, ask questions or seek added information. Maybe it's not as bad as it first sounded. Maybe the customer has some ideas or recommendations that will readily improve the situation.

3. If you intend to act on anything that you've heard, let the customer know.

4. If they're in a position to help you, ask for help. After all, if they understand the situation so astutely, they may have viable answers.

Better Left Unsaid or Undone

Here's a list of some things that you should avoid when faced with an angry customer.

1. Unless (and usually even if) you have compelling information, don't attempt to play point-counterpoint with a customer. If you need to rebut some of what's said, pick the most important or compelling issue and stay with that.

2. Don't offer your own list of criticisms of the customer in response. This isn't the issue, and it never helps.

3. Don't shuffle your feet, fidget, turn away, or make like you can't wait for the customer to stop, even though that's how you really feel.

Make It So
Assertive professionals develop good listening skills even if what they're hearing isn't necessarily pleasing to them. The venting of an angry customer will end, and you will have to seek resolution.

What Customers Want to Hear

After venting their spleens, irate customers basically want to know they won't get taken, that resolution is around the corner, and that you or your company acknowledges the legitimacy of the claim. So, be the big person that you are:

1. Take personal responsibility for resolution. "The ball's in my court, and I'll handle it."

2. Express regret over the situation. Note that I said *regret*, not sorrow or apology. It isn't always necessary for you to be apologetic. It is appropriate for you to regret whatever happened. This isn't skirting the issue, it's just using the most appropriate language for the situation.

3. State what you will do. "In order to alleviate this situation I intend to…"

4. Thank the customer for raising this issue. Again, this might be hard for you to do, but if you want to be professionally assertive, you also need to be professionally gracious. By that I mean that if somebody comes to you and presents a situation that perhaps was not easy for them to bring up, acknowledge them for bringing it up.

I'm Worthy—You're Worthy

Handle with Care
Everyone is "incomplete" in one aspect or another. That, however, has nothing to do with your ability to feel complete. They are two separate notions. You'd have to be a perfect human being to be complete in all aspects of your life. So far, human-kind hasn't produced anyone who fits that description. When you *choose* to feel complete, you automatically move in that direction. It's a wonderful process.

A friend of mine created an affirmation that she uses almost every day, particularly in situations in which she otherwise might feel a lack of confidence. The affirmation works well when dealing with customers, whether you're calling on them as part of a sales campaign, handling their complaints, and everything in between.

The affirmation is: *"I choose to easily feel worthy and complete."* Why this wording? By choosing to feel worthy, she's engaging in positive self-talk, which essentially says, "I am up to the challenge. No one else's experience, education, wealth, title, or position need intimidate me. I can hold my own with others. Moreover, I'm a worthy human being, just for being here. I don't have to go out of my way to prove myself; my worth is apparent."

This is a vital concept because if you feel incomplete, as if you lack something that's perpetually out of your grasp, you're not going to be assertive in the face of challenges related to customers.

Walk a Mile in These Spats

You can always rely on the time-honored notion of putting yourself in another person's moccasins. If you and an unhappy customer or client were to switch places, how would you like to be spoken to?

➤ What type of language would have the greatest impact on you?

➤ What tone of voice would be most effective?

➤ How would you like a situation to be approached?

➤ How would you like to be reminded to do something when, indeed, you need to be reminded?

➤ What facial expressions would appeal to you the most when someone makes a request?

The Golden Rule, "Do unto others as you would have them do unto you," or the Platinum Rule, "Do unto others as they would like to have done unto them" as described in Dr. Tony Alessandra's book, *The Platinum Rule,* work exceedingly well with customers. Put these Rules to use with someone the next time you feel challenged.

A Divine Alternative

Suppose you work in customer service and encounter someone who is giving you an exceedingly hard time. Consultant and professional speaker David Eastman suggests an approach that makes sense. "Instead of marshaling my energy to stand strong against opposing forces, I attempt to assertively use the energy of the other to find mutual solutions. First and foremost, this means that I have to see the divine in the other person, even if they're being a jerk!"

At the Conference of World Religions in Chicago way back in 1896, Swami Vivekananda advised attempting to see the divine in everyone. You don't have to be religious in any formal sense to respond openly and assertively with others. Indeed, to be strong, calm, and assertive, Eastman suggests that you attempt to see the divine in yourself as well as in others.

"Neither they nor I take precedence," Eastman says. "It's akin to Dr. Stephen Covey's definition of maturity, which is the balance of courage and consideration—'courage to speak the truth as I know it, and the consideration to be open to hearing and acting upon the other person's truth as well.'"

From this perspective, assertiveness is about clarity of purpose. It's amazing how well this approach to assertiveness works. It saves hurt feelings, energy, and reliance on any methodology or technique.

With Malice Toward None

Dave Yoho, a Fairfax, Virginia-based consultant to businesses worldwide and a renowned platform speaker, tells a tale about Alice Martin that contains a lesson for everyone. Alice is a customer service representative in the auto parts department of a large, metropolitan store. She is skilled in using assertive language.

One day, as Dave tells it, she receives a phone call from an irate customer who is seeking to exchange an expensive set of custom wheels; he's been back to the store twice already, and the latest set contains blemishes. While the customer is shouting and using vile language, Alice gets the necessary information to solve the problem. The customer, growing more impatient, eventually explodes.

"Lady," he screams, "you can take these wheels and shove 'em up your…" The remarks were uncalled for and in bad taste, but Alice keeps her cool.

Calmly she replies, "Sir, I appreciate your offer, but I'm already dealing with a stereo radio and set of hubcaps that were directed to the same part of my anatomy yesterday." Then she pauses.

The customer cannot believe his ears. He pauses, asks her name, and within 40 minutes is standing at her counter laughing. The wheels are exchanged and his problem is solved.

Alice retains a customer for her company—perhaps for YEARS—because of her assertive, effective language skills!

The Least You Need to Know

➤ Customers may not always be right, but they certainly do pay the bills.

➤ Emulating a person's communication pattern and body language enables you to quickly communicate with that person efficiently and effectively.

➤ You can't be all things to all customers, so identify which customers are vital to your business or practice.

➤ If you think there is a problem with a client or customer, there most assuredly is.

➤ Effective language skills can turn an irate customer into a customer for life.

Chapter 26

Collecting What's Yours

In This Chapter

➤ Convincing the slow payers to pay now

➤ Initial agreements, polite reminders, and aggressive strategies

➤ On not going overboard

➤ Small victories, big lessons

Some of your clients or customers, or perhaps even friends or relatives, may be trying to take you for a ride. I didn't want to have to be the one to break the news to you, but somebody's got to tackle the tough assignments. Without telling you in so many words, some people who owe you money may decide that you're going to have work hard to get it. This is when it *literally* pays to be assertive.

As you've seen in some previous chapters, it's sometimes necessary to go beyond the essentials of assertiveness, wherein everyone feels good about the encounter. As with poor customer service, un-neighborly neighbors, and harassment and discrimination, your interactions with slow or non-payers may not leave all parties with smiles on their faces.

Convincing People to Pay You

The nineteenth-century philosopher John Ruskin once said, "In touching money we touch the keystone of character." Wow, did he get that right. It's easy to get upset about the money others owe you, until you acknowledge that you train people how and when to pay you. You either have a coordinated, assertive policy in place, or you have a less than adequate approach to collecting what you've earned.

Make It So

To put it bluntly, you've got to convince the slow payers that the pain of paying you what they owe you will be far less than the inconvenience that they will experience—courtesy of you—if they don't pay!

That'll Be 60 Dollars

Have you noticed how many doctors and dentists have adopted a policy of asking you to pay right now, on your way out the door? Have you considered how many new opportunities there are to use your major credit card at places that aren't even oriented toward retail sales, from the pledge you make during a public television fund-raiser to the pre-made popcorn you order to help a local service organization?

Just the Facts

According to the Marist College Institute For Public Opinion, the number of Americans having money troubles is rising. In their 1995 survey, for example, 20 percent of respondents said that they always have money problems. A year later, 32 percent responded as such.

An Industry Unto Itself

There is a good reason for the demand for immediate payment and acceptance of credit cards as a form of payment. The experience of most businesses is that collecting payment is a difficult, time-consuming activity that is best avoided or, in some instances, left up to the credit companies that specialize in such activity.

Just the Facts

Collecting debts has become a large enough problem to merit its own industry; consider collection departments of sizable stores and companies, independent collection agencies, and accountants and lawyers who specialize in collection problems and litigation. Nationally, delinquent accounts turned over to collection agencies total far more than $20 billion per year, with an estimated additional $25 billion that businesses simply absorb. The collection industry estimates that between 3 and 5 percent of consumer debts and 2 and 4 percent of commercial debts go bad.

The paradox for businesses faced with collection problems is that if things are going well otherwise, it's not hard to overlook a few slow payers or non-payers. If things are going badly, who wants to devote an inordinate amount of time to a task hardly anyone finds enjoyable, especially when there are too many other things to do? When you have to collect from a friend or relative, it's easy to overlook the debt when you don't need the money, and perhaps embarrassing to handle when you do need the money back.

A Dollar Earned Is Not a Dollar Collected

Two women in Oregon started a firm called Northwest Communications. This was the first such firm in their small but growing city. They were able to fill a service vacuum with no competition, and things seemed rosy. The firm soon grew to four full-time staffers, many part-time employees, and a healthy roster of contractors who could be called upon as needed.

Traditionally, you don't ask for payment "up front" in this line of business or as a client is walking out the door. Rather, contracts are signed that include progress payments.

The company dutifully sent invoices as these segments were completed. When customers didn't pay and had to be re-invoiced and phoned, things really got crazy. "I didn't want, and couldn't afford, to work nearly full time chasing down bad accounts," one partner said, "but that's what was happening."

Two years into the business, the region's economy went into a tailspin. Debtors became slow to pay. Some clients filed for bankruptcy and never paid. Others paid their other creditors first, knowing that Northwest Communications would never spend the money or time to really "go after" them.

"The cash flow problem was our downfall," explained the partner. "Oddly enough, we had plenty of clients. We just didn't collect enough of what we earned to pay our bills in time. The business closed just before its third anniversary.

You too may find yourself awaiting repayment from others, funds that could help you when you're in a cash crunch.

The Slower an Account Becomes...

It's a truism of business (and of personal loans) that the slower-paying an account becomes—the slower someone pays on his bill—the more difficult it is to collect. The following table shows the percentages that companies actually manage to collect after certain amounts of time. The amounts unpaid are due to debtors simply refusing to pay any more and companies giving up.

Collection Difficulties Over Time

Time Overdue	Portion That Is Collectable
60 days	89%
6 months	67%
12 months	45%
24 months	23%
36 months	15%

If you can collect payment in full upon making a sale, you will eliminate much of the need to be assertive about collections later. If you're in a profession or industry where it's commonplace to extend credit, however, you'll need to take action to ensure that your customers are current in their payments.

Without getting too much into hard business, here are some options:

Handle with Care
Collecting quickly is usually to your advantage. There are exceptions, however. It's not wise to offend a possibly lucrative, long-term customer because of injudicious collection efforts. It is also bad business when industry norms and customer expectations call for an entirely different approach. Can you imagine trying to collect from a widow the day after the funeral?

➤ Obtain a credit report before you extend credit to someone. A party's credit report contains key information that indicates whether that party generally pays on time or not.

➤ Obtain at least a portion of the fee or charge right away. You might require a deposit, for example.

➤ Require progressive payments, such as one-third of the estimated fee at the start of a project, another third at some agreed-upon midpoint, and the final third upon completion.

➤ If you work on a retainer basis, arrange to have clients transfer your monthly fee into your business account via electronic funds transfer.

➤ Send out your invoices promptly.

➤ Reward prompt payers with an "early bird" discount.

➤ Levy a surcharge on late payers.

Different Kinds of Debtors

Going after people who owe you money is one of the world's greatest drags. Deadbeat accounts require a great deal of assertiveness, the kind that goes beyond having both parties feel good about the transaction. It often means letters, phone calls, and perhaps even aggressive tactics.

What Type of Debtor?

Debtors, whether in your business or personal life, can fall into one of four categories:

1. *Debtors who are negligent.* These debtors have the money and intend to pay, but need reminding.

2. *Debtors who are honest but confused.* Occasionally you encounter some debtors who would have paid on time if they had understood the terms.

3. *Debtors who won't show you the money.* These debtors have the money but make everyone wait or are under-financed and survive by paying slowly.

4. *Debtors who cannot pay.* These debtors say they are temporarily overextended, when in fact they are close to financial ruin.

Handle with Care
Collections usually generate a lot of frustration and plenty of dead ends. If you give up, you don't get paid. If you hang on, you spend a lot of time trying to collect, and you irritate those who hate to see you coming.

I Feel for You

Another way to categorize non-payers is according to how you *feel* about them, and hence how you'll proceed to collect your money. It's more emotional, but often works as well as more rational approaches.

1. *With kid gloves.* Clients who get the kid-glove treatment are those who represent a long-term, viable client who can reward you with more profitable business and/or referrals. With this group, you proceed slowly, carefully, and definitely politely. You treat the money owed as if it were simply an oversight and as if it represents no big deal to your business. You would, however, certainly like to "bring the account up to date."

2. *With shuttle diplomacy.* This approach is reserved for those slow payers who just miss the cut for the kid-glove approach. You're not sure if they represent more business or will provide good word of mouth. They are not contentious, however, and there's no need to jeopardize your relationship with them. You simply like to conduct your business efficiently, including receiving payment in a timely manner.

Handle with Care
Your closest relatives would probably be afforded the kid-glove or shuttle-diplomacy treatment (at least at first!)

3. *With boxing gloves.* You put on these gloves when there's little chance of repeat business, and you wouldn't want it anyway. With these holdouts you make contact frequently and forcefully, while remaining professional. Your objective and message

are clear—to get your money. Here you use a wide variety of tools including mail, phone, and fax in a swift flurry of punches.

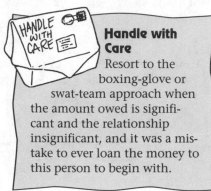

Handle with Care
Resort to the boxing-glove or swat-team approach when the amount owed is significant and the relationship insignificant, and it was a mistake to ever loan the money to this person to begin with.

4. *With the swat team.* You use swat-team techniques when boxing gloves don't work. The business relationship with this customer means absolutely nothing to you. It's your money and they're holding it. All weapons in your collection arsenal are assembled and lined up at the border. These include lawyers, hints of lawsuits, and collection agencies. You let the deadbeat know that you will never let up, the psychology being that it becomes less "painful" for them to pay you than to continue to be subject to your controlled but intense effort to get your money.

Collection Campaigns

There is no foolproof way to ensure that you get your money regardless of the category of debtor. Here's a system, however, that has worked for many people. Think of your collection campaign as having three chronological stages:

1. Initial agreement
2. Polite reminders
3. Aggressive strategies

Let's discuss each of these stages in more detail.

Handle with Care
A customer who is slow to pay for work or goods delivered is likely to be just as slow to pay for various parts of the work or goods during the life of the agreement. Consequently, you might end up in a position of "trying to collect" for one segment. Your leverage is that the customer may want to see the finished work or product badly enough to make segmented payments in a timely manner.

Initial Agreements

Depending upon the product or service in question, it may be possible, although time consuming, to work out an initial agreement about payment terms before work starts. This usually entails some mutually agreeable payment schedule, as discussed earlier. You can introduce such an agreement almost regardless of the size or clout of the customer.

Although the initial agreement may also carry a deadline for final payment (for example, 30 days after completion), don't expect to be immune from delays and excuses. Partial payments with friends or relatives can work, but they have their pitfalls—you might encounter someone who falls behind in making each payment. A written repayment schedule will help keep payments on track. Both parties should keep a copy.

Polite Reminders

Here is when you get to test your mettle. You issue polite reminders when someone starts to fall behind in what they owe you. You can start with follow-up letters, but keep in mind that too many people resort to letters when a polite personal phone call would be faster and easier, depending on the situation. (More on this shortly.)

Check Your Attitude at the Door

Your mental attitude is key to winning at collections both monetarily and emotionally: Try not to get discouraged or irritated. Your loss of temper or failure to control your emotions can creep into your letters and other communiqués and affect their quality.

If you are harsh, sarcastic, or whiny, you'll actually hinder your collection campaign. If your loan was to a friend or relative, you could irrevocably damage the quality of the relationship, even if *he* owes *you* the money and is the one holding up payment. Conversely, firmness and confidence bolster one another. Your quest is to apply pressure at distinct intervals in different degrees to vanquish the slow payer's resistance.

Make It So
Your notices are most effective when they're sent directly to the department and preferably to the correct individual in the company from whom you wish to collect. This person is probably *not* the individual or department you initially had contact with, so you will need to research the situation (see "Reach Out and Touch Someone," later in this chapter).

With Software to Guide You

"Debt collection" software is available today to assist you in your collection efforts. Many programs offer several copies of collection letters that you can readily adapt and send. If you model your letters after them, you can cut down on any chance of letting your emotions find their way into your letters. Some programs allow you to choose the order of letters and documents that you want to send, and then preselect what days they will be sent on. To see the latest programs that are available, visit a store like Walden Software or Egghead Software, or flip through the ads in *Entrepreneur, Inc.* or *Nation's Business* magazine.

Do not, however, necessarily proceed in your collection efforts at regular intervals. Many debtors understand such progressions and use the knowledge to delay payment for as long as possible. Thus, feel free to alter the strength and timing of your appeals.

Be Specific and Creative

To issue an effective polite reminder (that is, a collection letter) you need to do something other than merely copy the original invoice with "Payment Overdue" stamped on it. Instead, include specific information about the agreement, order, or contract for which payment is due, including:

➤ A description of the goods or services involved

➤ Details regarding the completion date and first invoice

➤ Details regarding any related written or oral agreements

➤ A self-addressed, stamped reply envelope

Use different letters, envelopes, sizes, shapes, colors, and so forth to keep the debtor off-balance. Many champion bill collectors have found it useful to add a personal, narrative letter with the collection letter. The personal letter appeals to the customer's sense of fair play, reputation, or self-interest. Such narratives may require your increasing assertiveness as overdue accounts linger on.

Use language that appeals to the other party's sense of fairness and justice. For example:

"A prompt remittance will be greatly appreciated."

"Please mail us a check, we've earned it."

"Please give this your attention today."

"Please! This account is past due and we'd like to complete the transaction."

"Would you please tell us the reason why you've withheld the payment?"

"As a reminder, paying bills promptly builds a good credit record."

"Credit is a sacred trust."

"The small profit we might have had in this transaction has been more than absorbed by our collection efforts."

"Whatever the reason, your check and an explanation from you would certainly be appreciated."

"Perhaps my earlier letters were not referred to you."

"You may have inadvertently overlooked this invoice."

"Evidently you've overlooked or forgotten our notice as we've had no word from you about your account. Will you assure us of your willingness to cooperate in this matter by sending us your payment now?"

Sometimes it's helpful to know why a payment is being withheld. If so, try to get the debtor to at least explain the delay by writing something back to you. This puts him into a person-to-person situation. You can also try using registered mail with a return receipt requested. The chances are that the debtor will read such a letter personally and perhaps make a response.

On a personal loan, you can bypass most of this stuff and simply call or ask about payment when you're face to face.

Personalized Collection Letters

Now, using these recommendations and insights, craft a friendly but specific and guilt-inducing letter that gets the other party right in the old conscience (assuming they have one!). For example:

```
Good morning, Bob Anderson...

I'm writing about the invoice for $1,800 we submitted to you on Febru-
ary 12th for the six cartons of widgets you ordered. Eleven weeks have
passed since you received shipment, and frankly, I'm concerned—I
haven't heard from you and haven't been able to get a return phone
call.

I don't have the financial capability to sustain a strong cash flow
when faced with outstanding payment due, or the desire to pursue col-
lection efforts. Like you, I've got a payroll to meet, considerable
overhead, and a host of other expenses.

Thus far, we haven't received payment from you, nor any indication of
why you have withheld payment for this long. I know you want to make
good on your financial obligations—we certainly hope to continue to be
your widget supplier.

I'd like to request payment in full at this time, or if that's not
possible, 50 percent payment and a call or note from you indicating
when you will send the balance. I think my request is fair and know
that you understand and appreciate our situation.

Here's to a great spring...I look forward to hearing from you.

Yours truly,

Looie DaMoneelenda
```

In addition to this letter, here is a wonderful catch-all phrase you can use if you suspect that the other party is on the verge of paying:

> "If you have already mailed your payment, please consider this a thank you instead of the friendly reminder it is intended to be."

Turn Up the Dial

If your letters are ignored, you may wish to turn up the dial on persuasive language. Here are some key phrases that I've used that can be marvelously effective:

"I am at a loss to understand why your account has not been paid." (With a friend or relative, you might say, "I'm at a loss to understand why you're putting me through this.")

"It was my understanding that you are an able professional, of the highest integrity who pays all bills promptly."

"I can't believe that you want this charge to be further overdue."

"I find it most difficult to write a reminder letter to a worthy customer such as you who has let his account run long overdue without any word of explanation."

Reach Out and Touch Someone

Phone calls can certainly also serve as polite reminders. You can use all of the language presented previously, adapted to how you speak and interact as part of the script during your call. Sometimes the mere act of calling and asserting yourself is all that's necessary. If you're dealing with a company, be aware that the larger the company, the more likely you'll have to make a number of calls before you find anyone who even knows about the account. Often that individual isn't likely to have the authority to actually pay the account.

> **Handle with Care**
>
> Be warned. The person with whom you speak may be well schooled in the "check is in the mail" run-around. His or her easiest tactic may be to agree, apologize profusely, get you off the phone, and ultimately, do nothing. Then, you wait for payment and start all over again, with more calls and letters.

You can use your fax machine to collect, if you keep your faxes very polite. If you know that the fax on the receiving end is in a public location, carefully consider whether using a fax reminder is appropriate for the situation, client, and sum in question.

If you have the correct person's e-mail address, a polite e-mail message could be the magic elixir.

Aggressive Strategies

When people owe you money and time is passing, say it's been three months or more, you may need to resort to aggressive collection strategies. These can be expensive, involving collection agencies and/or lawyers, and they often mean losing customers or clients who feel you are being difficult and heavy-handed. Some debtors, however, will only pay if *forced* to do so.

It's your money, and if you've got a customer who's swat-team material, it's pointless to beat around the bush any further. If you lose a client who doesn't pay, you're no worse off in many respects.

Pay, or Pay the Consequences

If you have reached a point where the debtor is totally uncooperative, tell them that you will be forced to bring in a third party to resolve the matter. At all times, avoid libelous statements in whatever you write. Without getting into heavy legal stuff, a libelous letter that passes through the hands of a secretary or clerk is considered "published" and can leave you (the letter writer) open to suit for damages for liability even if the statements are true. Also, don't write or put anything on the outside of the envelope that impugns the character or conduct of another, or that indicates it's a collection letter.

For example, these statements could be considered libelous:

> "We must assume from your silence that you do not intend to pay." (This implies you know something about the other party, which you cannot prove.)

> "The ABC Collection Agency knows how to handle non-payers." (This labels the other party as a non-payer, but if the party *does* pay, then the statement becomes false.)

Word Power
When what you write about another person is harmful or untrue, or intends to harm or malign them, your letter is said to be *libelous* and the other party can take legal action against you!

The following statements, however, are *not* liable, merely factual:

> "Unfortunately, our patience is exhausted."

> "If you send your check immediately, it will reach us in time to forestall any unpleasant action."

You can threaten a civil suit, but don't threaten to invoke any law that may call for criminal prosecution, because non-payment of an account on credit is rarely, if ever, considered a criminal act.

Weget Yourmoney Incorporated

In deciding whether or not to retain a collection agency, there are two factors to consider right off the bat:

1. Using an agency can take up a great deal of your time. You'll have to fill out forms, document your case, and spend more time on the phone with the agency.

Handle with Care
The older an account becomes, the more difficult it is to collect. Thus, use collection agencies quickly when circumstances warrant. As a general rule, however, don't use a collection agency unless you've exhausted all other means and you're prepared to sever business relations.

2. If you're assertive, a collection agency may not be any more effective than you could be.

Handle with Care

Avoid turning over dozens of slow-paying accounts to a collection agency right away—you need to get a feel for how the agency operates and how effective it is.

As in any industry or profession, there are many mediocre and poor collection agencies. Ask for referrals from others in business, your banker, accountant, or attorney. Also ask Small Business Administration Officials or your local Chamber of Commerce.

Ask collection agencies themselves for letters from satisfied clients or, barring that, names and phone numbers of satisfied clients. Then call the clients. If you're satisfied with the referrals, turn one or two accounts over to the agency. If you're pleased with the results, try more.

These days, many accountants and attorneys will undertake collection efforts for you, and some banks will assist you by writing a letter to the offending party on behalf of your business.

Whomever you may use, check out the company's policies and operations. Using a collection agency doesn't mean you can forget about the account and go back to work. After all, just like your overdue customers, they have to set priorities, and your collection may not be at the top of their list. You'll also want to track your collection agency's success rate. If you feel that they are not working hard enough, you may be better off on your own.

Weesue and Associates

When somebody has really owed you a lot of money for a long time, it's tempting to go too far in terms of threats and harassment. Watch out—the cost of collecting can exceed the payment due!

Here are some typical ways you can get into trouble that might end up being more costly than the money owed to you:

➤ Bringing suits for reasons other than collecting.

➤ Using overly aggressive collectors. Collectors who overstep their bounds leave the creditor wide open to legal action.

➤ Invading the debtor's right of privacy in attempting to get payment (such as showing up with a bullhorn outside the non-payer's house).

➤ Using threats that may be interpreted as extortion or blackmail.

As you escalate your attempts to collect, you may need to hire a lawyer to advise you of how far you can go and to keep you from overstepping the law. If you choose not to use an attorney, but want to stay on relatively safe ground, once again software can help. One program includes more than two dozen "legally sound" court documents you can use to speed up any legal claims you may wish to make. In any case, you need to avoid being sued yourself!

The Least You Need to Know

➤ It's easy to get upset about the money others owe you, until you acknowledge that you train customers how and when to pay you.

➤ The slower-paying an account becomes, the more difficult it is to collect.

➤ Segment your collections based on how you feel about the debtor.

➤ The three stages of collecting are the initial agreement, polite reminders, and aggressive strategies.

➤ Once you commit to aggressive collection strategies, prepare to sever the relationship with the customer.

➤ A variety of highly useful debt collection software programs are available.

Chapter 27

Assert Yourself, Now and Forever

In This Chapter

➤ Assert for the good of all

➤ Sometimes you'll be wrong

➤ Alternative forms of assertiveness

➤ The future belongs to the audacious

Once you put into practice the skills you've learned in this book, the payoff will come over and over again. You may one day find, however, that merely being assertive for yourself or your immediate family is not in itself fulfilling.

Soon enough, you'll realize that the true gift of assertiveness is being able to speak on behalf of a cause—for the downtrodden, the weary, the meek, or those who cannot speak for themselves. This wrap-up chapter will catapult you onto the path of speaking out to over-turn the injustices in everyday life. Heck, you might even become some group's spokesperson!

Practice Your New Skills for a Lifetime Payoff

My sister Nancy recently moved to Manhattan. One night she was having dinner with a friend when a customer at the take-out counter started speaking in a loud voice that disturbed the entire restaurant: "THAT'S NOT WHAT I WANTED!" "WHAT ELSE DO YOU HAVE?" "NO, NO, NO. CAN'T YOU GET ANYTHING RIGHT?" This "patron" started to leave the restaurant, but was still shouting at the person behind the counter. Everyone in the restaurant was aghast. As he made his way to the door, my sister finally said, "Hey, you can't talk to somebody like that. You ought to be ashamed of yourself." The man took a look at her across the crowded restaurant, and then left without saying anything more. My sister (without the benefit of this book!) asserted herself on behalf of the restaurant employee, to the relief of the patrons, and, when you think about it, for the good of society. Sure, the man could have been deranged, but in a crowded restaurant it's not likely that Nancy was in any danger.

What Do You See?

How many times do you see teenagers who act in ways in which any fully functioning adult would disapprove? How about kids who deface property? If you don't say anything, and the next adult doesn't say anything, guess what? They'll keep doing it!

Yes, I know there are arguments about butting in, and there are also safety concerns. But what if every time a teenager swore loudly publicly, numerous adults spoke up?

Suppose any time young children stepped out of line—did something that was clearly socially unacceptable—any number of adults were ready to step in and say, "Young man (or young lady), I don't think that's appropriate behavior"? Soon enough, in a year, perhaps a month, maybe only a week, much, if not all of the delinquency, truancy, and antisocial behavior that some youths exhibit would begin to dissipate. People would begin to toe the line.

Back of the Line, Jack

Once, I was waiting in line for a huge multi-family yard sale to begin.

I had been waiting for several minutes when another more recent line began to form across the street from us. The people in the new line had clearly arrived long after the people in the original line, and they pretended that they didn't see us. They milled about, waiting for the gates to open, so that they could rush in and be amongst the first.

I looked at the situation and was silently, mildly upset. Like the others in my line, I did nothing, for a while. Suddenly, my strategy came to me. I spotted an event organizer who was in full view of the phenomenon but who apparently chose not to make waves. I told her "Some of these people have been waiting here 30 to 40 minutes. Could you please say something to the people in the new line?" She agreed to. I went back to my place in line.

She walked over to the people in the new line, and I don't know what she said, but most of them went to the back of our line. Some still milled around, pretending they didn't hear her or see us. I wasn't going to be any more militant for the day.

As most of the renegade line broke up, a miraculous thing happened. The people in my line let out a round of applause and cheering. You see, everybody felt the same way, but no one wanted to assert himself. Hundreds of people in my line were willing to let this minor but clearly unfair situation exist. Yet any one of the individuals in my line could have done the same thing, and hence put the universe back in order, at least as far as this mini-drama goes.

Cross-Cultural Assertiveness

I didn't write this book merely so that you could gain your best advantage in work and in life. I wrote it so that society could improve, in little ways, here and there, one day at a time, for the long run.

The Welfare of Those Who Can't Speak

I was in Vietnam with my best friend Peter in February 1996. We were touring Saigon, now known as Ho Chi Minh City. We made our way to the zoo. Once inside, after strolling about for ten minutes, we saw some teenage boys who were apparently taunting one of the animals. I came up to them and in English said "All right, that's enough."

A couple of the boys looked as if they were drunk, even though this was mid-day. Their crazed look was a little scary. Again, I said to them, "That's enough." I didn't know whether they spoke English or not. They seemed to get the message. They moved on, joking and laughing, probably about those crazy Americans.

My friend said to me, "Jeff, this is their country and their zoo." Instinctively I said to him, "Peter, you know, though, abusing animals is wrong everywhere. I had to say it." He quickly understood.

Getting the Network in Place

Suppose those same kids went to another section of the zoo and did the same things, and somebody else came along and told them to stop. Suppose another day they did something else that clearly represented inappropriate behavior and somebody told them to stop. How long would it take before they got the idea that some of the behaviors they were exhibiting were not acceptable?

Suppose when they did something good an adult came along and said, "Nice job," "Good going," "Way to go," or "I appreciate your efforts"? How long would it take before they went out of their way to start doing things that got that kind of response? I think you're beginning to understand the whole enchilada. It's a simple psychological principle: Behavior that's rewarded is repeated.

If you are nervous about these tactics, start at home. If every parent took these tactics with their own children, we'd be off to a great start.

The Unlikely Event

There are situations where asserting yourself leads to trouble, but they are rare and fleeting. I recall playing volleyball on Monday evenings with the Washington D.C. Sports Club in the late 1970s. We played near the Lincoln Memorial almost overlooking the Potomac. It was a wonderful setting, and a wonderful time to be in Washington.

One evening, two men were playing volleyball on a court that was reserved for our group. One of them maintained a demeanor that was almost menacing. He was 6'3", built like a heavyweight prize fighter, and aggressive as all heck.

We told these two that it was time for our group to play. They didn't want to relinquish the court. They suggested that they play against our team. At first we didn't understand. They wanted to play two against six of us. As you can guess, we weren't happy about that.

We could have taken them but that wasn't the point. We play six against six. We would have let them join us had they been more accommodating. They decided, however, to stand their ground. They would not leave the court unless we agreed to play them six against two. They kept batting the ball back and forth to each other.

Time was passing, and the situation was getting ridiculous. I walked up to the big one and reached out to tap him on the shoulder as I said, "Say, don't you think that…" As fast as lightning, as I was tapping his shoulder, he whirled around to the left and hit me point-blank in the solar plexus.

I had no idea that this guy had a hair-trigger temper. As soon as he hit me, others jumped into the court, and while keeping their distance from him, verbally bade him to tone it down. In a couple of minutes, a member of the U.S. Park Police came by—apparently someone had flagged him down. The officer issued a citation and told the two to leave.

Make It So

Please don't let the long-shot odds of you being harmed diminish your potential for asserting yourself for the good of others around you and the good of society in general.

Two weeks later I appeared in court, somewhat concerned about encountering this guy again. Still, I felt it was important to see this thing through. He never showed. I asked the court what the procedure was, they said he would be picked up by the police and held until bond was posted. I left that evening, and fortunately never saw him again.

The point of all this? Every now and then, when attempting to assert yourself, you will encounter someone who flies off the handle. In my case, it's only been once in more than 40 years.

Yes, there are people who grab guns from their cars and shoot fellow motorists at California highways. Yes, there are people who spray bullets at passengers on New York subway cars. For the most part, these incidents do not occur in response to someone having asserted himself, verbally, moments before. The odds are that you'll never encounter any situation like that.

Good behavior that's rewarded is repeated. Antisocial behavior that is allowed in the absence of any other cues is also going to get repeated. For the good of society, go out and assert yourself all day long. Will you be wrong on occasion? Yes.

Will there be times when you shouldn't have put your two cents in? Yes.

Will some people say "Butt out"? Yes.

All of this and more will happen, but the net effect is that things will improve in your neighborhood, in your town, and all around you if enough people assert themselves responsibly as situations unfold.

A Variety of Alternatives

Suppose you're absolutely not going to speak out in a public place. Nevertheless, there are a variety of ways that you can assert yourself when you feel the situation merits it. Let's revisit some of the previous scenarios and see what else can be done.

Fortify Those Who Need It

In the case of the man berating the restaurant worker, maybe it's not your cup of tea to say anything to such an individual. What else could you do? How about going up to the person who was berated and offering some nurturing language such as the following:

➤ "He had no right to speak to you that way and I want you to know that everyone here was glad to see him go."

➤ "I don't know what started that, but it's clear that his manner and demeanor were uncalled for. By the way, we like the food and the service here—that's why we come so often."

➤ "I thought you handled that as well as you could under the circumstances. Who knows what that guy's problems are? You're doing a good job and there's no need to give that fellow a second thought."

Find Someone in Authority

Let's revisit the zoo situation. What else could you do? The most obvious action to take would be to go find a zoo official. Never mind all that stuff you heard when you were growing up about not being a "tattle-tale" on others.

Make It So
There are times when reporting inappropriate behavior of others to authorities is not only acceptable, but the right thing to do.

Too many books written in the last two decades blather on and on about how it's inappropriate to judge others and that the only true path to peace is to be nonjudgmental! This is, of course, unmitigated hogwash. Yes, self-help gurus and authors are prudent when they urge you to be less judgmental of others and more tolerant. It would certainly make for a better world.

315

Make It So
Do make judgment calls, at least as far as others' behavior is concerned. Go find a zoo official or security guard or whomever and report what you've observed.

Clearly, however, there is behavior of others that is socially detrimental. My mother told me when I was young that a good way to determine if the behavior of others is socially acceptable is to imagine that the behavior was repeated by everyone else. If everyone gave restaurant personnel a good tongue-lashing and then stormed out, it wouldn't be long before no one would enjoy themselves sitting in a restaurant and the entire industry would come to a halt. If everyone taunted and abused animals in zoos, it wouldn't be long before the very nature of the zoo-going experience would change, and the well-being and lives of the animals themselves would be in jeopardy.

Threaten to Boycott

Let's revisit the situation in which a mass of people have decided to form their own line to bypass others who have been waiting for a long time. Other than going up to an organizing official as I did, what else could you do? As an after-the-fact gesture, you could speak to the organizing hosts and suggest that you and others will not attend in the future unless some form of effective line control is installed. What isn't effective? Giving the people in the other line dirty looks—especially if they're not looking at you! Also, calling out to them from your line. That's likely to cause resentment and bitter feelings as opposed to resolving the situation amicably.

Letters to the Editor

Whether it's your local newspaper, an industry or trade magazine, or some other public printed forum, you always have the opportunity to send letters to the editor. Don't dismiss the potential power of this assertiveness vehicle.

In many magazines, the letters to the editor section represents public forums wherein lively debates ensue. When I peruse such publications, I frequently read the letters to the editor section first. Often I encounter well-crafted, thoughtful letters from obviously well-educated individuals. This stimulates my thinking, and on occasion even prompts me to change my opinion on some matter. Hence, the assertiveness of the author of the letter to the editor certainly prevailed in influencing me.

More Ways to Assert

Other options for asserting yourself, other than directly confronting specific individuals, are discussed in the following sections.

Voting

Undoubtedly you've heard stories about how one vote swung an entire election. One day, some place, perhaps at the local level, your vote will be the one. Until that time, it still makes sense for you to assert yourself via voting for several reasons:

1. All elections these days on the national, state, and local level are carefully examined by political pundits, reporters, campaign advisors, political action committees, special-interest groups, and the citizenry themselves. If you vote for a candidate who has particular views, even if that candidate loses, if he or she was able to garner a large following, information is imparted to others as to how a particular community, state, or entire country is moving. Hence, your vote can help to ultimately sway public opinion.

2. The mere act of voting often prompts you to take stands on other issues in other ways. Taking time out from work, or getting out of the house early some rainy Tuesday morning to cast your vote is a self-reinforcing gesture.

3. Perhaps most importantly, when you vote, and your particular candidate happens to win, you're more likely to feel as if you have a stake in government.

4. If your candidate doesn't win, perhaps you'll be more vigilant in examining the winning candidate's activities and record so as to hold the officer accountable.

Make Donations

If you support a political candidate, a group that's doing good work, or a cause in which you fully believe, assert yourself with your checkbook. If enough like-minded individuals do the same, even donations of $25 or $50 will have an impact.

Becoming Active

There is a wonderful book by Jeff Hollender titled, *How to Make the World a Better Place* (W.W. Norton, 1995). It shows you how you can make a difference in helping to achieve change on a local, national, or even global level. The book offers scores of simple strategies you can implement immediately, including:

➤ Making your community a safer place to live

➤ Helping the homeless

➤ Protecting the environment

➤ Reducing violence on television

➤ Controlling government spending

➤ Reducing discrimination

It also lists hundreds of civic, social, public, and philanthropic societies and includes names, addresses, and contact numbers so that you can follow through on your commitment.

Volunteer

Voting and making donations are useful and appropriate but relatively passive compared to becoming active and volunteering. *How to Make the World a Better Place* can also be a great resource if you're interested in volunteering your time or talents for a cause that you deem worthy.

Make It So

Action is invigorating. Go serve soup in a soup kitchen, or volunteer to answer the phone during pledge week at your public broadcasting station. You can't fix the whole world, but you can help a small part of it. You can assert yourself and make a real difference in an area that you deem worthwhile.

You can find such causes in your own community. Call your Chamber of Commerce, local United Way, town hall, editor of your newspaper's community page, or public affairs director of any local radio or television station to obtain names of groups seeking volunteers. Often, you'll have more than enough names and phone numbers of contact people within groups who are working in your community to make it a better place.

I know it's not easy to volunteer your time in this fast-paced society. Nevertheless, if you want to assert yourself in a highly-effective, hands-on, visible way, volunteering could be your cup of tea.

Encourage Others to Be Assertive

If you teach a course on public speaking, writing, making presentations, or interviewing for a job, you have the opportunity to help others to be effectively assertive.

Make It So

Are you a parent? If so, you have the opportunity to raise assertive children.

Perhaps you teach foreign-born students who are learning English as a second language. Maybe you're a counselor in a shelter for battered spouses. Or you're a Boy Scout or Girl Scout troop master. In all these cases, you have the opportunity to help other people to be more effective in their lives. Are you a columnist, or perhaps a book author yourself? If so, you have the opportunity to influence your readers.

Following is just a partial list of social, civic, and charitable groups you can join:

Active Corps of Executives	Jaycees
American Cancer Society	Kiwanis
American Heart Association	League of Women Voters
American Legion	Lions Clubs

Boys Club	Girls Club
March of Dimes	Masons
Catholic Youth Organization	Public Television
Civitans	Rotary Club
Easter Seal Campaign	Salvation Army
Elks	Scouts of America
Explorers	United Way
Garden Clubs	YMCA or YWCA
Goodwill Industries	VFW (Veterans of Foreign War)
Historical Society	Literacy Volunteers
Humane Society	

Practice Your New Skills for a Lifetime Payoff

Once you become comfortable asserting yourself in specific situations, look to expand your range. If you're good at speaking before a small group, look for the opportunity to speak to a larger group. If you're good at holding your own with co-workers, perhaps it's time to start being heard by some of the higher-ups in your organization.

In a different world, assertiveness skills wouldn't be so important. I wish the world were concocted differently. I wish that by doing a good job you would get the recognition and rewards that you deserve. I wish that people would see the real you without you having to help them. I wish the better-qualified, more worthy candidate always won in elections.

But since none of these is likely to happen with regularity, it behooves you and me to continually take advantage of opportunities to assert ourselves all the time.

Make It So
Each time you expand your repertoire—the range of situations in which you're able to effectively assert yourself—you're really laying the groundwork for creating a brand new you. When you put your skills into practice over and over again you're paving the way for a lifetime payoff.

Assert Until It's Second Nature

As with any new skill, at first things may seem a little shaky. If you work with computers, think about the first time you ever used word processing software on a computer. By contrast, think about your proficiency in using whatever word processing software you're using today. I'll bet you and your computer are almost one, and getting words down on a page is almost second nature to you. So it is with any skill, especially assertiveness.

If you keep stretching yourself, eventually you find that one bright morning you wake up, and not even thinking about it, you're a wholly assertive person. You can speak up when you want to and need to and even make the other party feel good about the interaction. In those few cases where you need to vigorously assert yourself regardless of how the other party will feel, you can do that as well.

There Is Genius in Boldness

In an increasingly crowded, over-communicated, frenzied world, it's not likely that your opportunity to stand out simply by being who you are and doing the job you're doing is going to increase. If anything, the odds are that without assertiveness skills, you may be lost in the shuffle, whether it's within your organization, community, or elsewhere.

I wish that things were different, but they aren't. I wish that shy and retiring types, the meek and mild, and the non-assertive people in general among us could comfortably traverse within society and attain the same benefits and rewards as their more assertive counterparts.

But until that day, which unfortunately, may not happen in your lifetime, the assertive shall prevail.

Boldly Go Where You've Never Gone Before

For the heck of it, if I were to ask you to jot down ten ways you can assert yourself where you once feared to, what might you come up with?

Here are some suggestions for you. This is a wild and crazy list and you may not entertain all of them. If, however, you can gravitate to even a handful of these suggestions, you'll stretch your assertiveness muscle.

➤ Run for public office.

➤ Stand up to your boss the next time you're chewed out.

➤ Directly confront movie patrons who are talking loudly.

➤ Go up to someone who you find remarkably attractive and engage in a pleasant, sustained conversation.

➤ Request that your bank give you a huge loan (presuming that you have a specific profitable business venture in mind).

➤ End a long-term friendship that lost all meaning, spark, and enthusiasm for you years ago.

➤ Defend your gender in the midst of substantial numbers of the opposite sex who've made unflattering remarks.

➤ March into your boss' office and ask for a raise and mean it, even if it's months away from the designated time in which raises usually occur.

➤ Serve on the honor court of your school, whereby you preside over cases where students have been accused of wrongdoing.

➤ Act as moderator for a publicly aired forum or debate.

➤ Volunteer to have a significant speaking part in your company's eight-minute promotional video.

➤ Visit an elected official and directly present your views on a controversial issue.

➤ Take an unpopular stand (but one that you believe is correct) in a letter to the editor in your local newspaper.

➤ Request that the manager at your supermarket remove the magazines and periodicals with lurid covers from the checkout area and out of the view of children.

➤ Tell the barber or stylist to stop cutting your hair as soon as you see that he or she is not giving you what you want.

➤ Thank those who have been helpful to you, such as a bus driver, police officer, mail carrier, or delivery person.

If you're thinking to yourself, gee, these aren't so wild, good! The task now is to put three or four of them into action in the next day or so. Then revisit the list and implement some others.

The Future Belongs to the Bold

Suppose you wanted me to summarize the whole book into one paragraph that covers when and where to you assert yourself.

➤ When does it make sense?

➤ When is it worth the effort?

I say when in doubt, let it out! In other words, the next time you're in a meeting or listening to someone and you're thinking to yourself, "Should I speak up here? Maybe it will be more trouble than it's worth," I suggest to you that that's probably a good time to assert yourself.

Trust the Inner You

Yes, occasionally you will go overboard and say too much. There will also be times when in retrospect it would have been better if you had said nothing. This will happen. This is life. You'll learn from those encounters and get better at training yourself to know when it's time to speak up. Still, heed your internal voice. If you think you ought to say something, the chances are extremely good that yes, this is an instance in which it makes

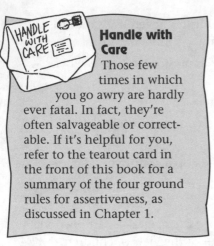

Handle with Care
Those few times in which you go awry are hardly ever fatal. In fact, they're often salvageable or correctable. If it's helpful for you, refer to the tearout card in the front of this book for a summary of the four ground rules for assertiveness, as discussed in Chapter 1.

sense for you to speak up. Don't let the handful of times where you err block you from the multitude of other times in which asserting yourself is appropriate.

I close with a memorable quote:

"This is the true joy in life, the being used for a purpose recognized by yourself as a mighty one; the being a force of nature instead of a feverish, selfish little clod of ailments and grievances complaining that the world will not devote itself to making you happy. I am of the opinion that my life belongs to the whole community and as long as I live it is my privilege to do for it whatever I can. I want to be thoroughly used up when I die, for the harder I work the more I live. I rejoice in life for its own sake. Life is no brief candle to me. It is a sort of splendid torch which I have got hold of for the moment, and I want to make it burn as brightly as possible before handing it on to future generations."

—George Bernard Shaw, *Man and Superman*

The Least You Need to Know

➤ The true gift of assertiveness is being able to speak on behalf of a cause—for the downtrodden, the weary, the meek, or those who cannot speak for themselves.

➤ Behavior that's rewarded is repeated.

➤ To determine whether the behavior of others is socially acceptable, imagine that the behavior was repeated by everyone else.

➤ Don't let the handful of times where you err block you from the multitude of times when asserting yourself is appropriate.

➤ You can't fix the whole world, but you can help a small part of it. You can assert yourself in an area worthwhile to you.

Further Reading

Ailes, Roger. *You Are the Message* (BusinessOne Irwin, 1986).

Alessandra, Dr. Tony. *The Platinum Rule* (Warner, 1996).

Bate, Barbara. *Communication and the Sexes* (Harper & Rowe, 1988).

Caposy, John. *Why Climb the Corporate Ladder When You Can Take the Elevator?* (Villard, 1994).

Carnegie, Dale. *How to Win Friends and Influence People* (Pocket Books, 1994).

Connor, Richard, and Jeff Davidson. *Marketing Your Consulting & Professional Services* (Wiley, 1997).

Daniels, Dr. Aubrey. *Bringing Out the Best in People* (McGraw-Hill, 1994).

Davidson, Jeff. *Blow Your Own Horn: How to Get Noticed and Get Ahead* (Berkley, 1991).

Davidson, Jeff. *Breathing Space: Living & Working at a Comfortable Pace in a Sped-Up Society* (MasterMedia, 1991).

Davidson, Jeff. *The Complete Idiot's Guide to Managing Time* (Macmillan, 1995).

Davidson, Jeff. *The Complete Idiot's Guide to Managing Stress* (Macmillan, 1997).

Davidson, Jeff. *The Speaker's Little Book of Wisdom* (ICS Books, 1998).

Dyer, Dr. Wayne. *How to be a No Limit Person* (Berkley, 1980).

Dyer, Dr. Wayne. *Pulling Your Own Strings* (HarperCollins, 1991).

Ellis, Dr. Albert, and Dr. Arthur Lang. *How to Keep People From Pushing Your Buttons* (Birch Lane Press, 1994).

Farrell, Dr. Warren. *Why Men Are the Way They Are* (McGraw-Hill, 1986).

Gallagher, Winifred, I.D. *How Heredity and Experience Make You Who You Are* (Random House, 1996).

Golding, William. *The Lord of the Flies* (Riverhead, 1997).

Hollender, Jeff. *How to Make the World a Better Place* (Norton, 1995).

Horn, Sam. *Tung Fu: The Art of Verbal Self-Defense* (St. Martin's, 1996).

Keyes, Ralph. *Nice Guys Finish Seventh: False Phrases, Spurious Sayings, and Familiar Misquotations* (HarperCollins,1992).

Moore, Thomas. *Care of the Soul* (Harper Perennial, 1994).

Morris, Dr. Desmond. *The Human Animal* (Crown, 1995).

Patterson, James, and Kim Peter. *The Day America Told the Truth* (Prentice Hall Press, 1990).

Powell, Colin. *My American Journey* (Random House, 1996).

Sabah, Joe. *How to Get the Job You Really Want and Get Employers to Call You* (Self-published, 1996).

Seligman, Dr. Martin. *Learned Optimism* (Pocket Books, 1992).

Shaw, George Bernard. *Man and Superman* (Viking, 1950).

Tannen, Dr. Deborah. *You Just Don't Understand: Women and Men in Conversation* (Ballantine, 1994).

Tannen, Dr. Deborah. *That's Not What I Meant!* (Ballantine, 1994).

Yoho, Dave, and Jeff Davidson. *How to Have a Good Year Every Year* (Berkley Books, 1991).

Index

C

Call for Action, 214
calls, 221-222, 228-232
  government agencies,
    221-222, 228-232
    chain of command,
      222, 231-232
    phrases, 230
    response time, 228-229
    tips, 228-229
    voice mail, 229-230
  holding, 205-206
  payment collection,
    303, 306
  shopping by phone, 206
career coaching, 80-81
cars
  buying, 216
  repairing, 215
chain of command,
  government agencies, 222,
  231-232
challenges
  businesses, 44-46
  non-native speakers,
    193-196
characteristics of
  assertiveness, 4-5, 78-79
children
  birth order, 155
  bossiness vs. assertiveness,
    teaching differences, 156
  communicating with,
    151-156
    guidelines, 152-153
    phrases, 153-156
    rewarding children,
      154-155
    techniques, 151-152
  guidelines, 198
  helping, appropriate
    situations, 31

parents/children, 157-160
  criticisms, 159
  guidelines, 158-160
practicing, 200
tips, 199-200
young adults, 198-200
see also family
city government
  *Directory of City Policy
    Officials*, 230
  *National Directory of
    Addresses*, 231
  see also government
clavicular-shoulder
  breathing, 62
clients, *see* customers
co-workers, 266-273
  criticisms, 269-271
  getting to know, 266
  groups
    becoming part of, 266
    strategies, 272-273
  listening, 267-268
  networking, 267
  non-assertiveness, 264
  perceptions, 39, 265-266
  phrases, 269
  rhetorical questions, 271
  tension between, 265-266
coaching, 80-81
collecting payments, 298-
309
  collection agencies, 298,
    307-308
  collection letters
    guidelines, 303-304
    libelous statements, 307
    phrases, 304, 306
    samples, 305
  customers
    relationships with
      businesses, 301-302
    types, 301

e-mail, 306
faxes, 306
legal aspects, 307-309
libelous statements, 307
phone calls, 303, 306
repayment schedules, 302
software, 303
time, 299-300
tips, 300
*Communication and the
  Sexes*, 121
communication techniques,
  see specific topics
competition, business
  strategies, 44
complaints, 164-165
  letters
    apartment/house
      problems, 210
    guidelines, 208-211
    samples, 209, 211
  purchases, 208
    Call for Action, 214
    company headquarters,
      finding, 208
    tips, 207-208
*Complete Idiot's Guide to
  Managing Stress, The*, 82
confidence,
  see self-confidence
confrontations with
  neighbors
    appropriate time, 170
    as a neighborhood,
      168-169
    legal aspects, 171-172
    mediation services,
      170-171
    record-keeping, 171-172
consumer situations
  cars
    buying, 216
    repairing, 215

T

U-V

A Little Knowledge Goes a Long Way ...

Check Out These
Best-Selling
COMPLETE IDIOT'S GUIDES

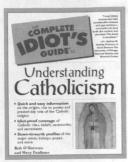

Understanding Catholicism

0-02-863639-2
$16.95

Learning Spanish on Your Own
SECOND EDITION

0-02-862743-1
$16.95

The Bible

0-02-862728-8
$16.95

Feng Shui
SECOND EDITION

0-02-864339-9
$18.95

Playing the Guitar
SECOND EDITION

0-02-864244-9
$21.95 w/CD-ROM

Personal Finance in Your 20s & 30s

0-02-862415-7
$18.95

Creating a Web Page
FIFTH EDITION

0-02-864316-X
$24.95 w/CD-ROM

Digital Photography
SECOND EDITION

0-02-864235-X
$24.95 w/CD-ROM

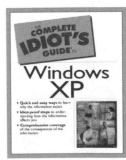

Windows XP

0-02-864232-5
$19.95

than *400 titles* in *26 different categories*
ble at booksellers everywhere

ALPH